HIKING THE
OREGON COAST
TRAIL

I hope this helps
your enjoyment of the outdoors.

Dad
2024

HIKING THE
OREGON COAST
TRAIL

**400 MILES FROM
THE COLUMBIA RIVER
TO CALIFORNIA**

Bonnie Henderson

**MOUNTAINEERS
BOOKS**

In memory of "Pirateboy" Jason Jensen (1971–2001), an early OCT inspiration:
"Pillage and plunder every treasure, every grain, every day."

 MOUNTAINEERS BOOKS is dedicated to the exploration, preservation, and enjoyment of outdoor and wilderness areas.

1001 SW Klickitat Way, Suite 201, Seattle, WA 98134
800-553-4453, www.mountaineersbooks.org

Printed in South Korea
Distributed in the United Kingdom by Cordee, www.cordee.co.uk
First edition: first printing 2021, second printing 2024

Copyeditor: Cooper Lee Bombardier
Design and layout: Heidi Smets
Cartographer: Pease Press
All photographs by the author unless credited otherwise
Cover photograph: *Arch rocks and natural bridges characterize the shoreline at Boardman State Scenic Corridor on the south coast; Section 5, Leg 6.* (Photo by Karsten Winegeart/Unsplash)
Frontispiece: *The trail south of Cape Falcon offers glimpses of Short Sand Beach and the waters of Cape Falcon Marine Reserve (Section 1, Leg 6).*

The background maps for this book were produced using the online map viewer CalTopo. For more information, visit caltopo.com.

Library of Congress Cataloging-in-Publication Data is on file for this title at https://lccn.loc .gov/2021011949. The ebook record is available at https://lccn.loc.gov/2021011950.

Mountaineers Books titles may be purchased for corporate, educational, or other promotional sales, and our authors are available for a wide range of events. For information on special discounts or booking an author, contact our customer service at 800-553-4453 or mbooks@ mountaineersbooks.org.

Printed on FSC®-certified materials

ISBN (paperback): 978-1-68051-327-1
ISBN (ebook): 978-1-68051-328-8

An independent nonprofit publisher since 1960

CONTENTS

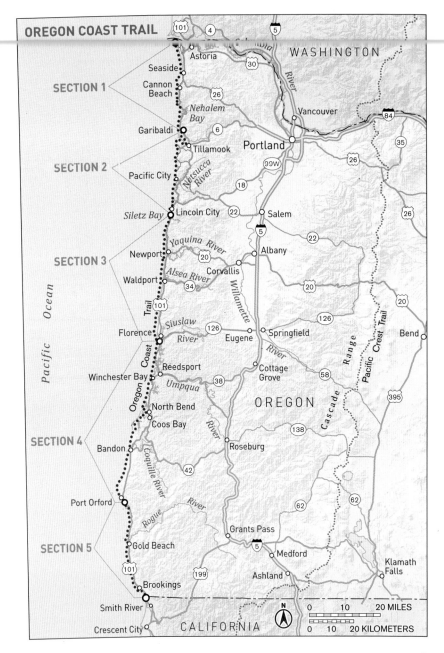

OREGON COAST TRAIL

SECTION 1
SECTION 2
SECTION 3
SECTION 4
SECTION 5

Pacific Ocean

Oregon Coast Trail

Astoria
Seaside
Cannon Beach
Nehalem Bay
Garibaldi
Tillamook
Pacific City
Netsucca River
Siletz Bay
Lincoln City
Yaquina River
Newport
Alsea River
Waldport
Corvallis
Florence
Siuslaw River
Reedsport
Winchester Bay
Umpqua River
North Bend
Coos Bay
Coquille River
Bandon
Roseburg
Rogue River
Port Orford
Grants Pass
Gold Beach
Medford
Brookings
Ashland
Smith River
Crescent City

WASHINGTON

Vancouver
Portland
Salem
Albany
Springfield
Eugene
Cottage Grove
OREGON
Bend
Pacific Crest Trail
Cascade Range
Willamette River
Klamath Falls

CALIFORNIA

N

0   10   20 MILES
0   10   20 KILOMETERS

INTRODUCTION

There is nothing in the world quite like the Oregon Coast Trail.

Nearly half of its roughly 400 miles is on the beach itself. Despite the fact that the trail rarely veers out of sight of the shoreline, the scenery changes constantly. Wide-open beaches are interspersed with forested headlands, and remote shorelines give way to busy tourist towns. It may rain on any given day, but the climate is fairly benign, at least during the spring-to-fall hiking season. An abundance of lodging allows inn-to-inn hiking along much of the route. I've hiked other long-distance trails, in the US and in Europe, but I keep coming back to the Oregon Coast Trail (OCT).

It's also still evolving. Where steep seaside cliffs or private property have created gaps in the trail, you will have to hike along the highway shoulder for a mile, maybe even several miles (or catch a ride, a bus, or a boat where available). You must be prepared to hike some long days and, sometimes, stealth camp or grab a motel room in sections where legal campsites are few and far between. To stay on the beach as much as possible, you'll want to arrange boat shuttles at some bay mouths—which will cost you a few dollars. And you may end up making a long walk around a big bay (or calling a cab or catching a bus) if your boat shuttle arrangements don't work out due to weather or some other circumstance. OCT thru-hikers and section hikers must be both self-reliant and flexible.

You don't need a guidebook to hike the OCT. People have been successfully thru-hiking the OCT for more than thirty years without relying on a guidebook, other than some self-published guides and the 2015 edition of my book *Day Hiking: Oregon Coast*, which provides OCT backpackers with some broad guidance. Oregon State Parks published a map, but it was very general. We all managed to figure it out.

But this guidebook will greatly increase your enjoyment of the OCT. You'll learn how to stay on the beach and off the highway. You'll discover where to camp, get good drinking water, and find a toilet. You'll know when and where to cross rivers and bays. Use it to help plan your trek; carry it with you to refer to trail tips and route hacks.

On my last long-distance hike on the OCT, I met a couple just north of Newport who were hiking northbound; they were hunched over, forging ahead into a strong north wind. They had no guidebook and not much in the way of

South of Rockaway Beach the OCT passes the offshore Twin Rocks; Section 1, Leg 8.
(Photo by Kat Riker)

maps. I urged them to take a bus up to the northern trailhead and finish the trail walking southbound.

"We're almost done!" the man said, though actually they had about a third of the trail left to go.

"We're from Ireland," the woman added. "We're used to wind!" Which was another way of saying, *We didn't do any homework before starting the OCT. And we're too stubborn to switch now.*

I met another hiker who later posted on his blog that 40 percent of the OCT was along the shoulder of US Highway 101. In reality, if you get boat rides across the major bay mouths and follow the route tips in this book, less than 10 percent of the OCT is currently along US 101—most of that in short hops of a mile or less. Construction of new trail stretches reduces a little more highway walking every year. But without good maps or good guidance, it can be hard to know how to stay on the beach and trail and off the highway. This book is designed to help you stay on the beach and trails, minimize your highway shoulder walking, and generally have the best possible OCT experience.

Using shuttle boats to cross bays and river mouths is one of the fun parts of walking the OCT.

AUTHOR'S NOTE

As I was finishing work on this guidebook, the 2021 hiking season was just starting to ramp up. The previous summer the COVID-19 pandemic had virtually shut down the Oregon Coast Trail and other long-distance trails; hiker-biker camps at coastal state parks had all been closed, and pandemic-related budget shortfalls had limited other services (including restroom and tap water access). After the initial lockdown that spring, many tourist services that hikers use later reopened, but differently (takeout replacing dining in, for instance). Some tourist businesses on the coast had their busiest summer ever; others struggled and eventually shut down. Then in September of that year a huge windstorm struck the state, downing trees and closing several stretches of the OCT; due to those same budget shortfalls, it was unclear when some of those trail sections would be cleared of windfall and would reopen to hikers.

Both of these events—the pandemic and the windstorm—serve to remind hikers that guidebooks such as this are just guides, and that the trails and the land they lead you through are ever-changing. The Oregon Coast is a particularly dynamic landscape; the OCT is subject to downed trees, landslides, and other natural phenomena. And it is not a wilderness trail but a route on which hikers frequently interact with the non-hiking world. If you are planning an OCT adventure, do your homework. Take a look at oregonstateparks.org to confirm that campgrounds—hiker-biker camps in particular—are open. Be sure to call ahead (or check websites) if you are counting on patronizing particular businesses, such as charter boat operators, and plan accordingly. I plan to post updates on the trail and its status on my website, hikingtheoct.com, but I may not have all the info you need—the onus is on you to prepare yourself and maintain public safety as you hike.

THE OREGON COAST TRAIL: AN OVERVIEW

The Oregon Coast Trail is a roughly 400-mile walking route that capitalizes on Oregon's 262 miles of publicly owned and accessible sandy beaches. Roughly half the route is on the beach itself. Another quarter follows footpaths over headlands, also publicly owned. The remaining quarter follows quiet side roads and, where unavoidable, the shoulder of US 101.

The trail began as a proposal by University of Oregon geography professor Sam Dicken. Dicken arrived in Eugene, Oregon, from Kentucky in 1947 to lead the University of Oregon's Department of Geography and Geology. Described by colleagues as a "muddy boots geographer," Dicken set out to explore every corner of Oregon. It was during a trip to Curry County in 1959 that he reportedly hatched the idea of a border-to-border coastal hiking route. A large chunk of the rugged coastline had come into public ownership, and he was struck by its beauty—and its inaccessibility to the public, due to a lack of trails. Constructing a few trails would allow people to get out of their cars and walk a short distance to see this coastline. Those trails, he realized, could link up with Oregon's publicly owned beaches and existing trails over headlands to create what he proposed as the Oregon Coast Trail.

With passage of the Oregon Recreation Trails System Act in 1971, money for planning and trail construction became available to make Dicken's vision real, and in 1988 Oregon State Parks—the agency that manages the OCT—declared the trail officially "hikeable." Hikeable, yes, but with about one-tenth of the route still following the highway shoulder (depending on how you count it), it's fair to say the OCT is still not complete.

Limited numbers of hikers thru-hiked it over the next few decades. Around 2017 a sudden spike of interest in long-distance hiking, spurred in great part by the book and then film *Wild*, by Oregon author Cheryl Strayed, coincided with difficulties or closures of parts of the Pacific Crest Trail (PCT)—first, high snow in the Sierra; later, wildfires in the Oregon and Washington Cascades—which

SIX THOUSAND YEARS ON THE OREGON COAST TRAIL

Humans have been traveling north and south on this coast for millennia. How long, exactly? Archaeologists long believed that the first humans to colonize North America came overland from Asia across Beringia—a land mass, now underwater, between present-day Siberia and Alaska that was exposed during the last ice age. Back then, so much ocean water was locked in sea ice at the poles that, worldwide, sea levels were as much as 450 feet lower than they are today. New research suggests that the first people more likely made their way around the Pacific Rim by boat some fourteen thousand years ago—or even earlier—taking advantage of the rich resources of the nearshore kelp beds and settling on the North and South American coasts before spreading inland.

But those earliest inhabitants walked a very different coast from the one we walk today. With sea levels so much lower, Oregon's coastline was west of where it is now—in some places many miles to the west. That's why archaeologists haven't found much evidence of human habitation on the Oregon Coast older than ten thousand years—because the charcoal, stone tools, bits of basket, middens, and other evidence of human life along the seashore would have been drowned by rising seas. Geologists believe that it wasn't until about six thousand years ago that the sea level along Oregon rose to where it is now, and what we think of as the Oregon Coast became the human thoroughfare we now enjoy.

The OCT route follows beaches, dirt paths, road shoulders, and boardwalks such as this one on the South Rainforest Trail over Cascade Head (Section 2, Leg 6).

resulted in hikers temporarily abandoning the PCT and moving over to the OCT. And word spread. Now OCT thru-hikers will find they have company on the trail and in hiker-biker camps.

The route is well-marked in some places and poorly marked in others, though it's constantly improving. Official maps and directions may not explain how to get around bay mouths with a boat shuttle, which, in my opinion, is key to enjoying the OCT, since it helps keep you on the beach and off the highway shoulder. The OCT has challenges unique to its dynamic landscape; you need to work with the tides and the topography and plan your day to avoid getting caught by the tide or having to wait out a tidal cycle to continue on your way. Knowing where you can find tap water and toilets is important on a trail where the surface water is sketchy and where squatting off-trail—on a busy tourist beach, for instance—may not be an option.

The Oregon Coast Trail is not a wilderness experience. The route will steer you through tony second-home neighborhoods, past phalanxes of oceanfront manses, and in and out of busy tourist towns. You will do some trudging on the highway shoulder as motor homes rush by. Camping on the beach itself is possible in some places but often is not; hikers typically overnight in developed campgrounds where available. Toilets and potable water are widely accessible in most places. Hikers can easily resupply from grocery stores along the way—not to mention restaurants, espresso shops, and wine and whiskey bars.

THE OCT VS. THE PCT

Have you left the Pacific Crest Trail to walk the Oregon Coast Trail? Here are a few key differences you should know about.

» PCT thru-hikers typically hike northbound to enjoy the desert in spring and to reach Canada before winter. Due to often strong prevailing north winds, OCT hikers typically hike southbound.

» You can't camp (or defecate) anywhere you choose on the OCT. Camping isn't allowed on the beach in many places. You may have to plan ahead more than you are accustomed to.

» The water in streams on the coast is not the pure springwater you find in the mountains. I strongly suggest drinking tap water (widely available) rather than filtering and drinking water from streams.

» Mail-ahead food boxes are unnecessary. You can resupply at grocery stores along the way.

» Expect to spend some money. Even if you eschew restaurant meals, and even if you manage to hitch rides with boaters rather than pay an outfitter for a boat shuttle, you are likely to camp in hiker-biker campgrounds—cheap, but not free.

It may not be a wilderness hike, but the Oregon Coast Trail is an adventure. You may have days where you don't see another human being. You'll need to watch the tides to avoid getting stuck on the wrong side of a river or a headland, or worse: stuck on a rock or sandbar, hoping for help from the Coast Guard. The river you thought would be knee-high might rise to your waist before you finish wading it. The river mouth you thought was a mile away may have shifted several miles away. You may find yourself flagging down a recreational crabber to catch a ride across a bay mouth. A large tree may have fallen across the trail, requiring a climb up and over, or through, a tangle of branches. Some trails are slow going due to roots, rocks, and mud. Another trail might be so brushy, or so laced with social trails, that wayfinding can be challenging. You will encounter landslides on trails and need to do some scrambling around or steeply up or down. You may end up needing to bivouac short of your day's planned destination. The weather is mostly benign in the summer, but there can be days where the rain never stops pouring down—and you end up having to wade more than one river. Inn-to-inn hiking is possible, but with no luggage transfer service (as of this writing), you still need to carry a backpack. The Oregon Coast isn't Disneyland, and the OCT isn't a perfectly manicured route. You'll need to keep your wits about you, and every day is different.

And don't be misled by the OCT's relative proximity to civilization: the Oregon Coast is a very dynamic landscape. Estuary boundaries are constantly shifting.

Sand volume on the beach varies year to year and with the seasons, with the highest sand depth usually in late summer. But it can change radically even within one hiking season, impacting how big your window of time is to get around headlands or across river mouths at low tide (more sand translates to a functionally lower tide). The locations of river and creek mouths change, wandering north and south, pushed by storms and prevailing ocean currents; they may not be exactly where indicated on the maps in this (or any) book, or even what Google Maps depicts. The mouth of the New River on the south coast is notorious for busting out in new locations or cutting a second outlet to the sea. Landslides on steep seaside hills are not uncommon; they tend to occur in the winter, but you'll have to manage the results in the summer when the trail you're on suddenly seems to disappear and you're left to scramble around the gap. What this means to you: the maps in this book may not precisely match what you encounter in the field, and OCT hikers must be prepared to roll with unexpected changes.

Most of all, the Oregon Coast Trail remains a work in progress. The first comprehensive master plan led by Oregon State Parks is under way as this book goes to press; it is designed to serve as a road map for eventually eliminating (or at least minimizing) highway shoulder-walking sections as well as developing more camping and otherwise making the trail more hiker-friendly.

THE OREGON BEACH BILL

In many coastal states the ocean beach is private property, except where it's been conserved for the public. In Oregon, all 262 miles of beaches and 64 miles of headlands are public lands, thanks to the 1967 Oregon Beach Bill. Fifty years earlier, Oregon's beaches had been declared public highways up to the high tide line. Then in 1966 several citizens complained to the state that they had been denied access to the dry sand beach in front of a Cannon Beach motel; the owner had fenced it off for the exclusive use of his guests. A state parks committee began examining the issue. In May 1967 a pair of helicopters carrying Governor Tom McCall and a gaggle of surveyors and scientists landed on the beach in a publicity event that ignited the public's imagination and support for the bill. Two months later Governor McCall signed it into law.

The Beach Bill declares that all "wet sand" within sixteen vertical feet of the low tide line belongs to the state of Oregon and grants the public "free and uninterrupted use of the beaches." Beach access points are also protected as public easements. The Oregon Beach Bill has become a point of pride for many Oregonians—and for those unaware of its history or existence, it is just another perk of living in Oregon.

HOW TO USE THIS GUIDE

This book was written primarily for Oregon Coast trail thru-hikers. But it can also be used by backpackers or inn-to-inn hikers who go out for a few days, or section hikers willing to walk up to a week at a time. The section boundaries are somewhat arbitrary, but each starts and ends at a town that can be accessed by public transportation. It can also be used by day-trippers, particularly those interested in a one-day hike with a shuttle; this guide notes the beach access points where you can typically leave a vehicle.

Each of the five sections begins with an information block. The **distance** is the overall mileage for the section, and **cumulative OCT mileage** is also noted. **Elevation gain/loss** tallies the cumulative ups and downs over the entire section, and **headland summits** lists significant headlands you'll need to climb, and how high the trail over it goes. **Max distance between campgrounds** refers only to developed campgrounds that allow tent camping; read the section narrative for suggestions about possible rough camping on the beach or dunes between campgrounds. **Max distance between lodging** may help you think about whether you're up for an inn-to-inn hike here. **Water availability** is noted as either good (at least one source of potable water available at or between campsites) or poor (limited potable water, requiring you to carry extra). **Boat shuttle** indicates whether there are big bays that need to be walked around or ferried across, and whether such a ferry may be available. Note that the shortest shuttles are currently running about $10 per person, with longer ones charging $40 for one and $10 for each additional passenger—and perhaps more for the longer shuttle to Charleston across Coos Bay. Each of the five sections is divided into **legs**. These divisions start and end at logical stopping points, but your hiking days may be longer or shorter than these legs.

An **elevation profile** gives you a quick visual on what to expect in the way of headland ascents and beach walking in that section. **Access** provides tips on parking and public transportation at both ends. **Suggested itineraries** aren't the only options for how to split up a trip on the OCT and where to camp or stay, but they make a good guide for planning, and they help you see where big gaps in camping or lodging might require extra-long days of hiking.

Each **leg description** also starts with an information block containing mileage and elevation figures. Following the trail description, you'll find mention of specific **hazards** to watch for, **camping** and **lodging** information, **boat shuttle**

After a few miles of highway walking, an OCT hiker follows a path to the beach south of Heceta Head (Section 3, Leg 7).

Neon yellow-green emergency beach access signs also serve as wayfinding markers for OCT hikers (but don't rely too heavily on them).

details, if any, and **food resupply** details (whether and where you can find groceries or restaurants). Campground price ranges refer to the best price available for OCT hikers: hiker-biker camps ($ for typically $7 to $11 per person in 2021) or regular tent camping sites ($$ for typically $15 to $25 per site in 2021). The leg description ends with a detailed **mileage log**. For details about campground reservations and parking passes, plus contact information for lodging, boat shuttle outfitters, and other private businesses mentioned in the text, check the Contacts section at the back of the book.

Each **leg map** indicates the route and other relevant details, including locations of toilets, potable water, and campgrounds (which also have toilets and water). The leg maps also include locations of **emergency beach access signs** (referred to by the abbreviation "BA" in the text). About two hundred of these neon greenish-yellow numbered signs have been installed all along the Oregon Coast by Oregon State Parks (note that the numbers on emergency beach access signs do not correspond to mileage). Their purpose is to get help quickly to people in an emergency. As a bonus, they're also very useful to OCT hikers as wayfinding aids. But don't depend too heavily on them: sometimes they're missing, and sometimes they are difficult to see from the beach. That said, they can be extremely helpful when, say, you're wondering where the best place to leave the beach is as you approach a river mouth, or you're trying to figure out if you've overshot your destination. The maps in this book don't include locations of every beach access sign; those that are irrelevant to the OCT have been omitted, and new ones may be added after this book is published.

PLANNING AND PREPARATION

As with any long-distance hike, a trek on the Oregon Coast Trail requires some planning and preparation. You'll want to train so that you're comfortable hiking 10 to 15 miles a day (the minimum distance you often need to hike between legal campsites). You may want to study the maps and tide tables before you pick the

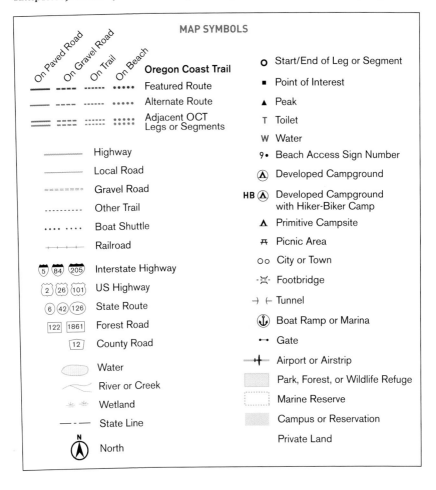

MAP SYMBOLS

On Paved Road | On Gravel Road | On Trail | On Beach

Oregon Coast Trail
Featured Route
Alternate Route
Adjacent OCT Legs or Segments

—————— Highway
—————— Local Road
========= Gravel Road
·········· Other Trail
···· ···· Boat Shuttle
++++++ Railroad

(5) (84) (205) Interstate Highway
(2) (26) (101) US Highway
(6) (42) (126) State Route
122 1861 Forest Road
12 County Road

Water
River or Creek
Wetland
— · — State Line
North

o Start/End of Leg or Segment
■ Point of Interest
▲ Peak
T Toilet
W Water
9• Beach Access Sign Number
Ⓐ Developed Campground
HB Ⓐ Developed Campground with Hiker-Biker Camp
▲ Primitive Campsite
Ħ Picnic Area
oo City or Town
-☼- Footbridge
→ ← Tunnel
⚓ Boat Ramp or Marina
•—• Gate
✈ Airport or Airstrip
    Park, Forest, or Wildlife Refuge
    Marine Reserve
    Campus or Reservation
    Private Land

KEY ADVICE FOR HIKING THE OREGON COAST TRAIL

» Plan your thru-hike June through September. Just because it rarely snows on the Oregon Coast doesn't mean you should, or can, hike the OCT in winter. Even if you don't mind rain, river levels are the major limiting factor; fall through spring, many rivers are too high to wade. This is especially important on the more remote south coast, where you might have to bushwhack inland for miles to reach a bridge. An April or May hike in Sections 1, 2, or 3 is possible, but the earlier you go, the more unsettled the weather can be.

» Figure on taking up to a month to hike the whole trail. Theoretically, you could take as long as you wish, but camping and lodging limitations mean you'll probably hike an average of at least 15 miles a day, meaning you'll probably complete this roughly 400-mile trail in less than four weeks. Pacific Crest Trail hikers accustomed to 25-mile days will finish even quicker. For what it's worth, the Fastest Known Time for an unsupported hike on the OCT is thirteen days (at this writing)—and just eight and a half days for a supported trek (read more at fastestknowntime.com).

» Hike southbound. People certainly do hike northbound, though mainly out of ignorance. Winds in summer prevail from the north-northwest, and they can be strong: 15 to 20 mph winds are common. It's not much fun hiking into that day after day. If for some reason you insist on a northbound hike, start walking early in the morning before the wind really kicks up.

» Don't count on camping on the beach. Half of the OCT is on the beach but for various reasons, camping is not allowed on many parts of those beach sections. Plan to use developed hiker-biker camps where you can, and beach camp primarily on the south coast, where there are fewer cities (and fewer restrictions).

» Read the introduction to this book. Whether you're deep into trip planning months in advance or you've already started your OCT trek and picked up this book along the way, stop and read up. The OCT is different in many respects from the PCT and other long-distance trails. It's not really a single trail but a combination of beaches, footpaths, roads, and boat shuttles. You can't camp (or crap) just anywhere. You need to watch the tides. You may need to make plans to avoid long highway walks around big bays. Awareness of public transportation options can keep you off the highway and save you money. Get to know this trail's quirks and you'll have a much better (and potentially safer) experience.

» Use the most recent edition of this book. And check my website, hikingtheoct .com, for updates. The OCT continues to evolve, with new trail sections being built and old ones rebuilt. The landscape itself is constantly changing.

dates of your trek to optimize your itinerary. You'll need to have good raingear and proper footwear. If you are counting on staying in lodging, you will want to make advance reservations (ditto for some private campgrounds). That said, hikers detouring off the Pacific Crest Trail (PCT) to the OCT typically do so with no advance planning, but they are already trail-hardened—physically fit and mentally flexible.

Overnighting on the OCT

Some OCT trekkers plan every overnight stop in advance; others figure it out day by day. I've done it both ways and can't say which is best. Planning limits your spontaneity but allows you to avoid surprises like unexpectedly long days of hiking or uncomfortable bivouacs or long waits for the tide to turn. And if things don't work out as planned, you may be able to step off the trail and catch a bus or taxi to your next destination. You'll find a lot of developed campgrounds, primitive campsites, and lodgings along the Oregon Coast Trail; most hikers depend on some combination of these over the course of a thru-hike.

Camping on the Beach. Uninformed folks may assume that hiking the OCT means camping on the beach every night. Not so. Camping is allowed on the beach in Oregon but with three big exceptions: (1) no camping adjacent to city limits of many towns, (2) no camping adjacent to a state park (whether or not there is a campground at that park), and (3) no camping in protected snowy plover areas. Those caveats severely restrict opportunities for beach camping in some sections—for instance, most of the areas included in Section 1.

You may decide that beach camping is overrated.

Specifically, beach camping is not allowed adjacent to Seaside, Cannon Beach, Manzanita, Rockaway Beach, Lincoln City, Newport, Bandon and Gold Beach. State parks also doesn't allow beach camping from Fort Stevens State Park south to Gearhart. Search your map app for the name of the city to find the city limits. The no-camping-adjacent-to-state-parks rule applies no matter what it's called (state natural area, state scenic corridor, etc.).

Personally, I think camping on the beach is overrated and not the best option on most of the OCT except where you have no other option. Sand has a tendency to get into *everything*. You must camp high enough up the beach to make sure high tide doesn't reach you overnight, which often puts you at a slant (and in very soft sand). This can keep you awake, giving you more time to worry about the tide. If it rains, it's even harder to keep sand out of your sleeping bag. The biggest problem with beach camping is that you don't have access to a toilet. In the mountains it's easy to find a private spot off-trail where you can squat and dig a "cat hole" and trust your feces will decompose nicely in the forest soil. Nothing about that is true on most of the Oregon Coast Trail (see Trail Hygiene).

Nevertheless beach camping is a highlight for many OCT hikers (some of whom don't realize their campsites are not strictly legal). A few possible sites are mentioned in the text. If you do camp on the beach, try for a location where you won't be too far from a toilet.

Hiker-Biker Camps. OCT hikers tend to overnight at hiker-biker camps whenever they can. These are sites within developed campgrounds that cater

Most hiker-biker camps in coastal state parks now provide phone charging stations and lockers for food and valuables, as well as tent sites, picnic tables, and access to toilets and showers.

to people arriving under their own power, either on foot or by bike. By definition they are drop-in sites (no reservations accepted) with flat spots for tents,
shared fire pits and picnic tables, and access to toilets and usually showers (no
extra fee). Every coastal state park campground has a hiker-biker camp, as do
a few county and Forest Service campgrounds. Cost tends to be minimal: $7 to
$11, except in Tillamook County, where an additional "reservation fee" brings
the cost to more than $20. Many state park hiker-biker camps now have lockers
where you can stash your belongings (including food, out of critters' reach) and
where you can charge your cell phone or other device; carry a small padlock
if you are concerned about security. Note that hiker-biker camps charge per
person, so two or three people hiking together may spend almost as much at a
hiker-biker camp as they would sharing a regular state park campsite (though
hiker-biker sites have the advantage of being drop-in).

Other Developed Camping. Some public (county or national forest) and
private campgrounds allow tent camping but do not have hiker-biker sites—in
other words, the campground may be full when you arrive. If you're a planner,
you may want to reserve a site in advance. If you're not, take your chances.
You're more likely to find an open spot on a weekday in June than a weekend in
August. Expect fees to be at least double the cost of a hiker-biker camp.

Dispersed Camping in the Forest or Dunes. There are a few areas where you
can wild camp in the forest or dunes rather than on the beach, such as the backpacker camp atop Tillamook Head (Section 1), in parts of Siuslaw National Forest in Section 3, and in the Oregon Dunes National Recreation Area (Section 4).

Stealth Camping. Stealth camping means spending the night where it is not
strictly legal. The fact is, the distance between developed campsites, even
between beaches where camping is allowed, is very great in a few places along
the OCT—too great for many hikers. Two examples are at the northern and
southern ends of the trail; there is no legal camping for 21.9 miles between
the campground at Fort Stevens State Park and the backpacker camp atop
Tillamook Head, nor along the 36.2 miles between the town of Gold Beach and
Harris Beach State Park. The State of Oregon has been actively promoting use
of the Oregon Coast Trail by long-distance hikers without tackling the problem
of insufficient campsites. In some places, but not all, you may be able to opt for
a motel room. I am definitely *not* suggesting you break the law. But if, simply
for safety's sake, you need to stealth camp once or twice, please follow strict
Leave No Trace guidelines: do not build a fire; properly bury your feces at least
six inches deep in dirt, not sand (or, if possible, wait and hike to the next toilet);
and leave your campsite looking like it did when you arrived (no garbage, no
vegetation impacted, etc.).

Hiking Inn-to-Inn. Many parts of the OCT—particularly in Sections 1, 2, and 3—lend themselves well to inn-to-inn hiking, meaning: hiking without a tent, sleeping bag, or stove, eating mostly in restaurants, and spending each night in a motel, hotel, hostel, or vacation rental of some kind. You will need to reserve your lodging in advance. Even on the north coast, you may have to hike some longish days between available lodging. Obviously hiking from inn to inn costs significantly more than backpacking, and it commits you to a schedule. Look for suggested itineraries in each section description. I am still waiting for an entrepreneur to begin offering daily luggage transfer service on the OCT, such as what you find on other long-distance trails with inn-to-inn walking, which allows hikers to carry only what a day hiker would need, and to have their suitcase waiting at their lodging each night.

Additional considerations for inn-to-inn hikers:
» When you are making reservations, make sure your lodgings are on (or a reasonable walking distance from) the OCT route. (Just because it's described as oceanfront or ocean-view doesn't mean it's easily accessible from the OCT; it may be high on a hill and a long walk off the trail.)
» Prices vary widely; they tend to be highest in popular north coast tourist towns.
» Some towns have only one or two lodging options; secure reservations there first before confirming the rest of your schedule.
» Some (but not most) accommodations on the coast require a minimum two-night stay during the high season.
» You may need to bring your own breakfast (and even dinner) if it is not provided by your lodgings and there are no cafés within walking distance; check when you make your reservations.

Drop-In Lodging. As busy as the Oregon Coast is in summer, backpackers seeking a night off from the trail may still find motels with vacancies, as I have in Pacific City in mid-July and in Gold Beach in early September. Call ahead or take your chances dropping in (and be prepared to camp if necessary). Less expensive lodgings in larger towns are your best bet.

Food Resupply

There is no need to mail yourself resupply boxes on the OCT, as you might on long-distance wilderness trails, as long as you are comfortable resupplying with what's available at grocery stores. Rarely will you need to carry more than a couple of days' worth of food. Grocery store availability is noted at the end of each leg description. Some hikers insist on carrying their preferred foods rather than eating what they can find in grocery stores, and people with food allergies may need to carry specific foods. But if your goal is simply good health,

Dozens of great coffee shops await you on the Oregon Coast's "Coffee Camino." (Photo by Jeanne Henderson)

consider the impact of that extra food weight on your joints and feet (and your general happiness).

SEASONAL SPECIALTIES ON THE OREGON COAST

One of the pleasures of the Oregon Coast Trail is enjoying locally grown, caught, or produced food. A few specialties to look for:

» Salmon, rockfish, Dungeness crab, and, in late summer, albacore tuna—on their own or in chowder. If the menu lists rockfish or lingcod fish-and-chips or tacos, don't pass it by.
» Razor clams—if they're fresh and cooked right; cooked too long, they get tough.
» Cheese: The Tillamook Creamery (on US 101 in Tillamook) is a popular tourist destination; you'll walk right by it if you follow the highway around Tillamook Bay. Otherwise look for their cheeses in stores. In Bandon, Face Rock Creamery is just off the OCT route; it specializes in cheddar from locally sourced cow's milk.
» Cranberries are grown on the south coast; look for them in candy and other products. You may find locally grown blueberries at markets in July.
» Brewpubs: Just about every town of any size has at least one microbrewery.
» Espresso: One OCT hiker found herself lured off the trail for a latte so often that she dubbed the route the "Coffee Camino."
» Fresh fruits and veggies: A dozen or so coastal towns have a weekly farmer's market in season. The Friday evening Manzanita Farmers Market is particularly bounteous and sociable.

Hiking Season for the OCT

The recommended months for hiking the OCT are June through September—or possibly as early as April or May. Two factors set the hiking season on the Oregon Coast: weather and river levels.

Weather. Summer on the Oregon Coast tends to be a series of fine but windy days punctuated by periods of rain and sometimes fog. Daytime highs are typically in the high sixties (though the temperature can shoot up into the eighties for short periods), and nighttime lows are in the low fifties. July and August are the warmest and driest months, each averaging one inch of rain. It's almost always breezy on the coast. Wind prevails from the north-north-west in summer, and it's not unusual to encounter afternoon winds of 15 to 20 mph (which are not a problem if you're hiking southbound). You may encounter a few days of cold fog and strong north winds, triggered by very hot weather in the inland valleys. Locals sometimes call this "fogust"; it will pass. In spring and fall you might catch a sou'wester: a storm with rain and strong winds from the south. Such storms are more characteristic of winter on the coast, however, and are one of the reasons to not attempt an OCT thru-hike October through March. In summary, the warmest, driest, least windy months are July and August, but June and September aren't bad. Earlier and later than that, you take your chances; by October you are likely to deal with a fierce storm or two.

River Levels. The OCT route crosses a number of rivers that you must wade. Rivers tend to drop to their lowest summer levels by mid-June and stay low until rains begin in earnest, typically in October or November. This is mainly an issue on the south coast. If you encounter a river too high to wade, even at low tide, in Sections 1, 2, or 3, there is always the option of crossing on a bridge (with perhaps a short detour). A number of rivers in sections 4 and 5 can be waded at low tide in summer but are uncrossable in winter and spring; some would require a very long detour (possibly over private land) to reach a bridge where you could safely cross. For that reason, I consider the hiking season on the north coast (assuming you're not afraid of a little rain) to be April through September, and on the south coast, June through September.

Sharing the Beach with Snowy Plovers. Periodically, Oregon Coast hikers will see fencing and signage referring to the western snowy plover: a small shorebird that nests on flat, open, sandy beaches just above the high tide line around active sand dunes, especially those with estuaries or ponds nearby. The snowy plover population in Oregon plummeted to just 28 breeding birds in 1992, causing it to be listed as a threatened species, mainly due to habitat loss from the introduction of European beach grass to stabilize dunes.

IF YOU REALLY, REALLY, REALLY WANT TO HIKE THE OREGON COASTAL TRAIL IN WINTER

» Plan to hike only as far south as Florence. South of Florence you will probably encounter rivers that cannot be crossed even at low tide (with no nearby bridge alternative).

» Don't count on boat ferries across bay mouths; outfitters may not be operating. Plan accordingly.

» A few private and public coastal campgrounds close in winter, including at least one state park campground and most US Forest Service campgrounds on the central coast. However, most state park and private RV campgrounds remain open.

Disturbance from people and dogs and predation by crows, raccoons, and foxes also hasn't helped.

A habitat conservation plan was put in place, and it seems to be working; 468 breeding birds were counted in 2017. That plan places some restrictions on OCT hikers during breeding season—March 15 to September 15—at sixteen sites in Section 1 (Nehalem Spit), Section 3 (Baker Beach), and Section 4 (several areas). These include:

» No camping.
» No beach fires.
» No dogs (even on leash).
» Walk only on the wet sand.

Timing Your Trek: Pros and Cons. Spring through fall, every month on the OCT is a little different.

April and May
» Pros: Weather can be good but unsettled. Lodging vacancies are more abundant and more affordable than later in the season.
» Cons: Rivers often too high to cross on south coast.

June
» Pros: Purple iris and other wildflowers are in bloom, wild strawberries and salmonberries are ripe, and songbirds sing in the trees. Lodging vacancies more abundant until mid-June.
» Cons: Not many boaters out yet, so fewer chances to hitch rides across bay mouths.

July and August
» Pros: The weather is more stable, and hitching rides across bay mouths with recreational crabbers is more likely. Ripe blackberries abound.
» Cons: You are less likely to find drop-in lodging vacancies.

September

» Pros: Weekday lodging vacancies are likelier. Presence of salmon fishermen could help you get rides across rivers.
» Cons: Weather is getting cooler and a little less settled.

Dogs on the OCT?

I don't recommend it—I say this as a dog owner and dog lover. Dogs make logistics trickier; you can't take a bus with a dog, and you'll have trouble hitching a ride if you're in a pinch. But the biggest problem is snowy plover restrictions: dogs are not allowed on many stretches of the Oregon Coast during plover nesting season from March 15 to September 15, even on leash.

If you *must* take your dog on an OCT thru-hike, start after about September 10; by the time you reach the first plover nesting sites south of Manzanita, the seasonal restrictions will be lifted. If you're section-hiking, you could go in the summer as long as you pick a stretch without plover restrictions:

» Mouth of the Columbia to Manzanita (most of Section 1).
» South of Sand Lake to Baker Beach north of Florence (in Sections 2 and 3).
» South of Floras Lake (Leg 5 of Section 4 plus all of Section 5).

Kids on the OCT?

Until more campsites are developed for backpackers, the OCT is not a great choice for family backpacking, simply because the distances required to hike between legal overnighting spots can be very long. The highway shoulder hiking is also an issue. One possibility for a multiday backpack trip with kids might be in Leg 1 of Section 4, at the Oregon Dunes National Recreation Area (NRA), but you would need to carry water or detour inland to campgrounds along the Siltcoos River or at Carter Lake for tap water, or—not recommended by this author—filter your water from surface streams.

Permits and Passes

Permits are not required to hike any portion of the Oregon Coast Trail; however, day-use permits are required to park at many, but not all, Oregon State Park and US Forest Service sites, such as trailheads in the Oregon Dunes NRA. If you plan to drive and leave a car overnight at one of these sites, you will need to arrange for a parking permit. If you use public transportation, you won't need any kind of permit or pass.

State Park Parking Permits. Overnight parking is by permit only. Arrange in advance by calling the specific park's main number (not the camping reservations 800 number). Find the phone number on the park's homepage at stateparks.oregon.gov or in the Contacts lists at the end of this book. You will be issued a permit that you can pick up on site and will be told where to park.

USFS Parking Permits. You can use a variety of permits to park overnight at Forest Service trailheads, such as at the Siuslaw National Forest sites or the Oregon Dunes NRA. One-day, five-day, and annual passes are available; some types can be used during the day at state parks too (but for overnight parking at state parks, follow the instructions above). A federal Senior Pass lets you park for free at Forest Service parking areas and camp for half price. See Contacts.

Calculating Costs

Part of the appeal of the OCT is the novelty of boat ferries across bay mouths, the opportunity to eat out rather than relying solely on snack bars and freeze-dried food, stopping for a latte or a pint of IPA here and there, and the possibility of finding relatively luxurious tent camping, with hot showers and flush toilets, at hiker-biker camps. You may end up taking a cab or a bus to avoid a highway hike. But it all adds up. There are a lot of ways to keep it cheap, such as attempting to hitch, rather than hire, boat shuttles. A monthlong trek for a solo hiker, staying in hiker-biker and other developed campsites, with a little wild camping in between, might set you back around $200 (excluding food), plus more than $100 if you pay for a few boat shuttles; sharing boat shuttles and campsites in developed campgrounds with a companion or other hikers you meet on the trail will cut down on those costs.

Accessing the OCT

Public transportation can get you close to the northern (and southern) trailheads; walk or take a cab to get the rest of the way.

Flying in and out of Oregon. Portland International Airport (PDX) is the closest airport to the northern trailhead. The Rogue Valley International–Medford Airport (MFR) in Medford is closest to the southern trailhead. Section hikers may consider flying in or out of Eugene (approximately two hours by bus from the coast) or North Bend–Coos Bay (basically on the trail).

Public Transportation to and from the Trailheads. From Portland International Airport to the northern trailhead: Take MAX light rail from the Portland airport to Union Station in downtown Portland. Bus transportation is available from Union Station to Astoria, stopping at other north coast towns along the way; do an internet search for details (they change too often to list here). To reach the trailhead, the simplest option is to call a local cab from Astoria (about

ABOUT CABS AND RIDE-SHARING APPS

Most towns of any size on the Oregon Coast have at least one taxi service. The quality varies. I've had very good experiences with cabs, but I've heard of other hikers who had to wait a long time for a taxi or for ones that never arrived. I recommend you call ahead to arrange your ride and confirm the cost, and that you be patient with these small-town taxi drivers, who are just trying to make a living.

Regarding ride-sharing apps, at this writing it appears that Uber and Lyft are not available anywhere on the Oregon Coast—but it also seems that they're seeking drivers in some towns, so these ride-sharing services may be coming soon.

a thirty-minute ride) or wherever you are. The closest you can get by bus is just outside Fort Stevens State Park; schedules and other details are at the NW Connector website (see Contacts).

From the southern terminus of the OCT south of Brookings, plan to spend the night in Smith River or Crescent City. Call a cab or keep walking 0.4 mile down the beach past the California state line to Pelican Beach, then walk 2.5 miles south on US 101 to Smith River Rancheria. There is limited bus service to the Medford airport from Brookings, the Lucky 7 Casino in Smith River, or Crescent City; it's a three-to-five hour ride, so plan ahead.

Note that Amtrak trains stop in Portland, Salem, Albany, and Eugene. Bus service is available between these stations and various points on the coast; buy your tickets online in advance. South of Eugene the passenger train route veers farther inland and is of no use to OCT hikers.

Driving and Parking. See details above under Permits and Passes for parking at state or federal sites. Leaving your car on a neighborhood street in a coastal town for a few days is another possibility, but you're better off parking with a permit at a park or other public site.

Public Transportation along the Coast. You may want to ride the bus to shuttle back to your starting point on a section hike, or to skip a highway walking portion, or to bridge the gap if you choose not to take boat shuttle across a bay mouth (or if your boat shuttle doesn't work out). The entire Oregon Coast is served by bus, though through a patchwork of operators. North of Yachats (most of Sections 1, 2 and 3), operators have consolidated their information under NW Connector, which makes things easier. Note that some bus operators will pick up and drop off at flag stops in addition to standard bus stops; call ahead to confirm and arrange, whether for pickup or drop-off. See Contacts for details.

GEAR AND CLOTHING

The OCT is a good place to practice ultralight backpacking. The mild climate and availability of food resupply means you can keep clothing, gear, and food weight to a minimum.

Gear

Ultralight gear (tent, sleeping bag, pad, and your pack itself) costs more, but every unnecessary ounce means shorter per-day distances, higher likelihood of blisters or joint problems, and less overall fun. Take the lightest tent you can, such as one with a mosquito net ceiling covered by a lightweight rain fly, since warmth is not really an issue. A tarp is even lighter, but you'll want the privacy of a tent at hiker-biker campgrounds.

The mild climate requires only a moderately warm sleeping bag (overnight temperatures don't dip much below 50 degrees in summertime). As for your sleeping pad, get either an insulated self-inflating pad of some kind (very compact, weight varies) or a closed-cell pad (very light but bulky; doesn't absorb water). I do not recommend an uninsulated inflatable mattress of any kind. It's a bummer when they stop holding air, which they always seem eventually to do.

I recommend using a waterproof pack or waterproof pack cover, and even then bring resealable plastic bags to keep valuables (and even clothing) dry. It doesn't typically rain often on the Oregon Coast in summer, but you can count on a drizzle or even full-on rainstorm or two in the time it takes you to walk the whole trail.

For cooking, all you really need is one pot with a lid and a backpacking stove with fuel. I am a convert to systems that integrate the stove and cookpot, such as the Jetboil; it's slightly heavier than a stove and pot, and I use it only to boil water, not to actually cook. But its wind-stopping baffles and insulation mean you carry less fuel. Some extreme backpackers even dispense with the stove and carry only food that doesn't require heating or cooking. Especially with the availability of restaurant meals (and even coffee shops) on the OCT, this approach is something to consider.

If you normally hike with trekking poles, then bring them! If trekking poles are part of the structure of your ultralight tent, you will have them. You don't need them on the OCT, but trekking poles come in very handy in the following situations (all of which you will encounter on the OCT):

» Where the trail is rough and rocky, they can help prevent tripping.
» They can help you catapult yourself over small streams and stabilize yourself when you're fording streams on fallen logs or stepping from rock to rock.
» When you're wading a river with higher water and a soft, sandy bottom, trekking poles can help you stay upright.
» Poles help take pressure off your knees on long downhill trail stretches.

Trekking poles can be very helpful on the OCT, especially for creek crossings—such as this one over a log to access the beach south of Yaquina Head (Section 3, Leg 3).

The Mountaineers' Ten Essentials. Even day hikers shouldn't go out without these items. The point of the Ten Essentials, originated by The Mountaineers, has always been to answer two basic questions: Can you prevent emergencies and respond positively should one occur (items 1–5)? And can you safely spend a night—or more—outside (items 6–10)? Use this list, which has been modified for use on the OCT, as a guide and tailor it to the needs of your outing.

1. **Navigation:** The five fundamentals are a map, altimeter, compass, GPS device, and a personal locator beacon or other device to contact emergency first responders. It's hard to get lost on the OCT, with the ocean always to the west and US 101 usually a short distance to the east; a phone with a compass app and electronic map app may be all you need. A personal locator beacon on a not-so-remote trail such as this is a matter of personal preference.

2. **Headlamp:** Include spare batteries. Alternately, carry a lightweight solar-powered lantern and hang it off your pack daily to recharge.

3. **Sun protection:** Wear sunglasses, consider wearing sun-protective clothes, and use broad-spectrum sunscreen rated at least SPF 30.

4. **First aid:** Basics include bandages; skin closures; gauze pads and dressings; roller bandage or wrap; tape; antiseptic; blister prevention and treatment supplies; nitrile gloves; tweezers; needle; nonprescription painkillers; anti-inflammatory, antidiarrheal, and antihistamine tablets; topical antibiotic; and any important personal prescriptions, including an EpiPen if you are allergic to bee or hornet venom.

5. **Knife:** Also consider a multitool, strong tape, some cordage, and gear repair supplies.

6. **Fire:** Carry at least one butane lighter (or waterproof matches) and firestarter, such as chemical heat tabs, cotton balls soaked in petroleum jelly, or commercially prepared firestarter. Even if you're not building campfires, it's good to carry firestarter materials for emergency use.

7. **Shelter:** In addition to a rain shell, carry a single-use bivy sack, plastic tube tent, or jumbo plastic trash bag.

8. **Extra food:** Carry at least one extra day's supply, for yourself or to share with another hiker in an emergency.

9. **Extra water:** Carry sufficient water. Consider carrying a few water purification tablets to use in an emergency.

10. **Extra clothes:** Pack additional layers needed to survive the night in the worst conditions that your party may realistically encounter.

Clothing

You don't need much warm clothing: just enough should the night turn cool or you get chilled after a rainstorm. You *do* need raingear. You also need sun protection. Think layers. Hiking pants with zip-off legs are handy on this trail;

PACKING LIST

The following is a comprehensive list of what I took on a solo two-week trip on the OCT. It amounts to the essentials plus just one or two small items of "contraband"—carefully and personally selected nonessentials. I handwashed socks, underwear, and T-shirts every couple of days. It seems like a long list, but I wore some of it, and the rest was very light or small. All of it fit into a small ultralight backpack. I've since added trekking poles to the list.

» Ultralight sleeping bag
» Three-quarter-length self-inflating sleeping pad
» Ultralight one-person tent
» Waterproof pack cover
» Backpacking stove and one cartridge of compressed gas
» Small backpacking pot and lid
» Spoon
» Camp cup
» Water bottles: three 1-liter soda bottles (used all three only when bivouacking without access to potable water)
» Ditty bag of minimal toiletries (biodegradable soap, toothbrush, toothpaste, floss, deodorant, skin lotion, medications)
» First-aid kit: ibuprofen, adhesive bandages, Neosporin, gauze, small roll of self-adhering bandage, a few alcohol swabs
» Blister kit: moleskin, KT tape, adhesive tape, blister bandages, small scissors
» Sunscreen and lip balm
» Camping towel (I use a light cotton dish towel: absorbs well, dries quickly)
» Ditty bag of "tools" (lighter, waterproof container of matches, multitool or knife, 15 feet of parachute cord for hanging food or drying clothes, a foot or so of duct tape folded into a small packet, half dozen safety pins, small sewing kit, emergency supply of water purification tablets, handful of firestarters)
» Emergency toilet kit (resealable plastic bag with backpacking spade, toilet paper, hand sanitizer, feminine hygiene products, and extra plastic bags for used TP)
» Cell phone (functions as compass, camera, GPS) and charger
» Wallet (I use a resealable plastic bag for ID, credit card, and cash)
» Glasses
» Paperback book
» Small journal for notes and sketching, pens, tiny watercolor set
» Two bandanas (multipurpose)
» Headlamp
» Maps and tide table printout (in resealable plastic bag)
» Ultralight waterproof jacket and pants

Lightweight hiking pants with zip-off legs
» Lightweight fleece jacket
» One quick-dry long-sleeve pullover shirt
» Two quick-dry T-shirts
» Underwear (minimal)
» Long underwear bottoms
» One pair running shorts

Three pairs wool socks (one reserved for camp)
» Flip-flops
» Lightweight wool hat
» Lightweight gloves
» Neck gaiter
» Sun hat
» Sunglasses
» Trail runners

due to almost constant wind, I've almost always worn long pants on the OCT, but now and then you get a hot day when shorts are appealing. One of my companions swears by her lightweight sun-protective long-sleeve hoodie; she says she never gets overheated, and she carries a lot less sunscreen.

Footwear. Trail runners or lightweight waterproof hiking boots are good choices on the OCT; both are lightweight and have gripping soles that will help you safely negotiate slippery rocks and roots. After years of backpacking in trail runners (the choice of many ultralight long-distance hikers), I've come to prefer lightweight waterproof boots on the OCT. They don't fill up with sand, and my feet stay dry even when pounding through shallow creeks (no pausing to take off shoes). Mine weigh just 4 ounces per shoe more than my trail runners, which isn't nothing but isn't bad. One downside of Gore-Tex boots on

These trail runners held up pretty well during a 200-mile hike on the OCT.

the OCT: sand can get worked into the layers of laminated fabric and lodge there forever. Wearing lightweight gaiters may help. Get shoes at least a half size larger than usual to avoid blisters, and be sure to train in the footwear (including socks) you plan to wear on the trail, preferably for a month or more prior to your trek.

Setting out on a long-distance hike wearing your favorite old pair of broken-in boots is a rookie mistake. You may find, too late, that the soles of your old boots no longer give you a good grip on muddy trails, or even worse, they may fall off. FedEx has been known to deliver to campgrounds, but that's a hassle you're better off avoiding. If you've come to the OCT after peeling off the Pacific Crest Trail, whatever footwear you were using there will work here.

ON THE TRAIL

Experienced backcountry backpackers will need to rethink some of their routines on this close-to-civilization trail. Ocean tides and the coastal landscape present unique challenges.

Wayfinding

Most of the route is marked with the blue-and-white OCT logo; look for it on trail posts, on street signposts, or even nailed to trees. The route markers are usually accurate, but they're not always where you need them to be. You may also see older wooden posts stamped with COAST TRAIL or OREGON COAST TRAIL, which aren't always up to date, so beware. FarOut Guides is developing a map app for the OCT in concert with this book; look for it at faroutguides.com. Because it provides real-time updates from users, it is especially helpful.

Oregon State Parks and the Oregon Coast Visitor Association (OCVA) both have maps posted online. However, OCVA maps include details targeted to day hikers, such as campgrounds that aren't actually on the OCT route, and they also lack beach access numbers so use them with care. If you use these online maps, I recommend using them in concert with this guidebook and the FarOut map app.

Know the Tides

Most of the time—when the beach is wide with no obstructions, or you're spending most of the day on headland trails—the tide isn't a concern on the OCT. But some points (smaller headlands) can be rounded only at low to mid-tide. The mouths of some creeks and smaller rivers can be waded only at low tide.

There are various sources of tide predictions available on the internet, including the handy free app Tide Alert (NOAA)-USA. Note that the timing of high and low tide varies significantly north to south. If you don't want to be

Look for this blue-and-white OCT logo to help you find your way; here, the sign indicates the path down to the beach at the mouth of Sixes River (Section 4, Leg 5).

checking your phone daily, consider printing out a tide chart from Hatfield Marine Science Center (search for "tides" at hmsc.oregonstate.edu); it gives tide predictions for the beach at Newport. In addition, you can save the chart on your phone. Then, depending on where you are, either add or subtract the minutes indicated in this chart to get a prediction for approximately when to expect high or low tide in your general location on the coast:

Tide Adjustments from Newport South Beach

Location	High tide	Low tide
Seaside	+6 minutes	+93 minutes
Barview	+1 minute	+22 minutes
Pacific City	+14 minutes	+38 minutes
Lincoln City	+7 minutes	+39 minutes
Newport South Beach	0 minutes	0 minutes
Florence (beach)	−12 minutes	−1 minute
Winchester Bay	−1 minute	−1 minute
Charleston	−11 minutes	−4 minutes
Bandon	−18 minutes	−6 minutes
Port Orford	−28 minutes	−23 minutes
Brookings	−40 minutes	−30 minutes

(Source: Oregon State University Hatfield Marine Science Center)

Hiking on the Highway Shoulder

If you're able to get boat rides across bays where they're available, less than 10 percent of your OCT hike will follow the shoulder of US 101. In most cases these are short stretches of a mile or so that get you around a steep cliff or allow you to access a bridge across a river that cannot be waded, for instance. But there are a few places where the highway shoulder hiking stretches to several miles. Efforts are under way to acquire land and construct new trails to minimize the highway hiking—but that's of no use to you setting out today. It's not all bad; it's often very scenic, but you need to keep your wits about you and watch out for wide vehicles such as motor homes and loaded log trucks. When the OCT route leads to US 101:

» Minimize your highway shoulder hiking by hitching rides, calling a cab, taking the bus, or arranging for boat shuttles across major bay mouths and by doing careful wayfinding so you don't miss a transition back to a trail or beach.

» Stay safe on the highway shoulder by walking single file, facing the traffic.

» Where the shoulder is very narrow (or nonexistent), you may have to walk in the bike lane, which is another reason to walk facing traffic; US 101 is a popular cycling route, and you'll need to step off for bikes.

» If possible, hike long highway stretches in the morning before traffic picks up.

Half of the road walking on the OCT isn't on US 101 but is on quiet side roads such as scenic Otter Crest Loop (Section 3, Leg 2).

Trail Hygiene

By trail hygiene, I'm referring mainly to defecation. There are a lot of toilets along the OCT. Toilet locations are noted on maps in this book. Where you see a toilet icon but no water icon, that typically means it is a vault toilet as opposed to a flush toilet. You may find additional portable toilets along the way in summer. Remember that the Oregon Coast is not a wilderness, so please use toilets whenever possible.

However, you should also carry the means to make an emergency pit stop: a lightweight trowel for digging, toilet paper, a resealable plastic bag for used TP, and hand sanitizer. Dig a hole at least six inches deep, preferably in forest soil, where feces will eventually break down, or in sandy dunes if you must. Make your hole in a remote location—not in someone's front yard, near the trail, or where children play—and refill it after you do your business. Please pack out your used TP, as it takes an extremely long time for buried toilet paper to decompose. Never attempt to burn used TP, which just creates a wildfire hazard. I have not explored the use of poop bags (the type designed for human use), as is required in some wilderness areas, but *you* could. I do not recommend burying your poo in the sand in the intertidal zone, although this is recommended on Northern California's Lost Coast; with steep cliffs down to the beach, apparently there is no other option there. You have a lot of other options on the OCT to properly dispose of your waste.

The sign says it all. There are a lot of toilets on the OCT; use them.

As for quick pee stops, that should not be a problem. If you're far from a toilet, you're probably on a remote stretch of beach and not on a crowded beach or in town. Women may find a pee cloth to be handy; this product is waterproof on one side, absorbent on the other, and you hang it off your backpack and rinse it out at night (for hygiene reasons, I wouldn't use just any rag). Or consider keeping TP and a resealable plastic bag handy or wearing a lightweight sanitary pad to absorb drips.

Drinking Water

I do not recommend drinking even filtered surface water while hiking the OCT, as backpackers typically do from headwater streams high in the mountains. By the time water has flowed down to the shoreline, it may have been contaminated by highway runoff and by herbicides or pesticides from agriculture and industrial tree farms, not to mention the usual contamination from animal (and human) feces.

Fortunately, there are a lot of sources of potable water along the OCT; they are marked on the maps in this book. The only places where you may have to carry more than a single day's supply of water are in the Oregon Dunes in Section 4 and in Section 5, where water sources are much fewer, as well as anytime you do dispersed camping. Take note of your day's water sources. Plan ahead and you will almost never need to carry more than a day's worth of water. Make sure at least one water bottle or bag you bring is short enough to fit under the faucet at rest area sinks.

Cell Phone Service and Charging

Depending on your service provider, you should have cell phone service on much, but not all, of the OCT. Coverage is worse on the sparsely populated south coast and when ducking into ravines or the shadows of headlands. Many (maybe eventually all) hiker-biker camps have cell phone charging stations. Otherwise, you'll need to be creative. I've recharged in park restrooms and behind the counter at friendly bars. You could carry a portable solar charger, but you'll have to balance the convenience and connectivity against the added weight.

Campfires

Beach fires are allowed on open sand, west of the vegetation line. What's not allowed are fires in or near piles of driftwood or against drift logs, which tend to keep burning long after you're gone. Keep your fire small. Public and private campgrounds typically have fire pits and have firewood available for purchase. Never build a fire without a fire ring if you camp in the forest and make sure all fires are fully extinguished before you leave.

Many hiker-biker camps have covered kiosks where you can charge your cell phone; hikers also sometimes repurpose RV charging posts, as this scene at Bullards Beach State Park attests.

LISTEN

The scenery is what draws most people to the Oregon Coast, but the sounds may be what you remember best:

» The chorus of Pacific tree frogs at dawn and dusk at a lakeside campground in the dunes.

» Varied thrushes and Swainson's thrushes singing at dawn in the forest on Tillamook Head.

» The syncopated moaning of the buoys at the mouth of Coos Bay drifting through the campground at Sunset Bay.

» The wash of waves that never ceases; even where the highway runs close to the coast, the ocean overwhelms the sounds of traffic.

Coastal Hazards

The ocean off Oregon may be colder and rougher than what you're used to. Some hazards are obvious, some less so.

Cold Ocean Water. Oregon's ocean ranges from about 47 degrees to 52 degrees Fahrenheit year-round, inviting hypothermia for anyone in it for very long. It's really not swimmable without a wetsuit. Take dips in freshwater lakes and small rivers instead.

Rip Currents (Undertows). Oregon's coast is prone to rip currents that pull unsuspecting swimmers away from shore. Should you get caught in one, try to stay calm and remain afloat in a horizontal position, swimming or drifting parallel to the shore until you get out of the current, then attempt to swim ashore at a different spot. Better yet, stay out of the ocean beyond wading.

Logs at the Surf Line. Avoid them. Incoming waves can lift them unexpectedly, throw you off if you've climbed on, and possibly crush you.

Rock Shelves along the Shore. They can be wet and slippery; if a wave rushes in and knocks you off your feet, you may be unable to climb out due to the cold water and turbulence.

Sneaker Waves. These are unusually large waves that surge up the beach from an otherwise calm ocean, catching beachgoers off guard with sometimes deadly results. Meteorologists have found that they are generated by far-off storms and they nearly always occur from October through April, peaking in November and March. This means that actual sneaker waves are not a big issue during the main OCT hiking season, but you can still be surprised by an unusually high wave in summer. It's always smart to keep an eye on the ocean while walking on the appealingly hard, wet sand close to the surf.

Creek and River Mouth Crossings. Heed the warnings in this book about which rivers must be crossed at low tide. Trekking poles can help you keep your balance if the water is knee-high or better. Avoid crossing while the tide is running out strongly.

Vehicles. Cars are not allowed on the beach on most of the Oregon Coast. The most notable exception is on Day 1 of a southbound hike, between Fort Stevens State Park and Gearhart. But don't be discouraged; beach driving has been outlawed almost everywhere else in Oregon. Where cars are allowed, keep your eyes open, as many drivers don't observe posted speed limits.

You are also likely to see (and hear) dune buggies, also known as all-terrain vehicles (ATVs) or off-highway vehicles (OHVs), in the vicinity of Sand Lake (Section 2) and in the Oregon Dunes (Section 4). Their use is strictly regulated to limited areas of dune and beach; in some places you may hear them but not see them. Unless you wander into the dunes in an OHV area, OHVs are a danger only to their own drivers and passengers.

Poison Oak. Poison oak is a native plant that, if touched, can cause a very unpleasant rash lasting ten days to two weeks. It is the only poisonous plant you need to watch for on the Oregon Coast, and then only south of Port Orford. It can appear as ground cover, a shrub, or a vine snaking up tree trunks: look for shiny, lobed leaves clustered in threes, turning bright red in the fall. The rash is caused by urushiol oil, which covers the leaves and stems. Don't touch it and don't let your clothes or shoes touch it, as the oil can rub off on your hands and cause a rash on any part of your body you then touch. Some people aren't sensitive to it; the rest of us get a rash that begins as itchy bumps

Poison oak leaves are lobed and arranged in threes. Watch for this plant south of Port Orford and do your best to avoid touching it.

Sometime in the next few hundred years there will be a large earthquake, followed by a tsunami, on the Oregon Coast. If the ground shakes, head inland and uphill.

about a day after exposure and can progress to weeping blisters (touching the blister fluid doesn't spread the rash; only contact with urushiol oil does).

If you do touch it, rinse off thoroughly with a lot of cold water as soon as possible. If you get the rash, there's not much you can do but ride it out, though calamine lotion or hydrocortisone cream might reduce itching and blistering, and an antihistamine may help relieve itching. In serious cases, consult a doctor.

Tsunami. You are certain to see signs along the highway and in state parks letting you know you're entering or leaving a tsunami inundation zone and directing where you should go if you feel an earthquake. Tsunamis are an extremely infrequent phenomenon on the Oregon Coast but one that hikers should be aware of: be prepared, not scared. Most tsunamis worldwide are triggered by earthquakes at fault lines on the ocean floor. Two very different types of tsunamis are known to occasionally strike the Oregon Coast.

A *distant tsunami* is one caused by a very large earthquake hundreds or thousands of miles away: for instance, on the coast of Japan or Alaska. These tsunamis take hours to cross the ocean to Oregon, and typically by the time they arrive they have diminished greatly. Many towns on the Oregon Coast have a system of tsunami warning sirens. If you are not near a town, be aware that arriving distant tsunamis are preceded by a sudden, significant withdrawal of water at the shore. If you notice the ocean suddenly receding far more than normal, simply move farther up or off the beach.

Distant tsunamis are rare and typically are only dangerous in bays and harbors or near the waterline on the beach. Other than the tsunami following the 2011 earthquake in Japan (which, by the time it reached Oregon, was perceptible in only a few harbors), the last distant tsunami large enough to do even minor damage to the region was in 1964, and prior to that possibly in 1899—both from earthquakes off of the coast of Alaska.

A *local tsunami* is an even less common but far more dangerous phenomenon, and the warning sign is unmistakable: It is preceded by a huge earthquake *here*. An underwater fault line called the Cascadia Subduction Zone runs just off the Pacific Northwest coast from Vancouver Island south to Cape Mendocino, California (south of Eureka), causing a megaquake here roughly every 250 to 700 years that, in turn, triggers a tsunami that strikes the coast twelve to thirty minutes later (quicker on the southern Oregon Coast). It's been 300-plus years since the last such quake. If you happen to be on the beach when a large earthquake strikes (four to six minutes of severe shaking), head as fast as you can to the highest ground you can reach and stay there for at least twenty-four hours. Read my book *The Next Tsunami: Living on a Restless Coast* to learn more.

Animals to Enjoy

Wildlife-watching is part of the pleasure of an Oregon Coast Trail trek. If you move quietly through the forest and are attentive on the beach, it will enrich your experience.

Elk. Elk are a common sight on the Oregon Coast, more common than deer, especially at dawn and dusk in open meadows such as those on the south side of Tillamook Head and on Cascade Head. Keep your distance, especially during the spring calving season; cow elk are fiercely protective of their young.

Birds. Bald eagles have made as strong a comeback on the Oregon Coast as they have elsewhere and can be seen year-round. In June and July masses of seabirds—common murres, cormorants, and more—nest on offshore rocks; Cannon Beach is known for the tufted puffins that nest in burrows on Haystack Rock. Gulls are common, of course, though the species you might see varies by place and season. Listen for the song of the varied thrush, Swainson's thrush, Pacific wren, and other songbirds in the forest.

Elk are a common sight on the edge of the Necanicum Estuary between Gearhart and Seaside.
(Photo by PacificLight Images)

Marine Mammals. Watch for seal heads peeking through the surf near river mouths. From high points, look for gray whales spouting offshore. Seals and sea lions can be seen lounging on offshore rocks.

Animals to Avoid

Most negative animal encounters involve food. To avoid such interactions and help protect animals from associating humans wih food, don't leave food sitting out; use critter-proof lockboxes in hiker-biker camps where available. Dispose of your garbage properly.

Raccoons, Rodents, and Jays. These animals have learned that hikers equal food; they are a scourge in developed campgrounds, where they will chew (or peck) through packs to get at any available food. The same is true in well-used backcountry campsites such as the backpacker camp on Tillamook Head. Store your food in lockers where available, such as at many hiker-biker camps;

otherwise consider caching your food in a sturdy stuff sack hanging from a branch or from a line you rig between two trees. There's no guarantee it won't be pilfered, but critters will go for easier pickings first.

Mosquitoes. Mosquitoes aren't much of a problem on the OCT, especially on the beach itself, but step into the moist dunes and you can get swarmed, especially in early summer. Carry a small container of insect repellant with 15 to 30 percent DEET, or your deterrent of choice. DEET has been shown to be safe at those levels even for pregnant women and children, but don't use it on infants under two months.

Ticks. In decades of hiking on the Oregon Coast, only once have I seen a single tick. It was while I camped in a grassy area in the Oregon Dunes. But I have friends who picked off multiple ticks while camping in the dunes. It's something to be aware of.

Black Bears. Bears on the Oregon Coast tend to be small—for example, females grow to just 5 or 6 feet long and 125–200 pounds. They are shy and mostly vegetarian; if you see one, it will probably be running away from you. But avoid getting between a bear and food, or a sow and her cub.

Cougars. They're around, but their presence should not overly concern you. There is no record of a cougar killing a human in modern history on the Oregon Coast. In the very unlikely event that you encounter one in the wild, stand your ground, maintain eye contact, and put on your pack to make yourself look larger. While continuing to maintain eye contact, back away slowly, and speak firmly. Don't run.

Blisters

Chances are you'll get at least one. I've observed that even if you don't get blisters during 6-to-8-mile training hikes, once you exceed 10 miles, particularly while carrying weight, things can happen to your feet that haven't happened before, including blisters. Here is my best advice.

Preventing Blisters. Blister prevention begins at the store when you're buying footwear and continues on the trail.

» Buy footwear at least a half size larger than usual. It might seem counterintuitive—feet sloshing around in big boots would seem to rub more—but your feet swell, and sloshing isn't as bad as rubbing. This is my number one piece of advice, based on personal experience, and it is echoed by the likes of trainers at the National Outdoor Leadership School.

If you're on the trail and you're getting blisters and you don't want to stop and buy bigger boots, try switching to lighter socks so your feet aren't stuffed so tightly into your boots.

» Break in your new footwear, preferably for a month or more, so your feet are used to your boots and your boots have adjusted to your feet. This is less an issue with trail runners; it is more of an issue with leather boots, which not many people wear anymore.

» Reduce your weight: pack weight and body weight, wherever and whenever you can. A lighter pack will definitely reduce your chance of getting blisters, especially if you're a big person who loves to hike and backpack.

» Keep your mileage reasonable. This is hard on the OCT, where you may have to hike many miles to get to legal camping. If you're on the larger side or you like to pack your luxuries, opt for a less ambitious itinerary.

» Keep your feet clean. If you stop to wade, use a bandana to dry your feet thoroughly and dust off sand before continuing.

» Consider socks, powder, or gel. You'll find a lot of opinions out there about wearing two layers of socks, powdering your feet, using blister prevention gel, or whatever. I say use what works. I wear one pair of lightweight wool socks. I put on a clean pair every morning. As long as my boots aren't too small or my socks too bulky, this works for me.

KT tape and craft scissors are the soul of a minimal blister prevention kit.

Treating Blisters. Carry tape and other supplies so you can quickly treat blisters while they're still small.

» At the first sign of a hot spot—any slight discomfort in your feet—stop and tape up. Anything will work, even duct tape. The best product is KT tape, which is stretchy and conforms well to the curves of toes and feet. I carry a small pair of craft scissors for this purpose.

» If an actual blister has formed, thick moleskin is the ticket. Use those scissors to cut a doughnut and fit it around the blister. Add a strip of adhesive tape across the top to keep it in place. Some Australian hikers I met turned me on to using a tuft of lambswool for extra padding. I reapply fresh moleskin every morning if blisters have established themselves.

» Bigger blisters may benefit from blister bandages, which are designed to be put on and kept on, for days even.

» To pop or not to pop? Opinions vary. You don't want to risk introducing bacteria and causing an infection. The following technique was taught to me by a medical doctor who learned it from other hikers on the Camino de Santiago in Spain. It works for me but use it at your own risk: Sterilize the blister area and a threaded sewing needle with alcohol. Insert the needle at the base of the blister and out the other side, close to the base of the blister, and draw the thread through, leaving an end hanging out each side. (If you do it right, puncturing only the blister and not tender skin beneath, it should not hurt.) Snip the thread so both ends are about a quarter of an inch long, and gently squeeze the blister liquid out. Leave the threads in place to keep the tiny needle holes from closing up, and let the threads eventually slough off on their own.

What's Your Long-Distance-Hiking Style?

Long-distance hikers tend to fall into one of two camps: EFI or Hike Your Own Hike.

EFI is short for Every F—ing Inch. Hiking EFI means never hitching a ride or calling a cab to avoid a highway shoulder walk. It means not taking that 5-mile excursion train—even if the timing is right and it sounds like fun. It means not lingering an extra day in a perfect spot with perfect weather if that means hitching a ride through the next leg to stay on schedule. EFI does give you bragging rights and a certain inner satisfaction. But EFI hikers should remember that the OCT route is not actually set in stone, and if you're unable to get a boat ride across a big bay, you'll be hiking miles of highway shoulder if you don't opt for a ride of some kind.

Hiking Your Own Hike, on the other hand, means making fun your prime directive. That may mean getting a ride to avoid walking through a tunnel with no sidewalks and too many motor homes or to avoid a long and unrewarding highway stretch. It may mean skipping entire legs because you have limited

Every September, North Coast Land Conservancy organizes CoastWalk Oregon, three consecutive days of hiking on a section of the Oregon Coast Trail, to raise funds for coastal conservation. (Photo by Carolyn Propst)

time and want to linger longer here or there. It may mean making one more espresso or brewpub stop than is entirely necessary and adjusting your plans accordingly. It may mean leaving the trail sooner than planned and returning another year to finish it off.

You choose. However you approach an OCT trek, I hope that you avoid comparing yourself to others, respect your limits, and listen to your body. Think about what you most want out of this trip and plan accordingly. And know that, at the trail's end at Crissey Field State Recreation Site, no one will be checking to make sure you hiked every inch or to confirm that you did it all in one go.

A Note about Safety

Safety is an important concern in all outdoor activities. No guidebook can alert you to every hazard or anticipate the limitations of every reader. Therefore, the descriptions of roads, trails, routes, and natural features in this book are not representations that a particular place or excursion will be safe for your party. When you follow any of the routes described in this book, you assume responsibility for your own safety. Under normal conditions, such excursions require the usual attention to traffic, road and trail conditions, tides, weather, terrain, seasonal closures, the capabilities of your party, and other factors. Because many of the lands in this book are subject to development and/or change of ownership, conditions may have changed since this book was written that make your use of some of these routes unwise. Always check for current conditions, obey posted private property signs, and avoid confrontations with property owners or managers. Keeping informed on current conditions and exercising common sense are the keys to a safe, enjoyable outing.

—Mountaineers Books

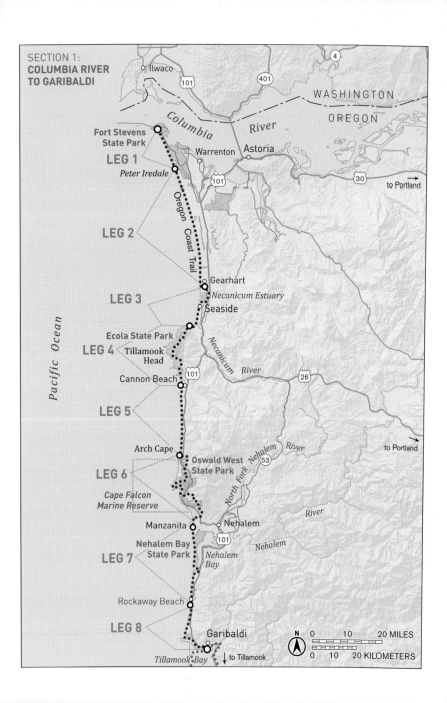

SECTION 1:
**COLUMBIA RIVER
TO GARIBALDI**

WASHINGTON

OREGON

Ilwaco

101

401

4

Columbia

River

Fort Stevens
State Park

Warrenton

Astoria

LEG 1

30

to Portland

Peter Iredale

101

LEG 2

Oregon Coast Trail

Gearhart

LEG 3

Necanicum Estuary

Seaside

Pacific Ocean

Ecola State Park

LEG 4 Tillamook
Head

Necanicum

River

101

26

Cannon Beach

LEG 5

Arch Cape

to Portland

Oswald West
State Park

Nehalem

River

53

LEG 6

*Cape Falcon
Marine Reserve*

North Fork

Manzanita

Nehalem

River

LEG 7

Nehalem Bay
State Park

101

Nehalem

*Nehalem
Bay*

Rockaway Beach

LEG 8

Garibaldi

N

0   10   20 MILES

0   10   20 KILOMETERS

Tillamook Bay

↓ to Tillamook

Depending on the tides, you may or may not be able to walk through the opening off Chapman Point (Leg 4) on your way to Haystack Rock at Cannon Beach.

SECTION 1
Columbia River to Garibaldi

Distance
68.3 miles

Cumulative OCT miles
Miles 0 to 68.3

Elevation gain/loss
+5000/–5025 feet

Headland summits
Tillamook Head (1200 feet), Arch Cape (540 feet), Cape Falcon (980 feet), Neahkahnie Mountain (1560 feet)

Max distance between campgrounds
21.9 miles (Fort Stevens State Park hiker-biker camp to Tillamook Head backpacker camp, Legs 2, 3, and 4) and 23.9 miles (Cannon Beach midtown to Nehalem Bay State Park, Legs 5, 6, and 7)

Max distance between lodging
17.1 miles (Arch Cape to Manzanita, Leg 6)

Water availability
Good

Boat shuttle
One (Leg 7)

Legs
1. Columbia River to *Peter Iredale*
2. *Peter Iredale* to Gearhart
3. Gearhart to Tillamook Head
4. Tillamook Head to Cannon Beach
5. Cannon Beach to Arch Cape
6. Arch Cape to Manzanita
7. Manzanita to Rockaway Beach
8. Rockaway Beach to Garibaldi

SECTION 1: COLUMBIA RIVER TO GARIBALDI

Not all long-distance trails start with this grand of an entrance. From the viewing platform at the trailhead, you gaze down Oregon's longest, widest beach to a distant blue hump—Tillamook Head, where you will make your first headland ascent. Section 1 of the Oregon Coast Trail is a great introduction to this epic trail because it offers a generous taste of what the OCT is all about. Spectacular views from beaches and high points abound, weather permitting. Popular coastal towns, beaches crammed with tourists, and main streets full of good restaurants and cafés contrast with lonely beaches and forested headlands with little-traveled trail stretches. One bay mouth is easily crossed by boat with no prior arrangements. There are lodging options for inn-to-inn hikers if you reserve ahead, though they may require some long days of hiking in between.

Section 1 also offers hikers some logistical challenges that, though unique to this stretch, are emblematic of the kinds of situations a hiker is likely to find on the Oregon Coast Trail and are atypical of other long-distance trails. Legal camping is scarce at the ends of Legs 2 and 5 as of this writing, and you may have to choose among stealth or dispersed camping, long days of hiking, or perhaps a night in an inn. You'll need to time your walk on Leg 5 carefully to avoid having to detour to the highway shoulder; but even so, it's only a 1-mile hike along the highway—and one of only two short highway stretches in this section.

If you're planning a thru-hike of the Oregon Coast Trail, this is almost certainly where you'll be starting; prevailing north winds during the ideal OCT hiking season (June–September) make a southbound trek the best choice by far. If you're planning a section hike, Section 1 is also a good choice if you can navigate the camping and lodging limitations.

But it's worth working out those kinks. Most of the route is on the beach, and the hard-packed sand—washed down the Columbia River over eons—makes for good walking. Beach stretches are separated by iconic headlands with well-established trails. Every day you'll reach a different beach town, each with its own personality. You'll encounter plenty of tourists on popular beach

The view south from the high point on Neahkahnie Mountain stretches to the mouth of Nehalem Bay and beyond (Leg 6).

stretches—and they'll quickly fall away as you walk on to more remote beaches or ascend a headland.

If you're coming from out of town, consider spending a night or two in Astoria before you start walking. It's about a half hour's drive east of the trailhead, but you can take a taxi from your lodgings to the trailhead when you're ready to start. Stock up on trail food in Astoria at a supermarket or at the well-stocked Astoria Co-op. The town is rich with history and is incredibly scenic, and it has more brewpubs and cafés than you'll have time to visit. Stretch your legs and see the length of the town on the Astoria Riverwalk. Visit the Columbia River Maritime Museum on the riverfront and check out the Astoria Column for a spectacular view of the lower Columbia region. With a car you can visit nearby Fort Clatsop, part of the Lewis and Clark National Historical Park, for one perspective on the region's human history. Alternately, you could stay in Cannon Beach, Seaside, or Gearhart and arrange a taxi to drop you at the trailhead your first morning.

Section 1 passes through the traditional homelands of the Clatsop and Tillamook people.

ACCESS

The northern trailhead for the Oregon Coast Trail is at Fort Stevens State Park, beach parking lot C, or, possibly through 2024, parking lot B. (See sidebar, "Construction—and Reconstruction—of the South Jetty.") There is no cost to park here, but you need to make prior arrangements to leave your car overnight, here or elsewhere in the park (see Contacts). Logistically it may be simpler to leave your car in a town such as Seaside and take a taxi or bus to your starting point, especially if you are returning via bus. The closest you can get by bus is Fort Stevens State Park campground, which is 4.8 miles from the trailhead. Accordingly, some hikers spend two nights at the hiker-biker campground here (a 1-mile detour off of the OCT); Day 1 they walk the beach north to the trailhead and back, doubling Leg 1. Then they start their actual southbound walk on Day 2 with Leg 2.

The southern end of Section 1 is at the town of Garibaldi. Cars may be left at the port for free for twenty-four hours, or up to seventy-two hours by prearrangement with the Port of Garibaldi. If you left a car at the north trailhead, return by bus and taxi. See Contacts for Port of Garibaldi and bus information.

SUGGESTED ITINERARIES

The mileage figures in the suggested itineraries below show mileage for each day's recommended hike, to the point where you leave the OCT route to head to camping or lodging. Your actual day's hike may be slightly longer, adding in mileage to lodging

The iron hull of the Peter Iredale *is a reminder of the hazards of ocean travel a century ago.*

or a developed campground (typically 0.1 to 0.3 mile; 1 mile to hiker-biker camp near the *Peter Iredale*). Limited legal camping in Section 1 requires hikers to either hike some very long days, stealth camp on the beach, or opt for lodging such as at a motel or hostel in Gearhart or Seaside.

5 Days Camping		Miles
Day 1	Columbia River to *Peter Iredale*	3.8
Day 2	*Peter Iredale* to Tillamook Head backpacker camp	20.9
Day 3	Tillamook Head to midtown Cannon Beach	6.6
Day 4	Midtown Cannon Beach to Nehalem Bay State Park	23.9
Day 5	Nehalem Bay State Park to Garibaldi	13.1

7 Days Camping + Lodging		Miles
Keep your daily mileage under 20 miles (and thus avoid stealth camping) by staying at a hostel in Seaside on Day 2 and reserving a room at an inn or vacation rental in Arch Cape on Day 5.		
Day 1	Columbia River to *Peter Iredale*	3.8
Day 2	*Peter Iredale* to Seaside Lodge and International Hostel	14
Day 3	Seaside hostel to Tillamook Head backpacker camp	6.9
Day 4	Tillamook Head to midtown Cannon Beach	6.6
Day 5	Midtown Cannon Beach to Arch Cape	5.5
Day 6	Arch Cape to Nehalem Bay State Park	18.4
Day 7	Nehalem Bay State Park to Garibaldi	13.1

7 Days Inn-to-Inn		Miles
Mileage will vary according to exact location of lodging.		
Day 1	Columbia River to 10th Avenue, Gearhart	14.4
Day 2	Gearhart to Avenue U, Seaside	5
Day 3	Seaside to 1st Street, Cannon Beach	11
Day 4	1st Street, Cannon Beach to Arch Cape	6.4
Day 5	Arch Cape to Laneda Avenue, Manzanita	17.1
Day 6	Manzanita to Rockaway Beach	8.5
Day 7	Rockaway Beach to Garibaldi	5.9

IN THE FOOTSTEPS OF LEWIS AND CLARK

In 1803, President Thomas Jefferson commissioned Captains Meriwether Lewis and William Clark to assemble a team of explorers to venture west from St. Louis to the Pacific Ocean, gathering as much information as they could about the people, the landscape, and the plants and animals they encountered. After an eighteen-month journey they reached the mouth of the Columbia, where they established Fort Clatsop, their home during the winter of 1805–6. Their journey accelerated colonization of the West by Euro-Americans—and accelerated the decimation of Indigenous communities, which had already been devastated by disease brought by the earliest seafaring explorers.

A visit to the reconstructed fort just south of Astoria provides insight to hikers about to set off down the Oregon Coast, a land that has been occupied by thriving communities of Native people for thousands of years but which was still terra incognita to the rest of the world in the early 1800s. As you walk along the highway between Gearhart and Seaside, you pass Ne-ah-coxie, which for millennia was a Native village site on the north side of the Necanicum River estuary; in 2020 ownership was returned to the Clatsop-Nehalem Confederated Tribes, who hope to build a traditional plankhouse here.

As you walk the beach past Seaside, you'll be passing the spot where members of the Lewis and Clark party operated a saltworks to preserve and flavor their meat during their stay at Fort Clatsop. When you ascend Tillamook Head and drop down to Cannon Beach, you'll be roughly following the route Captain Clark and other members of the party took to visit the Clatsop village along Ecola Creek (present-day Cannon Beach) to purchase some blubber that the Clatsops had salvaged from a beached whale. And you may relate to the sentiment of their indispensable interpreter Sacagawea, who insisted that she come along on the walk over Tillamook Head after her request was initially denied. As Clark recorded in his journal, "she had traveled a long way with us to see the great waters, and now that monstrous fish was also to be seen, she thought it very hard she could not be permitted to see either."

LEG 1   COLUMBIA RIVER TO *PETER IREDALE*

Distance	3.8 miles
Elevation gain/loss	-35 feet

The OCT's northern trailhead sits on the south jetty of the Columbia River. Look behind the restrooms for the trailhead monument marking the start of the trail along the jetty and down to the beach. (Note: Jetty construction has temporarily moved the trailhead to parking lot B (BA 1B), possibly through 2024. See sidebar, "Construction—and Reconstruction—of the South Jetty.")

The trail through the grassy dunes is crisscrossed with a few social trails; follow the most well-worn path eastward for about 0.3 mile until it winds down to the beach. From here the route is clear: follow the beach south. Enjoy this quiet stretch of beach fronting large Fort Stevens State Park. This leg ends at the *Peter Iredale* shipwreck (BA 2). This leg and the next together represent the longest uninterrupted beach walk on the entire Oregon Coast Trail.

At BA 2 you can access toilets, water, and a 1-mile path to the hiker-biker camp at Fort Stevens State Park. This is the last legal campsite before reaching the backpacker camp atop Tillamook Head, 21.9 miles south of BA2. For this reason, some hikers start their thru-hike with an afternoon hike to the hiker-biker camp here and start their real hike the following morning. Others spend two nights at the hiker-biker camp: They make an out-and-back hike from the camp north to the official trailhead on Day 1 (9.6 miles round-trip), then on Day 2, they pack up

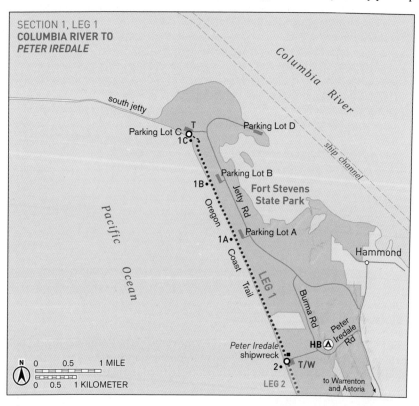

and start their southward journey from the camp. The Fort Stevens hiker-biker camp is near Coffenbury Lake, where you can take a swim, do more hiking, or drop a line if you have fishing gear.

CONSTRUCTION—AND RECONSTRUCTION—OF THE SOUTH JETTY

A major rehabilitation project on the Columbia River's south jetty is under way at this writing, blocking access to the northern OCT trailhead and observation tower at parking lot C (though the restrooms remain open). Possibly through 2024 you may need to start at parking lot B (BA 1B), cutting 1.9 miles off your first day's hike. Alternatively, just start your hike at the Fort Stevens State Park hiker-biker camp, 1 mile from the beach at BA 2. Visit the park's website and look for a "construction advisory" to confirm the current location of the trailhead before you head out.

Entering and exiting the mouth of the Columbia River used to be a dangerous proposition for mariners, with shifting sandbars and sometimes epic waves. A system of three "rubble-mound" jetties was constructed to help maintain a clear channel for seagoing vessels. The first to be built was the south jetty, the location of the Oregon Coast Trail's northern trailhead. Jetty construction began in 1885 using steamships and locomotives to move and place millions of tons of stone. Construction of these jetties caused sand to accumulate north and south of the river's mouth and are the reason the beach is so wide where you start beach walking.

Twin trailhead posts mark the start of the OCT on the Columbia River's south jetty in Fort Stevens State Park.

THE *PETER IREDALE* AND THE GRAVEYARD OF THE PACIFIC

On October 25, 1906, the iron-hulled, four-masted English sailing ship *Peter Iredale* ran aground—with no loss of life—on the beach a few miles south of the mouth of the Columbia en route from Mexico to Portland. It has remained on the beach ever since, rusting away ever so slowly. This shipwreck is one of more than two thousand marine vessels that have been lost near the mouth of the Columbia—it is the centerpiece of the "graveyard of the Pacific," a stretch of coastline from Tillamook Bay north to the northern tip of Vancouver Island. Unpredictable weather conditions, fog, shifting sandbars, tidal rips, and rocky reefs and shorelines have endangered marine vessels since European exploration of the area ramped up in the 1700s. Jetties, modern navigation techniques, bar pilots, a robust Coast Guard presence, and other factors have made passage past and into the Columbia River safer, but mariners know there are still no guarantees.

CAMPING

The only legal camping on this leg is at Fort Stevens State Park ($), which has a hiker-biker area near the ranger station where campers check in.

LODGING

There is no lodging on this leg.

FOOD RESUPPLY

The closest grocery store to Fort Stevens State Park is a mini-mart in Hammond, 1.4 miles from the hiker-biker camp.

Leg 1	Mileage between Waypoints
OCT north trailhead to *Peter Iredale* (BA 2)	3.8

LEG 2 *PETER IREDALE* TO GEARHART

Distance	11.5 miles
Elevation gain/loss	+30 feet

People are allowed to drive cars on the beach south of the *Peter Iredale,* so that's kind of a bummer for hikers. But don't let that turn you off from the OCT: this is the last significant stretch of beach in Oregon where cars are still allowed to drive. The few other stretches tend to be very short and just for immediate beach access, not for driving some distance, as on this leg. Stay alert for vehicles as you walk the beach; not all drivers observe the 25 mph speed limit.

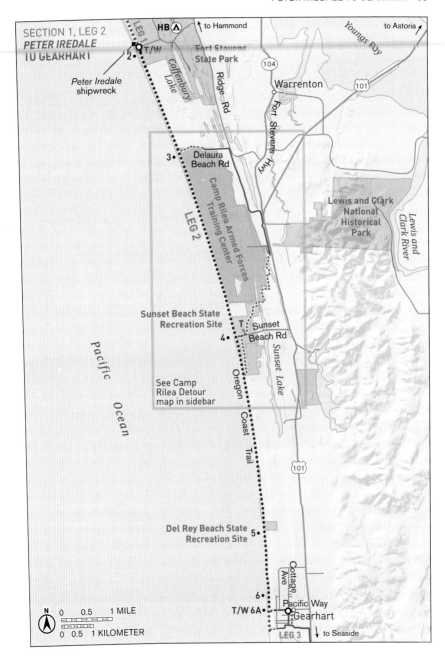

SECTION 1, LEG 2
PETER IREDALE
TO GEARHART

Peter Iredale
shipwreck

to Hammond

to Astoria

HB

LEG 1

T/W

Coffenbury Lake

Fort Stevens State Park

Ridge Rd

Warrenton

Fort Stevens Hwy

104

101

Youngs Bay

2

3

Delaura Beach Rd

LEG 2

Camp Rilea Armed Forces Training Center

Lewis and Clark National Historical Park

Lewis and Clark River

Sunset Beach State Recreation Site

Sunset Beach Rd

Sunset Lake

T

4

Pacific Ocean

Oregon Coast Trail

See Camp Rilea Detour map in sidebar

101

Del Rey Beach State Recreation Site

5

Cottage Ave

6

Pacific Way

T/W 6A

Gearhart

LEG 3

to Seaside

N

0   0.5   1 MILE

0   0.5   1 KILOMETER

You'll see cars, but you won't see houses. Virtually the entire shoreline from the south jetty to Gearhart is now under conservation protection by federal or state agencies or a private land trust and has no oceanfront housing.

About two miles past the *Peter Iredale* you'll reach the northwest corner of Camp Rilea (BA 3), a National Guard training camp that fronts 3 miles of ocean beach. Throughout its century-long existence—even, curiously, after passage of the Oregon Beach Bill, which guarantees the public access to the beach—the camp has taken it upon itself to close all 3 miles of its beach frontage when it is conducting live weapons training in the nearby dunes. This occurs frequently, year-round, more often in summer. During these closures, they take a fifteen-minute break once every hour to allow vehicles to drive through. Fortunately, the camp has recently changed some protocols to begin to accommodate OCT hikers, including sometimes closing only shorter stretches of beach. Hopefully you will breeze through and never see a soldier. But since you're reading up in advance, here is some helpful information:

Stopped by soldier, a hiker weighs waiting or making a fast hike across the soon-to-close stretch of beach adjacent to Camp Rilea.

The Fort to Sea Trail detour around Camp Rilea includes footbridges across dune swale lakes.

» The camp now announces planned beach closures on its website (see Contacts); check here to find out if the range will be "hot" (beach closed) or "cold" (beach open) when you plan to hike through. No guarantees, though; the schedule can change at the last minute.

» If the closure area is short (as little as 1.25 miles), soldiers may allow you to quickly hike through or even give you a ride during a break in firing. If the entire 3 miles is closed and vehicles are waiting to go through, consider hitching a ride in the back of a pickup truck during the next break in the firing.

» If you are stopped by soldiers at the northern boundary (BA 3), indicating the entire 3-mile beach is closed and will be for the rest of the day, and you don't want to try hitching a ride during a pause in the firing, consider taking a detour route around the camp. It's an interesting hike through the dunes and over a couple of dune swale lakes on substantial footbridges, but it adds 2.2 miles to your day.

DETOURING AROUND CAMP RILEA

You've just started your epic trek down the Oregon Coast Trail, and 5.8 miles in you are stopped by a soldier at BA 3. What to do? One option is to detour around the camp, adding 2.2 miles to your day's hike. The 5.9-mile route includes a portion of the Fort to Sea Trail, built to commemorate the 200th anniversary of the Lewis and Clark Expedition's arrival at the mouth of the Columbia in 1805; it roughly traces the route that expedition members took from their winter quarters at Fort Clatsop to the ocean beach, where they established a saltworks near the present-day town of Seaside.

Walk east, toward the BA 3 sign, onto Delaura Beach Road, a sand road with epic potholes filled with knee-deep water in winter but merely mid-calf-deep

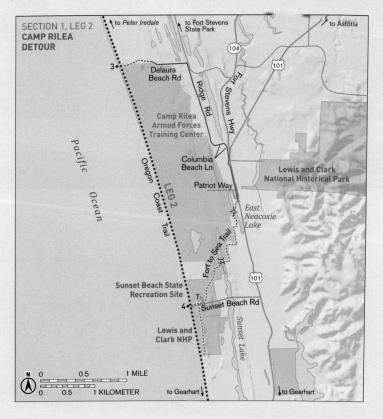

in summer, when you may be able to entirely skirt them. In 1 mile turn right onto (paved) Ridge Road. Follow it south, then east where it becomes Columbia Beach Lane, then briefly south again before reaching US 101. Walk the highway shoulder south 0.5 mile, cross Patriot Way, and walk down a mown grass strip to intersect the (paved, briefly) Fort to Sea Trail; follow it south (do not go east into the tunnel). Here you are 3.4 miles from where you left the beach. Follow the signed Fort to Sea Trail as it winds south and west 2.1 miles more across sand dunes, footbridges crossing dune swale lakes, pastures, and forest to emerge behind the restrooms at the Sunset Beach State Recreation Site parking area. Walk the road west 0.4 mile to return to the beach at BA 4.

At Sunset Beach (BA 4), you have the option of ducking into the trees for a bit. Take the access road east, then just behind the sign indicating a pedestrian crossing look for an unmarked trail heading south into the dunes. It runs for 0.7 mile through a stretch of land managed by the Lewis and Clark National Historical Park, ending at a T junction; follow the sand trail right to return to the beach.

Leave the beach at the 10th Avenue access (BA 6) if you plan to spend the night at McMenamins Gearhart Hotel. Otherwise, continue south to the Pacific Way beach access (BA 6A). You can't see the sign for BA 6A from the beach, so look for footsteps; you'll see the sign from the top of the foredune. Follow the path through the dunes to the end of Pacific Way. Just inland you'll find public restrooms next to the city tennis courts. The center of town is just a block farther, at Cottage Avenue, where you'll find one or two cafés. It's possible you will find a grocery store, but at this writing there isn't one here.

CAMPING

There are no developed campsites in this leg. But you have to sleep somewhere. Although state park officials urge hikers to not camp on the beach here, they do little enforcement, and state parks have not yet taken any steps toward developing legal camping options while continuing to promote use of the OCT. If you do camp, I advise that you do so in the vicinity of Sunset Beach (BA 4), where you can access the toilets at the parking area and where you are not in front of neighborhoods. You will need to carry water; none is available from the *Peter Iredale* to Gearhart.

LODGING

Most vacation rentals and other lodging in Gearhart seem to require a minimum two-night stay. An exception is McMenamins Gearhart Hotel, which also offers breakfast and dinner on-site.

FOOD RESUPPLY

McMenamins Gearhart Hotel has a full-service restaurant. Limited café and no grocery options in downtown Gearhart exist as of this writing.

Leg 2	Mileage between Waypoints
Peter Iredale to Delaura Beach Road (BA 3)	2.1
BA 3 to Sunset Beach (BA 4)	3.7
BA 4 to Del Rey Beach (BA 5)	3.5
BA 5 to 10th Avenue, Gearhart (BA 6)	1.3
BA 6 to Pacific Way (BA 6A)	0.5
BA 6A to Cottage Avenue	0.4

LEG 3   GEARHART TO TILLAMOOK HEAD

Distance	5.3 miles
Elevation gain/loss	+160/–30 feet

Gearhart is a quiet village with minimal tourist facilities besides golf courses. In contrast, Seaside is a lively tourist-oriented town with a lot of places to eat and sleep.

You might be tempted to follow the beach all the way to the end of the sand spit at the mouth of the Necanicum River. You might even be tempted to try to wade the Necanicum River mouth. Neither of these is recommended. Even at low tide in summer, the Necanicum is too deep to safely wade. And the mudflats at the edge of the estuary are soft and slow to walk in the best of circumstances. Rather than try to walk the edge of the estuary to the bridge on US 101, walk through Gearhart.

From the beach at BA 6A, follow Pacific Way a couple of blocks to the crossroads at the center of town. From here, walk south on Cottage Avenue to F Street, following the main traffic route; jog left, then right, then left again onto G Street and follow it east to US 101. If you miss BA 6A, you can also leave the beach at the west end of G Street, 0.6 mile farther down the beach.

Alternatively, instead of going south on Cottage Avenue, go east a half block and turn south on the Ridge Path, which follows a dune ridge through the trees and past cottages. Where it ends at F Street, follow the directions above to US 101.

Walk south on the highway shoulder for 0.6 mile, crossing Neawanna Creek, and immediately veer right on 24th Avenue, then left on N. Holladay Drive. At 12th Avenue, turn west and continue to the beach.

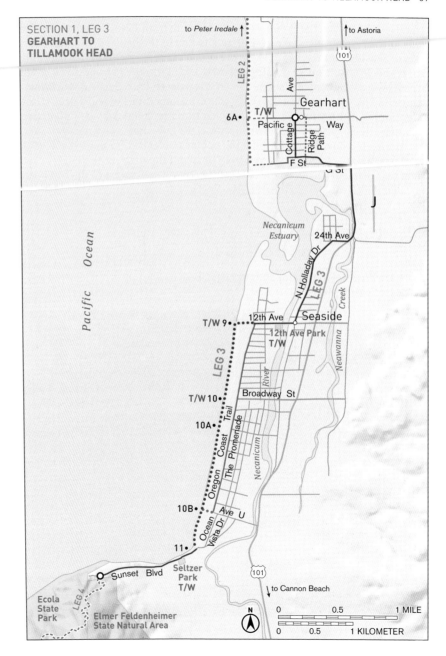

A raised sidewalk—the Promenade—runs south from 12th Avenue to Avenue U along the beachfront; you can walk this in lieu of the beach if you like. For a taste of Seaside's tourist heart, leave the beach or the Prom at the Turnaround, where the Prom juts out at a statue of Lewis and Clark (BA 10), and stroll down Broadway past the chowder shops and arcade palaces. It's 0.5 mile down Broadway to US 101, where just to the south there is a supermarket and a drug store.

Continuing south from BA 10, the beach turns to cobbles as you approach Tillamook Head; this spot is known locally as the Cove and is popular with surfers. At BA 11, follow a path through the cobbles to Sunset Boulevard. Fill your water bottles at Seltzer Park if you plan to spend the night at the backpacker camp on Tillamook Head. Follow Sunset Boulevard southwest to the trailhead for Tillamook Head.

HAZARDS
The mouth of the Necanicum River cannot be safely waded.

CAMPING
There are no developed campsites in Leg 2. Beach camping is not allowed anywhere on Seaside Beach.

The Ridge Path takes you off sidewalks and onto a dirt path past backyards in Gearhart.

A path snakes through the cobbles at the Cove on the way to the Tillamook Head trailhead.

LODGING

Seaside has plenty of lodging at a wide range of prices. Backpackers might consider a night at Seaside Lodge and International Hostel, on N. Holladay Drive 0.1 mile south of the OCT off of 12th Avenue. The hostel offers private and shared dorm rooms; let them know you are a walk-in and you'll get a discount on a dorm room.

FOOD RESUPPLY

Seaside has many eateries. There is a supermarket 0.5 mile from the beach on US 101 south of Broadway and a smaller grocery store three blocks east of the beach on Avenue U.

Leg 3	Mileage between Waypoints
Cottage Avenue, Gearhart, to US 101 at G Street	0.8
G Street to end of 12th Avenue, Seaside (BA 9)	1.7
BA 9 to Avenue U (BA 10B)	1.6
BA 10B to the Cove (BA 11)	0.4
BA 11 to north trailhead, Tillamook Head	0.8

LEG 4   TILLAMOOK HEAD TO CANNON BEACH

Distance	10.7 miles
Elevation gain/loss	+1870/–2030 feet

Tillamook Head is the OCT hiker's first headland ascent, one that slowly comes into focus on the walk south from the Columbia River. The head was logged beginning in the 1880s, but the shorefront was acquired by Oregon State Parks in the 1930s, forming the nucleus of what is today Ecola State Park. State Parks acquired more land, and nonprofit North Coast Land Conservancy has conserved hundreds of acres more. Now much of Tillamook Head is under conservation ownership. Listen for migrating songbirds—such as the flutelike notes of the varied thrush—and watch for elk prints; you may see elk at Ecola Point, particularly late or early in the day.

From the trailhead at the end of Sunset Boulevard, the OCT follows the Tillamook Head National Recreation Trail. About a half mile up the trail the grade steepens as the trail begins to switchback up the hillside. After reaching elevation, the trail rolls up and down along the headland, offering occasional ocean views. The moist climate here (the top of the head is often in a cloud) is hard on trails, so watch your footing on disintegrating boardwalks. You may have to scramble to get around a landslide that took out a chunk of trail 1.7 miles from the start of this leg. Approaching the backpacker camp, the trail descends slowly, switchbacks briefly, then levels out at a clearing in the woods with a covered picnic table and three log shelters arranged around a fire ring, each with four bunks. There is a vault toilet nearby but no water, so carry up what you'll need. Hang your food to keep it from critters accustomed to raiding backpacks here. I prefer sleeping in my own tent to the dark, dank shelters; there's a lot of level tent space. You never know who you'll meet up here: other thru-hikers, families on a first backpacking outing, homeless folks.

DETOUR TO A WORLD WAR II LOOKOUT

After Japan invaded Alaska's Aleutian Islands in 1942, the US Army Signal Corps set out to establish a chain of sixty-five secret radar sites along the West Coast; the remains of one is a 0.2-mile walk west of the Tillamook Head backpacker camp. The purpose of the site was to provide early warning and interception of approaching enemy aircraft and ships as well as to help friendly aircraft in trouble. It was deactivated shortly after the war. The operations building remains, built into the hillside, but its entrances are blocked with steel gratings. You'll also see concrete air intake vents and antenna piers, all draped with green moss.

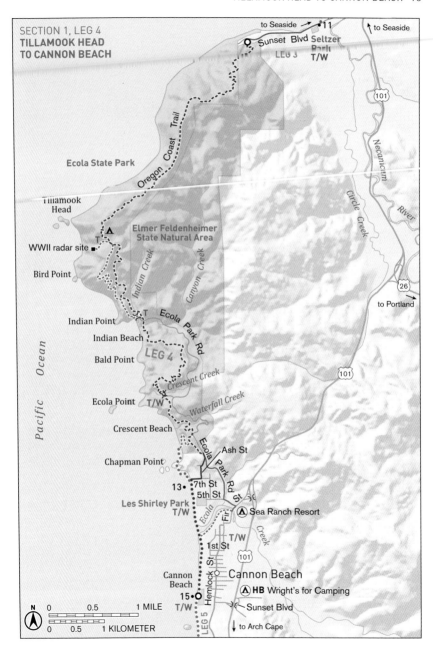

SECTION 1, LEG 4
TILLAMOOK HEAD
TO CANNON BEACH

to Seaside
11
↑ to Seaside

Sunset Blvd Seltzer Park T/W

LEG 3

to Seaside

101

Ecola State Park

Oregon Coast Trail

Necanicum River

Circle Creek

Tillamook Head

Elmer Feldenheimer State Natural Area

T

WWII radar site ■

Indian Creek

Canyon Creek

Bird Point

26

to Portland

Indian Point

Ecola Park Rd

Indian Beach

Bald Point

LEG 4

Pacific Ocean

Crescent Creek

Ecola Point T/W

Waterfall Creek

101

Crescent Beach

Ecola Park Rd

Ash St

Chapman Point

13

7th St

5th St

Les Shirley Park T/W

Ecola Creek

Sea Ranch Resort

Fir St

T/W

1st St

101

Cannon Beach

Cannon Beach

15

T/W

Hemlock St

Cannon Beach

HB Wright's for Camping

Sunset Blvd

to Arch Cape

LEG 5

N

0   0.5   1 MILE

0   0.5   1 KILOMETER

A glimpse of Chapman Point and Cannon Beach beyond from the trail to Crescent Beach
(Photo by Vickie Skellcerf)

TILLAMOOK ROCK LIGHTHOUSE

The offshore lighthouse you may glimpse from the trail over Tillamook Head is Tillamook Rock Lighthouse, or "Terrible Tilly" for its vulnerable location a mile offshore and the violent waves and weather that batter it in winter. Demolition of the top of the rock began in late 1879, and construction of the tower was completed a year and a half later, miraculously with no loss of life except for the engineer who initially scoped out the project; he slipped off the rock and drowned. The lighthouse must have saved untold lives in its seventy-six years of service warning sailing ships transiting the "graveyard of the Pacific" to stay away from the headland. After Tilly was decommissioned in 1957, it went through a series of private owners and became a columbarium to house cremated remains. The rock itself is now part of Oregon Islands National Wildlife Refuge and serves as an important stopover and breeding ground for seabirds.

From the backpacker camp, follow the trail south 0.2 mile to where it splits; the left-hand trail (Indian Creek Road, or Clatsop Loop Trail) follows a gravel service road to the parking area at Indian Beach. The right-hand Lighthouse Trail follows an often muddy but more scenic footpath with views of Tillamook Rock Lighthouse. This route is 0.1 mile longer. It descends to a footbridge before meeting the service road and hitting the parking area.

Pick up the trail again on the south side of the Indian Beach parking area. It winds south along the shore, then at about 0.3 mile veers east. This is the start of a trail that replaced a former shoreline trail destroyed by a landslide in 2016. The trail now swings farther inland to avoid the slide-prone area and reconnects with the old trail just north of a prominent ocean view. It crosses Crescent Creek just before reaching the Ecola Point parking area.

The trail resumes behind the restrooms at the southeast corner of the parking area. It leads up some steps and out to the road briefly before continuing as a footpath west of the road. Soon you'll reach a clearing with a view south; here you can scope out whether you can successfully detour down to the beach and walk around Chapman Point (see sidebar, "Minus-Tide Beach Walking"). From this point the trail rolls, steeply in places, south through the forest. At 1 mile from the Ecola Point parking area you reach a trail junction. A right turn leads down the steep hillside to Crescent Beach. Take this trail only if it's low tide and you could see, from that last viewpoint, that the tide is low enough to allow you to squeeze through the opening between the headland and offshore rock at Chapman Point—and you are game to do some wading, if necessary. Depending on how the waves have rearranged the sand at Chapman Point, you may get through here with dry feet, or you may need to wade through a pool of seawater anywhere from ankle- to hip-deep, even at low tide.

This Sitka spruce was perhaps too small to cut when loggers passed through a century ago; now it's protected within Ecola State Park.

The safer bet is to turn left at that trail junction and skip the detour to Crescent Beach. In that case, continue on the trail 0.1 mile to where it ends at Ecola Park Road at the park boundary. Follow the road south 0.25 mile to Ash Street at 8th Street, then follow Ash south (it becomes a steep pedestrian-only path) to 7th Street. Take 7th Street west up and over the foredune to Chapman Beach south of Chapman Point (BA 13). Continue down the beach 0.8 mile to the mouth of Ecola Creek, which should be wadeable during the hiking season. Directly inland are stairs leading up the seawall to downtown Cannon Beach. BA 15, at midtown, is 0.9 mile farther, just north of landmark Haystack Rock.

If you don't want to wade Ecola Creek, stay on Ecola Park Road past Ash Street, continue south to the end of the park road at 5th Street, turn left, and then turn right over the road bridge spanning Ecola Creek. A bark-chip footpath at the south end of the bridge leads through NeCus' Park and back to the beach, or follow sidewalks to the center of town.

Cannon Beach is a lively town year-round; it's flat-out overcrowded in summer. Browse art galleries and boutiques or stop for coffee, a beer, a glass of wine, or a meal. Haystack Rock, just offshore, is part of Oregon Islands National

Wildlife Refuge (see Leg 5). If you love solitude, hope that you don't find your-self walking down Cannon Beach during the annual Sandcastle Contest day in June or on Oregon Corgi Beach Day in July. If you do, take the crowds in stride. Cannon Beach and Seaside are the beaches closest to Portland. You'll hear a lot of different languages, and it's fun to see all kinds of people enjoying the coast and each other.

There are two main commercial areas, both with shops and eateries: down-town (centered on 2nd Street) and midtown (centered on Gower Avenue). There is a grocery store downtown and a second one near the Tolovana Park beach access (see Leg 5).

CAMPING

The primitive backpacker camp on Tillamook Head is fr~~ ~~~~~ ~~~~ ~~~ ~~~ ~~~ and has a vault toilet but no water. Camping is not a lowed on the beach at Cannon Beach (strictly enforced). Two private campgrounds in Cannon Beach offer tent camping. Sea Ranch Resort ($$), at the edge of downtown, has a lot of amenities (espresso, massage) but no hiker-biker area; sites can (and prob-ably should) be reserved in advance. Look for it at the north end of Ecola Creek Bridge off Fir Street. Wright's for Camping ($) is about 1 mile farther south in midtown; leave the beach at BA 15 and follow Sunset Boulevard east, under US 101. It has a chill vibe and a small drop-in hiker-biker area plus amenities such as showers and laundry. Both are walking distance to grocery stores and a variety of eateries.

MINUS-TIDE BEACH WALKING

For a few days during some years, it's possible to walk the beach from Indian Point all the way to Cannon Beach rather than along the official route of the OCT, which follows roads and trails above the beach. Typically, it happens only during very low "minus tides," when the low tide is forecast to be below 0 in height, and only if the sand volume that summer happens to be especially high. Southbound OCT hikers wanting to try it may need to depart the backpacker camp on Tilla-mook Head very early—the lowest tides in summer occur early in the morning.

From the parking area at Indian Point, follow the trail down to Indian Beach and head south. Even if you can get around Bald Point, there's no guarantee that you'll make it around Ecola Point. If the tide is too high to get around Ecola Point, you'll have to backtrack. If you make it past Ecola Point onto Crescent Beach, you're nearly home free. You'll probably be able to slip between the rocks at Chapman Point (though you may get your feet and legs wet) and continue on to Cannon Beach. If necessary, you can hike the Crescent Beach trail up the hillside and follow the traditional OCT route to Cannon Beach.

Wright's for Camping, just east of midtown Cannon Beach, is a great, low-key private campground that accommodates drop-in hikers and cyclists.

HAZARDS

The trail over Tillamook Head can be rough, with mud, roots, rotted wooden boardwalks, and landslides.

LODGING

Cannon Beach is a popular vacation destination with a lot of lodging options; expect to pay more here than in Seaside or Rockaway Beach. Virtually all accommodations are within walking distance to food.

FOOD RESUPPLY

Cannon Beach has a wealth of eateries, from downtown at the north to Tolovana Park at the south. There is a grocery store in downtown Cannon Beach.

Leg 4	Mileage between Waypoints
Tillamook Head north trailhead to backpacker camp	4.1
Backpacker camp to Indian Beach parking area	1.2
Indian Beach to Ecola Point parking area	2.2
Ecola Point to Chapman Beach (BA 13)	1.5
BA 13 to 1st Street, Cannon Beach	0.8
1st Street to BA 15 (Midtown Cannon Beach)	0.9

LEG 5   CANNON BEACH TO ARCH CAPE

Distance — 5.9 miles
Elevation gain/loss — 0 feet

This leg requires a little planning around the tides. It's a long, scenic beach walk that begins on busy Cannon Beach and slowly leaves the crowds behind. A series of short headlands jutting into the ocean beginning with Silver Point may block your way at high tide, so plan to hike this leg at mid-tide or lower (or you'll need to detour to US 101).

Hug Point is the biggest obstacle. A crude road was blasted into the rock here in the early 1900s to allow stagecoaches and, ultimately, motor vehicles traveling down the beach to get around this point. But depending on the sand volume, the rock road itself is still only accessible within about an hour of low tide. If it looks like you're going to miss that window, leave the beach at Arcadia Beach State Recreation Site (BA 17), then walk the highway shoulder 1 mile to the entrance to Hug Point State Recreation Site, where you can return to the beach south of the point itself. From here you still have a couple of rocky points to get around, but unless it's high tide you'll probably manage.

This leg ends at BA 19, which you'll see as you near the wall of rock that is Arch Cape. But if you're staying in Arch Cape, you'll stop before you get to BA 19. The advantage of overnighting in Arch Cape rather than Cannon Beach is that you're fresh for what comes next: a fairly long and rigorous hike to reach Manzanita.

HAZARDS

Time your beach walk to hit Silver Point by mid-tide and Hug Point within an hour of low tide, or plan to walk the highway shoulder.

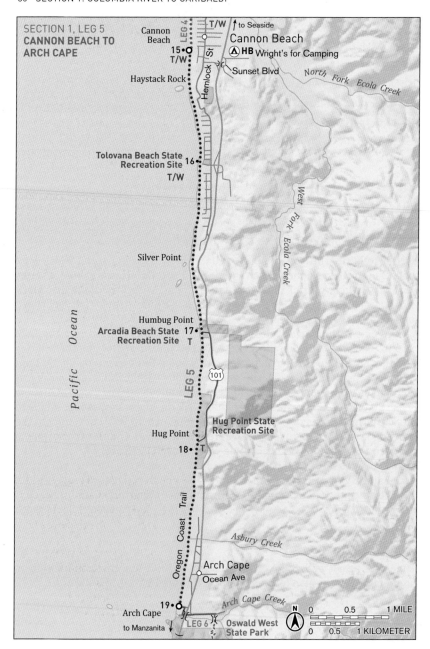

SECTION 1, LEG 5
CANNON BEACH TO ARCH CAPE

LEG 4

T/W → to Seaside

Cannon Beach

Cannon Beach

HB Wright's for Camping

15 • T/W

Haystack Rock

Sunset Blvd

Hemlock St

North Fork Ecola Creek

Tolovana Beach State Recreation Site   16
T/W

West Fork Ecola Creek

Silver Point

Pacific Ocean

Humbug Point
Arcadia Beach State   17
Recreation Site   T

LEG 5

101

Hug Point State Recreation Site

Hug Point

18 • T

Oregon Coast Trail

Asbury Creek

Arch Cape
Ocean Ave

Arch Cape Creek

19 •

Arch Cape
to Manzanita

LEG 6

Oswald West State Park

N

0   0.5   1 MILE

0   0.5   1 KILOMETER

Find a serene stretch of beach and a waterfall just south of Hug Point.

CAMPING

There are no developed campsites on this leg. Beach camping is technically legal south of Cannon Beach city limits as long as you're not adjacent to state park property—so, south of Silver Point to Arcadia Beach State Recreation Site, or south of Arcadia to a short distance north of Hug Point. If you do camp here, note that there are homes nearby, and use toilets at Arcadia Beach or Hug Point access.

WILDLIFE-WATCHING AT HAYSTACK ROCK

If you spend the night in Cannon Beach, you'll start Leg 5 by walking past Haystack Rock, with its vast tide pools and tufted puffins flying in and out of their burrow nests high on the rock. You may also see red-vested volunteers with the Haystack Rock Awareness Program. They set up spotting scopes to get better views of the puffins and vigorously defend the tide pools from clambering humans. Those tide pools are protected as Oregon marine gardens, and Haystack Rock is part of Oregon Islands National Wildlife Refuge, which protects every rock and reef off the Oregon Coast as well as a handful of mainland areas. No climbing is allowed on Haystack Rock, and if you have the opportunity to explore the tide pools, do so with care and respect for the sea anemones and sea stars, limpets and mussels, and dozens of other animals and plant species that inhabit the intertidal zone.

The kites come out to play on the beach at Arch Cape.

LODGING

There are a couple of small inns as well as vacation rentals and B&Bs in Arch Cape; all need to be reserved in advance, and some may require a two-night stay in summer. If you stay at an inn on Ocean Avenue, look for an unmarked path leaving the beach about 0.3 mile south of Asbury Creek and follow it to Ocean Avenue. There are no restaurants or grocery stores in Arch Cape, so make sure your lodgings provide breakfast, and bring your own dinner (and breakfast, if necessary).

FOOD RESUPPLY

There is a bakery, tavern, restaurant, and grocery store in the vicinity of Tolovana Wayside; no services in Arch Cape.

Leg 5	Mileage between Waypoints
Midtown Cannon Beach (BA 15) to Tolovana Beach State Recreation Site (BA 16)	0.9
BA 16 to Arcadia Beach State Recreation Site (BA 17)	1.9
BA 17 to Hug Point	1
Hug Point to BA 19 north of Arch Cape Creek	2.1

LEG 6 ARCH CAPE TO MANZANITA

Distance   18 miles
Elevation gain/loss   +2860/–2860 feet

This leg is almost entirely off of the beach. It mostly follows narrow forest trails through lush, forested Oswald West State Park. You'll walk out to the tip of Cape Falcon and to the top of Neahkahnie Mountain, which provides one of the Oregon Coast's most spectacular vistas, and reach the town of Manzanita, a smaller-scale version of Cannon Beach. Just south of town is Nehalem Bay State Park. There is no developed camping or lodging on this stretch until you reach Manzanita (lodging) at 16.7 miles or Nehalem Bay State Park campground slightly farther, at 18 miles.

From the beach north of Arch Cape, leave the beach at BA 19 or continue a bit farther to where you see Arch Cape Creek tumbling onto the beach; a sand trail leads off the beach just north of the creek. Either way, follow neighborhood roads to the creek and under the US 101 bridge, then go east onto Shingle Mill Lane. About a half mile up the road, watch for an OCT post on your right; turn here, down what looks like a driveway, to reach a suspension footbridge over Arch Cape Creek and the start of the trail over Arch Cape.

When the trail reaches US 101 at 1.4 miles from the footbridge, cross the highway and walk the shoulder south a short distance to where the trail resumes. In 0.6 mile the trail crosses Falcon Cove Road. It winds upward for the next 1.4 miles, crests the cape, then begins winding down about 2 miles to a grand viewpoint where the trail makes a sharp left turn. In another 0.6 mile you'll reach a short spur leading west to tip of Cape Falcon.

Back on the main trail, you'll hit a junction; go straight (a left leads out to US 101). In 0.4 mile the trail drops down to a picnic area at Short Sand Beach, a popular surfing venue with flush toilets and water. This section of trail is well-worn; expect mud, roots, and possibly rotting boardwalk in places.

Continuing along the trail, follow OCT signs south on a footbridge across Short Sand Creek. At each of the next three trail junctions, turn right. The last

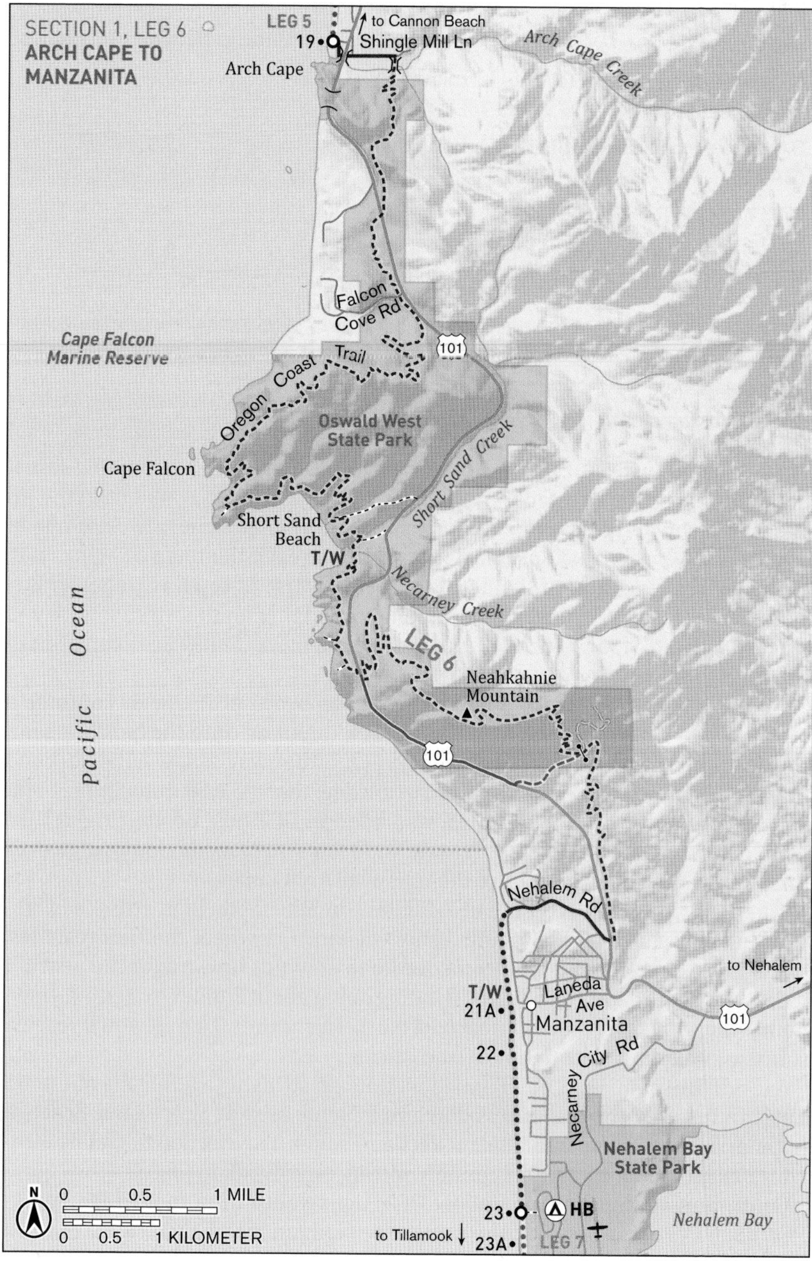

SECTION 1, LEG 6
ARCH CAPE TO MANZANITA

LEG 5
to Cannon Beach
19 • Shingle Mill Ln
Arch Cape

Arch Cape Creek

Falcon Cove Rd

101

Cape Falcon Marine Reserve

Oregon Coast Trail

Oswald West State Park

Short Sand Creek

Cape Falcon

Short Sand Beach
T/W

Necarney Creek

Pacific Ocean

LEG 6

Neahkahnie Mountain

101

Nehalem Rd

to Nehalem

101

T/W
21A • Laneda Ave
Manzanita
22 •

Necarney City Rd

Nehalem Bay State Park

Nehalem Bay

N
0   0.5   1 MILE
0   0.5   1 KILOMETER

23 • HB
to Tillamook ↓   23A •   LEG 7

Leg 6 starts with a walk across a suspension footbridge over Arch Cape Creek.

one takes you across another footbridge, this one over Necarney Creek. At the next trail junction, make sharp left (right leads to beach). After emerging into a grassy meadow known as Elk Flats, follow the main trail as it winds leftward up to US 101 (not the right-ish side, which leads out to the cliffs above Devils Cauldron). At this point, you've completed 1650 feet of this leg's elevation gain—and you haven't even tackled Neahkahnie Mountain yet.

Cross the highway and pick up the trail heading up Neahkahnie Mountain (or not; see sidebar, "Neahkahnie Mountain Shortcut"). It begins in an open hillside meadow and leads into a deep, airy forest, ascending with a series of long switchbacks before finally emerging from the trees at a viewpoint just below the summit knob. You could scramble to the top for bragging rights, but it's steep and traverses a fragile wildflower field; the view is just as good from the trail. Continuing on, follow the trail as it makes a switchback behind the ridge, then leads south across a gravel service road and descends to the Neahkahnie Mountain south trailhead.

At the tip of Cape Falcon you'll find yourself looking down on nesting and roosting seabirds.

NEAHKAHNIE MOUNTAIN SHORTCUT

If you're tuckered out, you can skip the ascent of Neahkahnie Mountain and instead hike along the west side of US 101 for 1.3 miles, then up the gravel access road to the south Neahkahnie trailhead, cutting 2 miles and nearly 1000 feet of elevation gain from your day. The highway portion of this route follows a scenic sidewalk most of the way; only at the south end must you briefly follow the highway shoulder before crossing the highway and taking the gravel road to the Neahkahnie south trailhead (0.6 mile, 230 feet up) to return to the OCT.

From the south trailhead, walk up the gravel road about 100 yards, rounding a gate, to where the trail resumes on your right. This trail section descends through second-growth forest for 1.3 miles nearly to US 101, offering occasional views of the Nehalem Valley, then it parallels the highway 0.6 mile more to end across the highway from Nehalem Road. Cross the highway and walk along Nehalem Road down to Ocean Road. Follow Ocean Road to the left, and immediately return to the beach. To reach Laneda Avenue, the main street running through Manzanita, leave the beach at BA 21A. Continue south on the beach 1.3 miles to reach a trail to the hiker-biker camp at Nehalem Bay State Park at BA 23.

CAMPING

There was once a wonderful hike-in campground in Oswald West State Park at Short Sand Beach (that's why you see flush toilets and so many little trails); it was closed to camping after one of the old-growth trees here suddenly fell one night, barely missing a family in their tent. Overnight camping is now prohibited in the former campground and is enforced by park staff. If conditions force you to bivouac along the trail in the park, you might find a trailside spot in the vicinity of the tip of Cape Falcon.

Nehalem Bay State Park campground ($) south of Manzanita has a hiker-biker area; take the spur trail over the dune at BA 23.

LODGING

There are a lot of lodging options in Manzanita, from small, posh inns to less expensive motels and vacation rentals.

FOOD RESUPPLY

There are several eateries and two grocery stores in Manzanita, one three blocks up Laneda Avenue from the beach and another at US 101 and Manzanita Avenue.

Short Sand Beach is a popular surfing venue.

Leg 6	Mileage between Waypoints
Arch Cape (BA 19) to footbridge over Arch Cape Creek	0.5
Footbridge to US 101 crossing	1.4
US 101 crossing to spur trail, Cape Falcon	4.6
Cape Falcon to Short Sand Beach picnic area	1.7
Short Sand Beach to Neahkahnie north trailhead	1.7
Neahkahnie north trailhead to trail summit	2.2
Neahkahnie trail summit to Neahkahnie south trailhead	1.3
Neahkahnie south trailhead to US 101 at Nehalem Road	1.9
Nehalem Road to beach access off Ocean Avenue	0.9
Beach access to end of Laneda Avenue (BA 21A), Manzanita	0.5
BA 21A to trail to hiker-biker camp, Nehalem Bay State Park (BA 23)	1.3

THANK GOVERNOR OSWALD WEST

Oregon's fourteenth governor, Oswald West, was an early and forceful advocate of public land. In 1913 he convinced the state legislature to designate all of Oregon's ocean beaches a public highway, which, in fact, they had always been and still were at that time. From the day the first migrants from Asia reached this coastline thousands of years earlier until the late 1920s, when the Oregon Coast Highway—US 101—was substantially completed, the beach was the only practical north–south route on the Oregon Coast, traveled by foot, horse, wagon, and eventually automobile.

Of course, the beaches were more than roads, and thanks to this legislation, no individual in Oregon could then claim to own any part of them. "I pointed out that thus we would come into miles and miles of highway without cost to the taxpayer," West famously told a reporter. "The legislature and the public took the bait—hook, line and sinker." In this way West, for whom the park that includes Cape Falcon and Neahkahnie Mountain was named, set the stage for the even more comprehensive Oregon Beach Bill in 1967.

Downtown Manzanita offers hikers groceries, lodging, good dining and imbibing, and historical perspective.

LEG 7   MANZANITA TO ROCKAWAY BEACH

Distance   7.2 miles
Elevation gain/loss   +30/–30 feet

There's no headland to ascend on this leg: just miles of beach, interrupted by an easily arranged boat ferry across the bay and a walk along the Nehalem Bay south jetty. Be aware that dogs are not allowed on the beach south of the Nehalem Bay State Park day-use area during snowy plover nesting season.

From BA 23 at the state park, follow the ocean side of Nehalem Spit, the long finger of sand that encloses Nehalem Bay. As you approach the north jetty at the end of the spit, watch for a trail signpost in the dunes 0.1 mile north of the jetty itself. Follow that sand trail 0.2 mile, turn right at the junction, and continue on the trail through a tangle of Scotch broom another 0.3 mile to the edge of the jetty. This might be the best spot to clamber down boulders to the beach, or follow the jetty upstream, looking for a safe spot to pick your way down to the beach below.

Continue up the bay beach until you can see the marina at Jetty Fishery across the water. This small business has been ferrying OCT hikers across the Nehalem for decades. Wave to hail a skiff or call them (see Contacts); they may ask you to walk a little farther up the river beach to where they prefer to pick up passengers. After a short trip across the water, consider pausing at a Jetty Fishery picnic table for a cold beverage or a bite of fresh-cooked Dungeness crab.

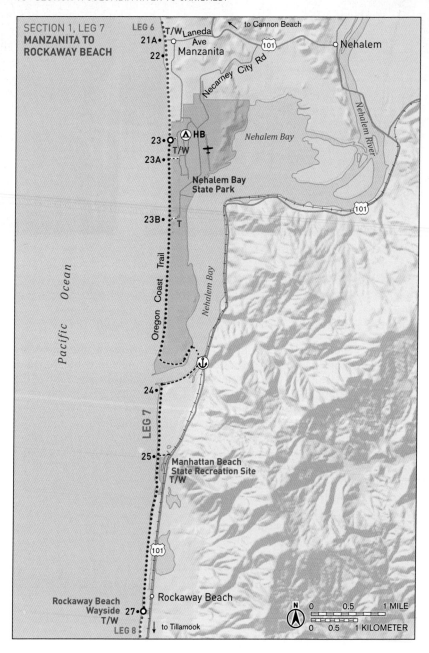

SECTION 1, LEG 7
**MANZANITA TO
ROCKAWAY BEACH**

LEG 6

T/W Laneda
21A Ave
22 Manzanita

to Cannon Beach

101

Nehalem

Necarney City Rd

Nehalem River

Nehalem Bay

23 HB
T/W

23A

Nehalem Bay
State Park

101

23B   T

Oregon Coast Trail

Pacific   Ocean

Nehalem Bay

24

LEG 7

25

Manhattan Beach
State Recreation Site
T/W

101

Rockaway Beach
Wayside 27
T/W

Rockaway Beach

LEG 8   to Tillamook

N   0   0.5   1 MILE

0   0.5   1 KILOMETER

Find a path through the rocks to the top of the Nehalem's south jetty, then head west. (Photo by Carolyn Propst)

To continue, walk out to the highway, crossing the railroad tracks, and follow the shoulder south 0.8 mile to a neighborhood tsunami escape path down the hill, over the tracks, and out Riley Street to the beach. (Map points to walking on the jetty, but Jetty Fishery no longer allows access.) Take care—the highway shoulder varies from wide to nonexistent. Walking the tracks south would be safer, especially since they're used only for special occasions, but the train operators discourage it.

Walk the beach to the town of Rockaway Beach. The main beach access here (BA 27) has toilets and is a good spot to access services such as a grocery store.

HAZARDS
Watch for potholes in the Nehalem Bay south jetty. Take care scrambling through the driftwood approaching the beach.

CAMPING
Jetty Fishery offers tent camping and efficiency cabins. Beach camping is not allowed along the beach here. There are more camping options ahead in Leg 8.

LODGING
There are a handful of motels plus vacation rentals in Rockaway Beach.

floating in the harbor near the public restrooms; that's where you may be able to arrange a ride across Tillamook Bay at the start of Section 2.

PIER'S END PIER

Have energy for a little more walking in Garibaldi? Walk out the Pier's End Pier; at 700 feet, it is the longest over-water pier in Oregon. Locals crab and fish from the pier. It leads to Garibaldi's historic US Coast Guard Lifeboat Station. When it opened in 1936, the boathouse could accommodate two thirty-six-foot motor lifeboats and one twenty-six-foot oar-powered surfboat. A system of rails allowed fully manned lifeboats to be rapidly launched. The boathouse served the USCG Tillamook Bay Station until it was decommissioned in the early 1960s. After sitting empty for many years, the boathouse was restored by a citizens' group and transformed into the Tillamook Bay Heritage Center at Pier's End. It tends to be open only for special events.

Rockaway Beach is wide and long. The offshore Twin Rocks, in the distance, are about halfway between Rockaway Beach Wayside and Tillamook Bay.

CAMPING

Barview Jetty County Park ($$) has a drop-in hiker biker area and is a decent enough place to camp, but Tillamook County charges roughly twice the state park hiker-biker rate. Old Mill RV Park ($$) at 201 3rd Street in Garibaldi is a welcoming private RV campground with tent sites just a short walk from restaurants and other services. Consider reserving ahead on summer weekends.

LODGING

Hikers will find several lodging options in Garibaldi.

FOOD RESUPPLY

There are several restaurants in Garibaldi and a grocery store on US 101 just west of the Port of Garibaldi.

Leg 8	Mileage between Waypoints
BA 27 at Rockaway Beach to Tillamook Bay north jetty (BA 28)	3.1
BA 28 to US 101 at Barview Jetty County Park	0.9
Barview to Garibaldi Marina	1.9

OR TAKE THE TRAIN

The Oregon Coast Scenic Railroad operates an excursion train on the shoreline between Rockaway Beach and Garibaldi; if you like, take the train on this stretch. You'll save energy, but not much time; it's very slow moving. The nonprofit railroad is a labor of love; vintage cars, some of them open-air, are pulled by old steam or diesel engines. Southbounders can leave the beach at Rockaway Beach (BA 27) and pick up the train right there. Unfortunately, there is no flag stop at Barview Jetty County Park, where hikers could use one to avoid a walk on the road or railroad tracks. Schedule and ticket details are online (see Contacts).

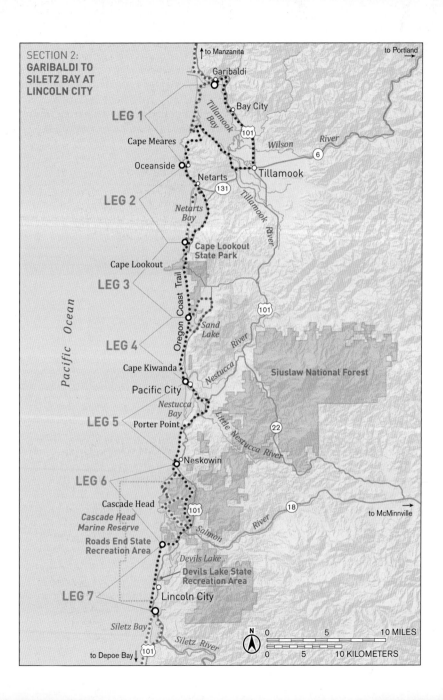

SECTION 2:
GARIBALDI TO SILETZ BAY AT LINCOLN CITY

↑ to Manzanita

to Portland →

Garibaldi

Bay City

Tillamook Bay

101

Wilson   River

6

LEG 1

Cape Meares

Oceanside

Netarts

131

Tillamook

Tillamook River

LEG 2

Netarts Bay

Cape Lookout State Park

Pacific Ocean

Cape Lookout

Oregon Coast Trail

101

LEG 3

Sand Lake

LEG 4

River

Siuslaw National Forest

Cape Kiwanda

Pacific City

Nestucca

River

Nestucca Bay

Porter Point

LEG 5

Little Nestucca River

22

Neskowin

LEG 6

Cascade Head

101

18

to McMinnville →

Cascade Head Marine Reserve

Salmon   River

Roads End State Recreation Area

Devils Lake

Devils Lake State Recreation Area

LEG 7

Lincoln City

Siletz Bay

Siletz River

to Depoe Bay ↓ 101

N

0   5   10 MILES

0   5   10 KILOMETERS

The forest on Cape Meares has some of the biggest Sitka spruce in Oregon (Leg 1).

SECTION 2
Garibaldi to Siletz Bay at Lincoln City

Distance
73.1 miles (60.9 with boat shuttle across Tillamook Bay)

Cumulative OCT miles
Miles 68.3 to 141.4

Elevation gain/loss
+4800/−4800 feet

Headland summits
Cape Meares (490 feet), Cape Lookout (831 feet), Cape Kiwanda (90 feet), Cascade Head (1340 feet)

Max distance between campgrounds
27.4 miles (Webb County Park, Pacific City, to Devils Lake State Recreation Area, Legs 4, 5, and 6) and 24.9 miles, or 18.3 miles with boat shuttle (Garibaldi to Cape Lookout State Park, Legs 1 and 2)

Max distance between lodging
16.4 miles (Tillamook to Netarts without boat shuttle, Legs 1 and 2) and 17.6 miles (Netarts to Cape Kiwanda, Legs 2, 3, and 4)

Water availability
Good

Boat shuttle
Two (Legs 1 and 2)

Legs
1. Garibaldi to Oceanside
2. Oceanside to Cape Lookout State Park
3. Cape Lookout State Park to Sand Lake
4. Sand Lake to Pacific City
5. Pacific City to Neskowin
6. Neskowin to Roads End, Lincoln City
7. Roads End to Siletz Bay at Lincoln City

SECTION 2: GARIBALDI TO SILETZ BAY AT LINCOLN CITY

The Tillamook Coast has the most remote beaches and trail hiking on the northern Oregon Coast Trail. With wide beaches, deep forests, and long sand spits separating the ocean from large bays, it's gorgeous. This section of the Oregon Coast Trail begins in what's called the Three Capes region, for the trio of headlands that begin at the south end of Tillamook Bay: basalt Cape Meares and Cape Lookout followed by sandstone Cape Kiwanda. Soon you encounter another looming cape—Cascade Head, the site of Oregon's only United Nations Biosphere Reserve—and then one more headland south of the Salmon River before hitting the long beach at Lincoln City.

There are also a number of river and bay mouths that present challenges to OCT hikers. To begin with, there's the mouth of Tillamook Bay. Then you meet Netarts Bay, Nestucca Bay, and the Salmon River, all of which must be dealt with by catching a boat ride—not a sure bet at any of these crossings—or walking, busing, hitching, or taxiing around. For most of this section, US 101 is far inland, but there are local roads that offer access if needed.

Views from the headlands are spectacular, as are the forests and the long beaches, on some of which you will probably be alone. There are a lot of lodging and camping options, though some are far apart.

Section 2 passes through the traditional homeland of the Tillamook people.

ACCESS

If you are able to arrange a boat ride across Tillamook Bay, you can leave your car at the Port of Garibaldi for free for up to seventy-two hours by pre-arrangement with the port (see Contacts). For longer periods, try street parking. You can return to Garibaldi by bus. Otherwise you could leave a car at the Bayocean Spit parking area, though leaving a car for several nights at this remote site might invite vandalism.

The southern end of Section 2 is at the mouth of Siletz Bay, at the southern end of Lincoln City. There is beach parking here at the west end of SW 51st Street, but overnight parking is not allowed; leave your vehicle, if you must, on a side street. See Contacts for options for return travel by bus.

From the saddle atop Cape Kiwanda, bear west to return to the beach (Leg 4).

SUGGESTED ITINERARIES

Mileage figures here reflect distances on the OCT route only; distance to lodgings or a campground may add 0.1 to 0.7 mile to your day's hike. These itineraries assume you will wade Sand Lake outlet; add 6.5 miles if you walk around the estuary (consider breaking it up with a vacation rental in Tierra del Mar). This is a good section for inn-to-inn hiking if you can manage the daily distances.

5 Days Camping with Tillamook Bay Boat Shuttle	Miles
Section hikers could shorten Day 1 by starting at Oceanside or Netarts.	
Day 1 Garibaldi to Cape Lookout State Park	18.3
Day 2 Cape Lookout State Park to Webb County Campground at Cape Kiwanda (BA 37)	12.1
Day 3 Cape Kiwanda to bivouac site on North Rainforest Trail, Cascade Head Scenic Research Area	13.6
Day 4 North Rainforest Trail bivouac site to Devils Lake State Recreation Area	13.8
Day 5 Devils Lake State Recreation Area to Siletz Bay	3.1

7 Days Camping with Tillamook Bay Boat Shuttle	Miles
Day 1 Garibaldi to Cape Lookout State Park	18.3
Day 2 Cape Lookout State Park to beach south of Cape Lookout	4.1
Day 3 Beach to Webb County Campground at Cape Kiwanda (BA 37)	8
Day 4 Cape Kiwanda to beach at Porter Point	7.7
Day 5 Porter Point to bivouac site on North Rainforest Trail, Cascade Head Scenic Research Area	5.9
Day 6 North Rainforest Trail bivouac site to Roads End beach	10.7
Day 7 Roads End to Siletz Bay	6.2

7 Days Camping and Lodging	Miles
Day 1 Garibaldi to Tillamook Bay City RV Park	5.6
Day 2 Tillamook Bay City RV Park to Cape Meares vacation rental	11.5

Day 3	Cape Meares to Cape Lookout State Park	13.4
Day 4	Cape Lookout State Park to Webb County Campground at Cape Kiwanda (BA 37)	12.1
Day 5	Cape Kiwanda to bivouac site on North Rainforest Trail, Cascade Head Scenic Research Area	13.6
Day 6	North Rainforest Trail bivouac site to Devils Lake State Recreation Area	13.8
Day 7	Devils Lake State Recreation Area to Siletz Bay	3.1

6 Days Inn-to-Inn		Miles
Day 1	Garibaldi to Tillamook	8.6
Day 2	Tillamook to Netarts	16.4
Day 3	Netarts to Cape Kiwanda (BA 37)	17.6
Day 4	Cape Kiwanda to Neskowin	11.1
Day 5	Neskowin to Roads End, Lincoln City	13.2
Day 6	Roads End to Siletz Bay	6.2

5 Days Inn-to-Inn with Tillamook Bay Boat Shuttle		Miles
Day 1	Garibaldi to Netarts	12.8
Day 2	Netarts to Cape Kiwanda (BA 37)	17.6
Day 3	Cape Kiwanda to Neskowin	11.1
Day 4	Neskowin to Roads End, Lincoln City	13.2
Day 5	Roads End to Siletz Bay	6.2

LEG 1 GARIBALDI TO OCEANSIDE

Distance   22.6 miles
Elevation gain/loss +940/−950 feet

Ideally, Leg 1 begins with a boat shuttle from Garibaldi to Bayocean Spit; it's a fun way to start the leg, it keeps you on the beach and off the highway, and it cuts the leg's mileage from 22.6 miles to just 10.4 miles. Since we can't assume you'll be able to arrange that, the mileage figures here are based on the official route: walking the shoulder of US 101 around Tillamook Bay to the city of Tillamook and beyond, to the north side of Cape Meares. For details on walking Leg 1 with a boat shuttle, see sidebar, "Get A Boat Shuttle Across Tillamook Bay."

GET A BOAT SHUTTLE ACROSS TILLAMOOK BAY

From Garibaldi, rather than hiking the highway shoulder, the ideal way to proceed south is with a boat ride to Bayocean Spit, either by hitching a ride from the port with a recreational boater or by paying for a prearranged ferry. Garibaldi Marina has been shuttling hikers across the bay for years; typically, they'll only do it closer to high tide than low tide, and not as the tide ebbs. Fog or high winds will also rule out this 1-mile-plus crossing.

If you can arrange a boat ride to Bayocean Spit, you'll want to get dropped off in the vicinity of Crab Harbor. From here, look for the wide gravel trail just above the bay beach and follow it south. You'll meet a trail heading west at mile 1.8; take it 0.2 mile out to the beach (or continue south 1 mile more and take another trail west 0.3 mile to the beach). Continue south past the residential community of Cape Meares. At mile 4.3 (EBA 30), continue south on the beach as described in the main text.

Alternate Leg 1—Across Tillamook Bay	Mileage between Waypoints
Garibaldi to Bayshore Drive, Cape Meares, via boat shuttle and beach	4.9
Bayshore Drive to Cape Meares State Scenic Viewpoint parking	2.6
Cape Meares SSV to Symons State Scenic Viewpoint (BA 31A)	2.9

From the harbor at Garibaldi, follow US 101 as it winds east and south, along the edge of the bay, 4.6 miles to the town of Bay City. From here the highway veers away from the bayshore, passes the popular Tillamook Creamery, and reaches downtown Tillamook in 5.4 miles. Turn right on 3rd Street (becomes State Route 131) and right again in 1.8 miles on Bayocean Road NW after crossing the Tillamook River. Continue 5.3 miles, among dairy farms and then along the bay, past Bayocean Dike Road and becoming NW Meares Avenue, to the beach at EBA 30. (Alternatively, take a bus south from Garibaldi and rejoin the OCT in Netarts or Oceanside, skipping the ascent of Cape Meares; see Leg 2.) There is currently no direct bus to the community of Cape Meares, but one may be added in summer 2024. Check for updates at nworegontransit.org.

Continue past the residential community of Cape Meares (at BA 30), where there are no shops or cafés. Approaching the bottom of Cape Meares, cross a field of round boulders, then scramble over a rock ledge (or around, if the tide permits) and continue to a gully at about 0.5 mile. Climb up the gully and

REMEMBERING BAYOCEAN

In 1906, a real estate broker from Kansas City envisioned a second Atlantic City on the sand spit separating Tillamook Bay from the Pacific Ocean. By 1914, Bay Ocean Park had become a bustling community complete with a hotel, a dance hall, a thousand-seat theater, a natatorium, and a gas station. Early travelers arrived by steamship after a rough bar crossing, so residents chipped in to help build a jetty at the end of the spit to ease the passage. But the presence of the jetty also triggered erosion on the spit's beaches. Winter storms began encroaching and washed away houses and buildings, including the natatorium in 1932. The last house fell into the sea in 1960. All that is left today of the once-vibrant resort are a few commemorative signs. Today, Bayocean Spit is mostly owned by Tillamook County and is frequented by hikers, mountain bikers, and bird-watchers, who wander the beach and the forested bayside trail. Primitive camping is allowed.

catch the 1-mile trail leading up to the entrance to Cape Meares State Scenic Viewpoint.

Bayshore Drive used to be the OCT route to the top of Cape Meares (shown on the map as an alternate), and you may still be able to follow the old road

The crew at Garibaldi Marina can run you over to Bayocean Spit if conditions permit.

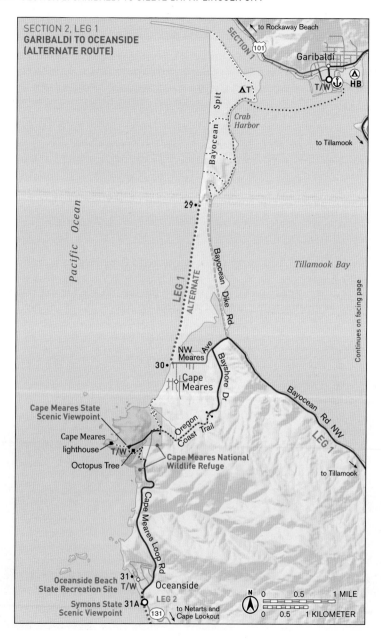

SECTION 2, LEG 1
**GARIBALDI TO OCEANSIDE
(ALTERNATE ROUTE)**

to Rockaway Beach

SECTION 1

101

Garibaldi

T/W ⚓ Ⓐ HB

Bayocean Spit

▲T

*Crab
Harbor*

to Tillamook

29•

Pacific Ocean

Tillamook Bay

Bayocean Dike Rd

LEG 1
ALTERNATE

Continues on facing page

NW
Meares Ave

30•

Cape
Meares

Bayshore Dr

Bayocean Rd NW

LEG 1

**Cape Meares State
Scenic Viewpoint**

Oregon
Coast Trail

to Tillamook

Cape Meares
lighthouse T/W

Octopus Tree

**Cape Meares National
Wildlife Refuge**

Cape Meares Loop Rd

**Oceanside Beach 31•
State Recreation Site** T/W

Oceanside

LEG 2

**Symons State 31A•
Scenic Viewpoint**

131

to Netarts and
Cape Lookout

N

0   0.5   1 MILE

0   0.5   1 KILOMETER

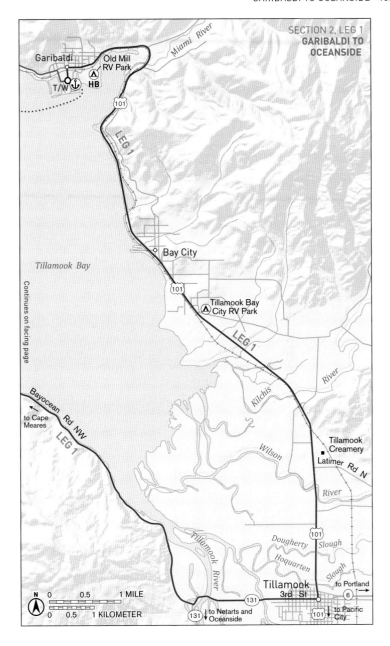

Miami River

Garibaldi

Old Mill
RV Park

T/W HB

101

LEG 1

Tillamook Bay

Bay City

101

Tillamook Bay
City RV Park

LEG 1

Kilchis River

Continues on facing page

Bayocean Rd NW

to Cape
Meares

LEG 1

Wilson

Tillamook
Creamery

Latimer Rd N

River

Tillamook River

Dougherty Slough

Hoquarten Slough

101

Slough

to Portland

Tillamook
3rd St

6

131

131 ↓ to Netarts and
Oceanside

101 ↓ to Pacific
City

N

| 0 | 0.5 | 1 MILE |

| 0 | 0.5 | 1 KILOMETER |

to the top of the cape. But the road has recently been rebuilt and rerouted for cars, and the trail described here is now the official OCT route. Mileages listed in the mileage tables will vary slightly as a result of these changes and updates to this book.

From the park entrance atop Cape Meares, you could turn south and follow Cape Meares Loop Road 2.5 miles to the beach, but the OCT detour down into the park is worth doing for the views (and possibly the restroom). Follow the park road 0.6 mile down to the parking area, where viewing platforms offer grand shoreline views and the chance to spot nesting seabirds, falcons, and even whales, and a short path leads to a nineteenth-century lighthouse.

To continue, follow signs past the restrooms to the Octopus Tree, a large Sitka spruce with no central trunk. The OCT continues on the other side of the Octopus Tree as a possibly unsigned path leading 0.7 mile through the clifftop forest to emerge at Cape Meares Loop Road. Walk the road shoulder south 2.1 miles to where it meets SR 131 at the shoreline. "Downtown" Oceanside is 0.2 mile north on this road; there you'll find a couple of cafés, a small inn and vacation rentals, and beach access. Otherwise, Symons State Scenic Viewpoint is 0.1 mile south; here, take a scramble trail to return to the beach.

CAMPING

If you must hike the highway, tent camping is available at Twins Ranch ($$) and Tillamook Bay City RV Park ($$), both about 6 miles south of Garibaldi, past Bay City. You may find other private RV parks with tent camping in the area. Otherwise, the only camping on this leg is dispersed camping on Bay-ocean Spit, particularly in the vicinity of Crab Harbor, for those who get a boat shuttle across Tillamook Bay or highway hikers who don't mind detouring north to the spit to camp. The beach at the community of Cape Meares is narrow and doesn't lend itself to camping.

LODGING

Lodging options in the city of Tillamook include two large chain hotels on US 101 about 1.4 miles north of downtown. Vacation rentals are available in the community of Cape Meares, but there are no motels. Bring your own food. There are limited accommodations in Oceanside, where you'll find a couple of cafés but no groceries.

BOAT SHUTTLE

Garibaldi Marina ferries hikers from Garibaldi to Bayocean Spit, typically in the morning depending on weather and tide. Call one to two days ahead to arrange, and hope for good weather. A boat ride is typically $30 per person.

FOOD RESUPPLY

You'll find supermarkets and restaurants in Tillamook, if you take the highway route to Cape Meares. If you get a boat shuttle, there are no markets and limited cafés on this leg.

CAPE MEARES IS FOR BIRDS

A lighthouse was built atop Cape Meares and put into service in 1890. For seventy-three years it served as a navigation landmark for the mouth of Tillamook Bay, 5-plus miles to the north. At thirty-eight feet, it's the shortest lighthouse in Oregon, as it stands at the edge of a sheer cliff two hundred feet above the sea. The lighthouse and land that surrounds are now part of Cape Meares State Scenic Viewpoint. Take the paved path west 0.2 mile from the parking area to tour the lighthouse (open daily April to October).

Surrounding the state park is Cape Meares National Wildlife Refuge, which protects a spectacular old-growth spruce and hemlock forest. The vertical cliffs and rocky outcroppings here serve as nesting sites for several species of seabirds, including common murres, pigeon guillemots, pelagic cormorants, and black oystercatchers. Peregrine falcons nest here as well.

There are a lot of theories about why the Octopus Tree on Cape Meares has multiple trunks—maybe nature, maybe nurture.

Leg 1	Mileage between Waypoints
Garibaldi to Bayshore Drive, Cape Meares, via US 101	17.1
Bayshore Drive to Cape Meares State Scenic Viewpoint parking	2.6
Cape Meares SSV to Symons State Scenic Viewpoint (BA 31A)	2.9

LEG 2   OCEANSIDE TO CAPE LOOKOUT STATE PARK

Distance   7.9 miles
Elevation gain/loss   +530/–500 feet

From Symons State Scenic Viewpoint south of Oceanside, you can walk the beach most of the way south to the boat landing at Netarts at low to mid-tide; if the tide is high, follow the shoulder of State Route 131 to Netarts Bay Drive, turn right, and go 0.2 mile to the boat landing. Or start on the beach but, if necessary, leave the beach and get on the road in 1.5 miles at Happy Camp (BA 32). If you walk on the beach, as you approach the breakwater at Netarts, take the little trail leading off of the beach to reach the boat landing.

At the Netarts boat landing you may be able to hitch a ride with a recreational boater across Netarts Bay to Netarts Spit or possibly arrange a ferry (see Boat Shuttle, below). If so, you'll get dropped off near the end of the spit. Walk around the end of the spit and down the remote ocean beach for 5 miles to the campground at Cape Lookout State Park. Leave the beach at BA 33C, which is just south of the hiker-biker camp.

If you can't get a boat ride across Netarts Bay, walk south on Netarts Bay Drive, which becomes Whiskey Creek Road. It's about the same distance to the state park campground as the walk down the spit, and it's not a bad road walk. The shoulder is narrow much of the way, but there's not much traffic. You'll pass oyster farms and a gourmet salt company, and you get glimpses of the bay through the trees.

CAMPING

The hiker-biker camp at the south end of the Cape Lookout State Park campground ($) is one of the most appealing on the coast. Beach camping is not allowed on Netarts Spit.

LODGING

There are some modest motels north of the Netarts boat landing. To access them, leave the beach at Happy Camp (BA 32). Otherwise the only lodging on

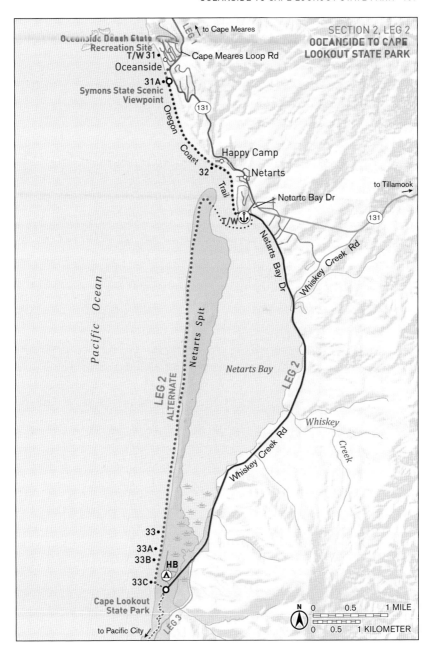

to Cape Meares

Oceanside Beach State
Recreation Site
T/W 31
Oceanside
Cape Meares Loop Rd

31A
Symons State Scenic
Viewpoint

131

Oregon Coast Trail

Happy Camp
32
Netarts

to Tillamook

Netarts Bay Dr
T/W

131

Netarts Bay Dr

Whiskey Creek Rd

Pacific Ocean

Netarts Spit

LEG 2 ALTERNATE

Netarts Bay

LEG 2

Whiskey

Whiskey Creek Rd

Creek

33
33A
33B
HB
33C

Cape Lookout
State Park

LEG 3

to Pacific City

N

0   0.5   1 MILE

0   0.5   1 KILOMETER

Netarts Spit encloses a long, narrow bay.

The hiker-biker camp at Cape Lookout State Park is close to the base of the headland and deep in the forest.

this leg for those who walk around the bay rather than boat across it is a few vacation rentals along Whiskey Creek Road. Cape Lookout State Park has yurts and deluxe cabins, but they tend to get booked quickly.

BOAT SHUTTLE

Big Spruce RV Park used to offer boat rides across Netarts Bay from the Netarts boat landing; they've suspended regular hiker ferries. But give them a call from the landing (see Contacts); it's possible they'll be able to give you a ride. Hopefully regular hiker ferry service will resume here in the future. On a sunny weekend you may be able to hitch a ride across with a recreational boater.

FOOD RESUPPLY

There are a couple of cafés in Oceanside, a short detour off the OCT route. A small grocery store is located on the highway a few blocks off of the OCT at the north end of Netarts.

Leg 2	Mileage between Waypoints
Symons State Scenic Viewpoint (BA 31A) to Netarts boat landing	2.4
Netarts to BA 33C at Cape Lookout State Park hiker-biker camp	5.5

LEG 3 CAPE LOOKOUT STATE PARK TO SAND LAKE

Distance   8.3 miles
Elevation gain/loss +960/–970 feet

The OCT route south from the Cape Lookout State Park hiker-biker camp starts as a gravel road, crosses a creek, and narrows to a path leading up the north side of the cape. Watch your footing next to the wire-and-rock gabion built alongside the creek a short distance up the trail. Bear right where a spur trail from the highway comes at about 1 mile; shortly after that you'll cross a long suspension footbridge over Cape Creek.

The trail tops out at a trailhead parking area; take the trail heading due west, then make an immediate left to continue south on the OCT. (The trail straight ahead leads 2.5 miles to the tip of the cape. See sidebar, "Detour to the End of Cape Lookout.") From this junction the OCT descends gently on long switchbacks to the remote beach at the foot of the cape. Walk the beach south, passing a Boy Scout camp (watch for the flagpole in the dunes). Beginning at BA 34, about a half mile north of the Sand Lake outlet, you may encounter off-highway vehicles on the beach—you'll almost certainly hear them in the dunes.

When you reach the mouth of the Sand Lake outlet you have two choices: either wade the outlet or follow the water's edge inland about a half mile to Fisherman Day Use Area at Sandbeach Campground, where you'll find a toilet, potable water, and campground options.

DETOUR TO THE END OF CAPE LOOKOUT

The 5-mile roundtrip hike to the end of forested Cape Lookout is one of the most rewarding hikes on the Oregon Coast; if you can work it into your OCT hike, you won't regret it. The cape jabs like a gnarled finger into the Pacific, with steep cliffs on either side. The trail is in good condition for the first 1.2 miles but gets muddy and root-covered in its gradual descent to the four-hundred-foot-high viewpoint—a good spot for whale watching—at the trail's end. Return as you came.

SECTION 2, LEG 3
**CAPE LOOKOUT STATE PARK
TO SAND LAKE**

to Netarts

HB

LEG 2

33C

Cape Lookout Rd

Jackson Creek

Cape Lookout
State Park

Cape Creek

Siuslaw
National
Forest

Cape
Lookout

T

Cape Lookout Rd

Camp Meriwether
Boy Scout Camp

to Tillamook

Pacific Ocean

Sandlake Rd

Siuslaw
National
Forest

Oregon Coast Trail

LEG 3

Galloway Rd

Sand Creek

LEG 3

East Dunes CG

34

Sandbeach CG

HB

Fisherman's
Day Use Area

T/W

Sandlake Rd

Sand Lake outlet

Clay Myers State
Natural Area

Whalen Island
County Park

LEG 4

Sand Lake
estuary

Siuslaw
National
Forest

34A

Sitka Sedge
State Natural
Area

T/W

Reneke Creek

N

0   0.5   1 MILE
0   0.5   1 KILOMETER

to Pacific City

The outlet to the Sand Lake estuary can be crossed only at low tide in summer, when the creeks feeding it slow to a trickle—even then it can be challenging. There are two ways to approach it. One is to cross at the mouth, almost in the surf, at low tide, where the water may still be up to your waist. The other is to cross to Whalen Island, the forested upland southeast of Fisherman Day Use Area, but only if the tide is low enough to expose the sandflats. Walk about 150 yards upstream from the day use area to where the channel tends to be shallowest, wade the channel, then walk south-southeast along the sand to Whalen Island. Look for a trail just above the shore and follow it south to toilets and a bridge to Sandlake Road (see below).

Some hikers choose to skip this crossing and walk the rural roads around the estuary. If so, leave the beach at Fisherman Day Use Area and follow Galloway Road and Sandlake Road to Sitka Sedge State Natural Area. From here, follow trails leading west to the beach. This road route adds 6.5 miles to the mileage listed here. On the plus side, the trail walk through Sitka Sedge is lovely, and the route leads you past an additional camping option (see sidebar, "Conservation of the Sand Lake Estuary").

Cross a footbridge to begin the hike to the top of Cape Lookout.

CONSERVATION OF THE SAND LAKE ESTUARY

Like Netarts Bay back in Leg 1, Sand Lake is what's called a bar-built estuary. It's the kind formed not at the mouth of a major river but where sandbars are built up by ocean waves and currents and the resulting bay is fed only by small streams. The Sand Lake estuary may be Oregon's best-conserved estuary, thanks to collaborative efforts by the State of Oregon, the US Forest Service, and private conservation organizations such as North Coast Land Conservancy and The Nature Conservancy. In the middle of the estuary is Whalen Island, accessible across a road bridge (for those hiking around the estuary). It's the site of Whalen Island County Park, which has a small campground, and adjacent Clay Myers State Natural Area at Whalen Island, which has a short loop trail. In 2014, Oregon State Parks also acquired the former Beltz Farm, which occupies a large area of land on the south side of the estuary. It's now known as Sitka Sedge State Natural Area. If you wade the mouth of Sand Lake you'll walk by it; if you walk around the estuary, you'll follow trails through Sitka Sedge to return to the beach.

CAMPING

Beach camping is possible in this stretch; the best place is just south of Cape Lookout (north of the Boy Scout camp and OHV area). The Forest Service recently developed a small walk-in hiker-biker campsite ($) near Fisherman's Day Use Area at the edge of the Sand Lake estuary; at this writing, it was unclear whether reservations would be needed and what the cost would be. Check the website for information (see Contacts).

Developed camping is available at nearby Sandbeach Campground ($$), also managed by the Forest Service and primarily for use by OHV riders, on an as-available basis (or by advance reservation), but there are no showers. The Forest Service does not allow dispersed camping in the dunes here.

If you decide to walk around Sand Lake, consider camping at Whalen Island County Campground ($$), off Sandlake Road 5.6 miles from Fisherman's Day Use Area. It is not a hiker-biker camp, but accommodating camp hosts may find a spot for you even if the campground is full.

LODGING

Since the 2021 closure of Sandlake Country Inn, on Galloway Road 2.5 miles from Sand Lake outlet, there is no lodging on this leg.

FOOD RESUPPLY

There are no grocery stores or cafés on this leg.

Leg 3	Mileage between Waypoints
Cape Lookout State Park hiker-biker camp to top of Cape Lookout	2.3
Top of Cape Lookout to beach at foot of cape	1.8
Beach at foot of cape to the Sand Lake outlet	4.2

LEG 4 SAND LAKE TO PACIFIC CITY

Distance	5.1 miles
Elevation gain/loss	+110/−120 feet

Once you're across the outlet to Sand Lake, continue south on the beach. If you walked the road around Sand Lake, return to the beach via Sitka Sedge State Natural Area; from the parking area, take the main trail (atop the dike) west, following signs toward the beach at all junctions. It's about 0.8 mile from the parking area to the beach, landing you at BA 34A, about a mile south of the Sand Lake outlet.

Walk the beach south toward sandstone Cape Kiwanda and climb its sandy saddle. At the top, stay on the sand but veer just to the right of the grassy dunes; soon you'll see a clear sand path down to the beach. Do not venture west of the fencing atop Cape Kiwanda; it's illegal and dangerous. Cape Kiwanda beach access (BA 37) is popular with surfers as well as dory boat fishermen, who launch into the surf here. It's also a popular spot for an espresso, a meal, or a brew.

Continue south on the beach to BA 37A. Nestucca Spit stretches nearly 3 miles to the south, but the mouth of the Nestucca River is deep and cannot be waded, and there is no easy boat crossing (but there is a possible boat shuttle; see Leg 5). The spit is protected as Bob Straub State Park; there is no campground.

At BA 37A, head east onto Pacific Avenue a short distance to Brooten Road, at the center of Pacific City.

CELEBRATE THE 100-MILE MARK

Just completing any long-distance trail is an accomplishment; completing the big three in the US—the Pacific Crest Trail, the Continental Divide Trail, and the Appalachian Trail—makes you a triple-crowner. Will "Akuna" Robinson is among that elite group. Wherever he hikes, he says, hitting the 100-mile mark is always a cause for celebration: he knows he's on his way to completion. On the OCT, you'll hit 100 miles—depending on some route decisions you've made—right about at Pacific City. Congratulations!

Sunrise and morning mist create a magical mood at the Sand Lake estuary. (Photo by Carolyn Propst)

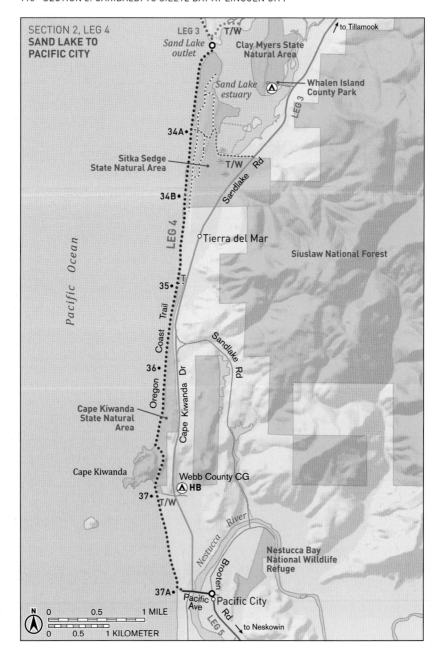

SECTION 2, LEG 4
**SAND LAKE TO
PACIFIC CITY**

LEG 3   T/W

*Sand Lake
outlet*

Clay Myers State
Natural Area

↗ to Tillamook

*Sand Lake
estuary*

Ⓐ   Whalen Island
County Park

LEG 3

34A•

Sitka Sedge
State Natural Area

T/W   Sandlake Rd

34B•

LEG 4

○Tierra del Mar

Siuslaw National Forest

Pacific Ocean

35•

Sandlake Rd

Oregon Coast Trail

36•

Cape Kiwanda Dr

Cape Kiwanda
State Natural
Area

Cape Kiwanda

Webb County CG
Ⓐ HB

37•
T/W

Nestucca River

Nestucca Bay
National Wildlife
Refuge

37A•

Pacific
Ave   ○Pacific City

Brooten Rd

LEG 5

→ to Neskowin

N
0   0.5   1 MILE
0   0.5   1 KILOMETER

CAMPING

Webb County Campground ($$) is an uninspiring and overpriced campground with a hiker-biker area in a great location if you're looking for a restaurant meal and grocery resupply. It is tucked right behind the Inn at Cape Kiwanda. Beach camping between Sand Lake and Cape Kiwanda is possible, but it's not very remote.

A surfer heads for the water on the south side of Cape Kiwanda.

LODGING

There are a lot of lodging opportunities here, from more expensive ocean-view inns at Cape Kiwanda to less expensive motels in Pacific City, plus vacation rentals.

FOOD RESUPPLY

There are small grocery stores at Cape Kiwanda and "downtown" Pacific City.

Leg 4	Mileage between Waypoints
Sand Lake outlet to base of Cape Kiwanda	3.2
Base of Cape Kiwanda to Cape Kiwanda beach access (BA 37)	0.6
BA 37 to BA 37A at Pacific Avenue	1
BA 37A to Pacific Avenue and Brooten Road	0.3

LEG 5 PACIFIC CITY TO NESKOWIN

Distance	9.8 miles
Elevation gain/loss	+520/–520 feet

Continuing south from Pacific City, most OCT hikers follow the official route: follow Brooten Road to US 101, walk the highway shoulder to Winema Road, and take Winema Road back to the beach, for a total of 6.4 road shoulder miles.

Alternately, board a midmorning Tillamook County bus (see NW Connector under "Bus Transportation" in Contacts) at Cape Kiwanda or downtown Pacific City headed toward Lincoln City. Ask the driver to let you off at Winema Road; follow Winema Road 0.6 mile to return to the beach next to a church camp.

Continue south on the beach to the community of Neskowin. If the tide is high, leave the beach at BA 39A, which leads to Mount Angel Avenue; take an immediate right on Breakers Avenue and follow it south to Salem Avenue, which leads two blocks east to Neskowin Beach State Recreation Site. If the tide is low, you can continue down the beach to check out Proposal Rock, a tree-topped sea stack (or even walk all the way around it at very low tide). From Proposal Rock backtrack a bit (possibly wading up Neskowin Creek) to BA 39B and a trail leading out to the state recreation site.

CAMPING

There is no developed camping on this leg but there are camping options 0.8 and 2.4 miles ahead in Leg 6. Beach camping is possible north of Neskowin; the best (most remote) spot might be at Porter Point, about 0.75 mile north of your

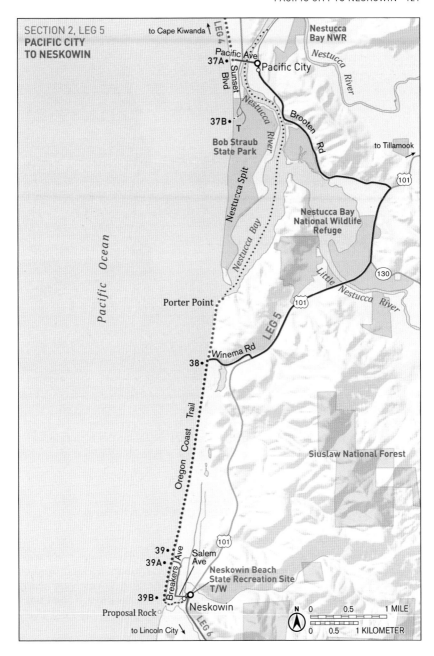

SECTION 2, LEG 5
**PACIFIC CITY
TO NESKOWIN**

to Cape Kiwanda

LEG 4

Nestucca
Bay NWR

Pacific Ave

37A•

Sunset Blvd

Nestucca River

Pacific City

Nestucca River

Brooten Rd

to Tillamook

37B• T

Bob Straub
State Park

Nestucca Spit

Nestucca Bay

101

Nestucca Bay
National Wildlife
Refuge

130

Little Nestucca River

Pacific Ocean

Porter Point

101

LEG 5

Winema Rd

38•

Oregon Coast Trail

Siuslaw National Forest

101

39•
39A•

Breakers Ave

Salem
Ave

Neskowin Beach
State Recreation Site
T/W

39B•

Neskowin

Proposal Rock

LEG 6

to Lincoln City

N

0   0.5   1 MILE

0   0.5   1 KILOMETER

Porter Point is just north of the Winema Road beach access.

return to the beach at Winema Road, if you feel confident the high tide won't reach you. In summer, the church camp typically provides a portable toilet at BA 38 as a courtesy to the public.

LODGING

There are condos and other vacation rentals available in Neskowin.

BOAT SHUTTLE

Nestucca Adventures is a kayak and stand-up paddleboard business in Pacific City. You may be able to arrange a ride in a Zodiac from its dock on Brooten Road (a short walk north of the traffic light in Pacific City) downstream nearly 4 scenic miles to the beach just inside the mouth of the Nestucca, if conditions and schedule permit. Morning, before the business opens, is the most likely time to arrange a shuttle.

FOOD RESUPPLY

There is a café and a deli with limited grocery options in Neskowin.

Leg 5	Mileage between Waypoints
Pacific Avenue to US 101 via Brooten Road	2.7
Brooten Road to Winema Road via US 101	3.1
Winema Road to BA 38	0.6
BA 38 to Neskowin (BA 39A)	2.9
BA 39A to Neskowin Beach State Recreation Site	0.5

LEG 6   NESKOWIN TO ROADS END, LINCOLN CITY

Distance   13.2 miles
Elevation gain/loss +1730/−1740 feet

The route of the Oregon Coast Trail over Cascade Head and the Salmon River is currently in flux—in a good way. All the land managers in this area, particularly those at Siuslaw National Forest, have been working hard to improve the OCT over Cascade Head so OCT hikers no longer have to hike along the highway for miles and miles. And they've also been working to provide hikers with legal campsites in the forest. Until this point, no camping has been allowed within Cascade Head Scenic Research Area. They've made great progress, but more progress has probably been made since this book was published. I suggest checking my website and the Siuslaw National Forest website for route updates (see Contacts).

As of press time, the following route will keep a southbound OCT hiker on the quickest route with the fewest highway miles. But this route bypasses some amazing views on the gorgeous undeveloped headland, so consider incorporating the detour and alternative routes also suggested in this leg.

From Neskowin Beach State Recreation Site, walk south along the highway 1.9 miles until you see a possibly unmarked berm on your right; just beyond it you'll see a trail heading into the forest. (It's possible the trailhead may eventually be moved 0.7 mile closer to Neskowin, in the vicinity of the road leading to the town's sewage lagoon, 0.4 mile south of the RV park; watch for OCT signs.)

Follow the Cascade Head North Rainforest Trail as it rolls along Fall Creek; at 0.6 mile it makes a sharp left and steepens into a steady ascent of the north side of the headland to gravel Forest Road 1861. Cross the road to pick up the Cascade Head South Rainforest Trail heading down the other side, first through a forest of large Sitka spruce and then alder-dominated woods. It ends near the intersection of Three Rocks Road and US 101.

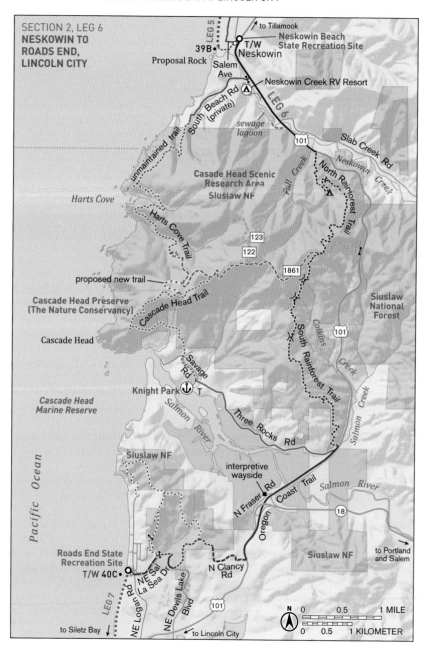

SECTION 2, LEG 6
**NESKOWIN TO
ROADS END,
LINCOLN CITY**

to Tillamook

**Neskowin Beach
State Recreation Site**

T/W
Neskowin

39B

Proposal Rock

Salem
Ave

Neskowin Creek RV Resort

South Beach Rd
(private)

sewage
lagoon

LEG 5

LEG 6

101

Slab Creek Rd

Neskowin Creek

**Casade Head Scenic
Research Area
Siuslaw NF**

Fall Creek

North Rainforest Trail

Harts Cove

Harts Cove Trail

123

122

1861

proposed new trail

Cascade Head Trail

**Cascade Head Preserve
(The Nature Conservancy)**

Cascade Head

Calkins Creek

**Siuslaw
National
Forest**

101

South Rainforest Trail

*Cascade Head
Marine Reserve*

Savage
Rd

Knight Park   T

Salmon River

Three Rocks Rd

Salmon Creek

Pacific Ocean

Siuslaw NF

interpretive
wayside

N Fraser Rd

Oregon Coast Trail

Salmon River

18

to Portland
and Salem

**Roads End State
Recreation Site**

T/W 40C

NE Logan Rd

NE Sal
La Sea Dr

NE Devils Lake Blvd

N Clancy
Rd

Siuslaw NF

LEG 7

101

to Siletz Bay

to Lincoln City

N

0   0.5   1 MILE

0   0.5   1 KILOMETER

The South Rainforest Trail begins in deep Sitka spruce forest.

To cross the wide Salmon River floodplain, you must walk south along the highway for 3.8 miles to the north end of Lincoln City. Leave the highway at NW 40th Street and follow signs west to Chinook Winds Resort and beach access (EBA 41A). The map shows a route up N. Clancy Road, but public access is unclear. At this time I recommend that you remain on the highway shoulder to 40th Street and return to the beach 0.9 mile south of Road's End State Recreation Site. (By the time you read this, a connector trail may have been built that starts at a small interpretive wayside off N. Fraser Road, cutting more miles off your highway shoulder walk.)

DON'T HURRY OVER CASCADE HEAD

Cascade Head is one of the most special places on the Oregon Coast. But you wouldn't know it by sticking to the official route of the OCT, which bypasses the craggy shoreline, most of the old-growth forests, and the high coastal meadows of Cascade Head on its inland route. Consider taking a detour to explore the best parts of this wild headland and to take in the spectacular views along the shoreline.

In 1974 nearly ten thousand acres here were designated Cascade Head Scenic Research Area (CHSRA) by the federal government. It was the first such non-wilderness designation in the US to protect the scenic, ecological, and scientific values of a large area of public and private land. The landscape within CHSRA includes salt-spray meadows harboring rare plants and butterflies, deep forests of Sitka spruce and western hemlock, and the Salmon River estuary. It lies at the heart of a United Nations Biosphere Reserve, one of fewer than thirty in the entire country.

The best-known destination on Cascade Head is a preserve run by The Nature Conservancy (TNC) that protects the open grasslands on the southwest portion of the headland. The view of the Salmon River estuary and coastline stretching south from here is not to be missed, but you *will* miss it if you stick to the official route.

Instead of crossing Forest Road 1861 on your hike over the headland, consider following this gravel road west 2 miles to the Nature Conservancy trailhead, then follow the trail 0.9 mile through the forest to the viewpoint at the top of the grassy knoll. (Alternatively, consider taking the "back way" over Cascade Head; see sidebar, "The Back Way Over Cascade Head.") At this writing, plans call for moving the main trailhead 0.5 mile up the road, where a larger parking area could be built, and rerouting the trail. Since you don't need to park a car, you could use the old trailhead and trail, which will be retained as an accessible trail.

Return as you came to continue on the official OCT route, or follow TNC's Cascade Head Trail 3 miles down to Three Rocks Road, and take the road 2.5 miles back to US 101 and the official OCT route. Note: TNC is rethinking the layout of its popular trail system here; by the time you visit, you may find the trail down to Three Rocks closed or rerouted.

Important update: Forest Road 1861, the gravel road running east–west on Cascade Head and providing access to Harts Cove and The Nature Conservancy's Cascade Head Preserve trails, is closed to vehicles possibly permanently following massive landslides in 2021. You can still walk the road, but it is not being maintained; expect to find your way around fallen trees and other obstacles.

The view south from the summit of Cascade Head is well worth a detour.

CAMPING

Neskowin Creek RV Resort ($$) allows hikers and bikers to tent camp by res-
ervation. Traditionally, no camping has been allowed on Cascade Head, but
Siuslaw National Forest plans to develop a rustic campground off of FR 1861,
not far from the Nature Conservancy trailhead and possibly also a backpacker
camp off FR 123 (north of FR 1861). Check my website or the Siuslaw National
Forest website (see Contacts) for updates. Another option for a solo hiker or
possibly a pair is a small, flat area about 0.6 mile from the northern end of the
North Rainforest Trail, right where the trail turns and steepens; Forest Service
officials have told me they don't mind if OCT hikers bivouac here. Alternately,
consider camping on the remote-ish beach north of Roads End.

LODGING

There are vacation rentals in the vicinity of Roads End, and many more lodging
opportunities just to the south (see Leg 7).

FOOD RESUPPLY

The next grocery stores and cafés are in Leg 7.

Trails through public land at the north end of Lincoln City return you to the beach at Roads End.

THE BACK WAY OVER CASCADE HEAD

Important update: Hikers are now advised not to use the following alternative route. Since Forest Road 1861 closed in 2021 due to landslides, the road has not been maintained, nor have the trails that it accesses, making wayfinding more difficult and creating hazards for hikers.

One great frustration for OCT enthusiasts is that there actually is an alternative shoreline-hugging route through national forest land over Cascade Head that adds about 4 miles to your hike over the headland. However, the Forest Service doesn't maintain it, so routefinding can be challenging. And the trailhead is at the top of a gated community.

If you can overcome that obstacle—such as by overnighting in a vacation rental in the neighborhood—and you are up for an adventure, consider this alternative route. This route is officially off-limits January 1 to July 15 (Harts Cove Trail and Forest Road 1861), though that may have changed by the time you read this.

From the beach at Neskowin, cross Neskowin Creek and look for a little trail leaving the beach directly across from Proposal Rock, which should put you on Proposal Rock Loop. Follow it 0.25 mile to South Beach Road, turn right, and follow South Beach Road uphill, passing a water tower to where the road ends at a second water tower, a total of 1.5 miles from the beach. (Alternatively, you can access this route by turning west onto gated South Beach Road from US 101.) A narrow trail heads into the woods behind this second water tower. Take it.

Most of your elevation gain is already done; from here, the trail rises about 200 feet over the next mile, then descends gradually for 0.8 mile to meet the Harts Cove Trail just east of where that trail breaks out of the forest and into a seaside meadow signaling the trail's end. The trail over the head is faint and maintained only by local residents; you may need to scramble over fallen logs, and one spot in particular can get a little confusing. I recommend using GPS to help you stay on track toward Harts Cove.

From here, follow the Harts Cove Trail south about 2.7 miles to the trailhead at the end of FR 1861. The trail grade rolls pleasantly until the last 0.5 mile, which is relentlessly uphill. Walk the road 0.9 mile to the Nature Conservancy trailhead (or less; plans call for moving this trailhead 0.5 mile up the road toward the Harts Cove trailhead).

From here continue on the road 2 miles to pick up the OCT route leading down the headland to the intersection of Three Rocks Road and US 101 for a total of about 11.4 miles versus the 7.9 miles of the standard route. Add more miles and more scenery by detouring through The Nature Conservancy's preserve (see sidebar, "Don't Hurry Over Cascade Head").

LODGING

There are vacation rentals in the vicinity of Roads End, and many more lodging opportunities just to the south (see Leg 7).

FOOD RESUPPLY

The next grocery stores and cafés are in Leg 7.

Leg 6	Mileage between Waypoints
Neskowin Beach State Recreation Site to Cascade Head North Rainforest Trail	1.9
North Rainforest Trail to FR 1861	2.5
FR 1861 to Three Rocks Road and US 101 via Cascade Head South Rainforest Trail	3.5
Three Rocks Road to N. Clancy Road	1.9
N. Clancy Road to start of connector trail	0.7
Connector trail to first trail junction	0.9
Trail junction to NE Devils Lake Boulevard	0.9
NE Devils Lake Boulevard to trailhead at cul-de-sac	0.2
Cul-de-sac to NE Sal La Sea Drive	0.2
Sal La Sea Drive to beach at Roads End State Recreation Site (BA 40C)	0.5

LEG 7   ROADS END TO SILETZ BAY AT LINCOLN CITY

Distance	6.2 miles
Elevation gain/loss	+10 feet

From Roads End, walk the beach south. Midway to Siletz Bay you'll pass D River State Recreation Site (BA 45). If the little D River is running too high to wade or jump across and you don't want to take off your shoes, leave the beach north of the large restaurant building just north of the creek, walk around it to the highway, and cross the highway bridge to return to the beach south of the D River with dry feet. Continue south, past the big hotel at Spanish Head, to where the beach runs out at the bay mouth. Walk past the BA 49 sign to the Taft Beach parking area.

CAMPING

There is a hiker-biker camp at Devils Lake State Recreation Area (see Contacts), though it's close to the traffic noise of US 101. To get there, leave the beach at

An off-season kite flyer has the beach to herself at D River State Recreation Site, where the sky is usually full of colorful kites on summer days.

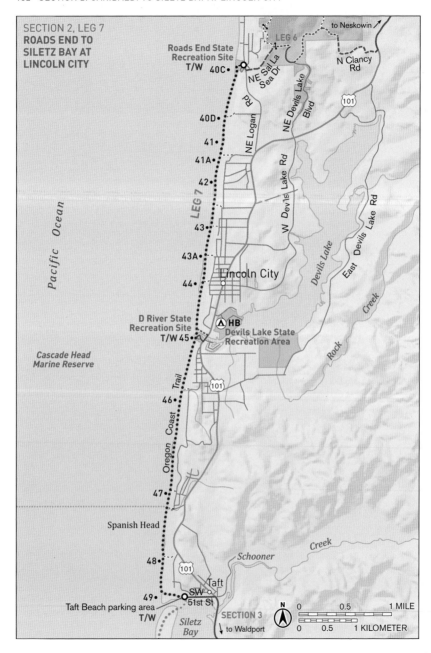

SECTION 2, LEG 7
**ROADS END TO
SILETZ BAY AT
LINCOLN CITY**

LEG 6

to Neskowin ↗

N Clancy
Rd

Roads End State
Recreation Site
T/W 40C

NE Sal La
Sea Dr

NE Devils Lake Blvd

NE Logan Rd

101

40D

41

41A

42

W Devils Lake Rd

East Devils Lake Rd

LEG 7

43

43A

Devils Lake

Lincoln City

44

Rock Creek

D River State
Recreation Site
T/W 45

⛺ HB
Devils Lake State
Recreation Area

Pacific Ocean

Cascade Head
Marine Reserve

Oregon Coast Trail

101

46

47

Rock Creek

Spanish Head

Creek

48

Schooner

101

Taft

49
Taft Beach parking area
T/W

SW
51st St

SECTION 3
↓ to Waldport

Siletz
Bay

N

0   0.5   1 MILE

0   0.5   1 KILOMETER

Roads End is the northernmost neighborhood in 6-mile-long Lincoln City.

the mouth of D River (BA 45), cross US 101, and walk north a short distance to NW 1st Avenue. Follow it east to the boardwalk trail leading north into the park campground, 0.2 mile from BA45. You may be able to camp on the beach north of Roads End (north of the Lincoln City limits).

LODGING

Lincoln City is a popular tourist destination; a large number of lodging options are available along this entire leg.

FOOD RESUPPLY

There are several grocery stores arrayed along US 101 in Lincoln City, including some within a couple of blocks of the end of this leg at Taft.

Leg 7	Mileage between Waypoints
Roads End State Recreation Site (BA 40C) to D River SRS (BA 45)	3.1
BA 45 to Taft Beach parking area, Siletz Bay (BA 49)	3.1

LINCOLN CITY: SEVEN COMMUNITIES, ONE TOWN

Until the mid-1960s, what is today Lincoln City was a string of seven distinct coastal communities, from Roads End at the north to Taft at the mouth of Siletz Bay. Motorists now experience it as one nearly continuous strip mall. For OCT hikers, it's just a long, fairly wide beach fronted with houses and hotels. With so many restaurants and businesses of all kinds, it may be a good place to resupply and possibly lay over.

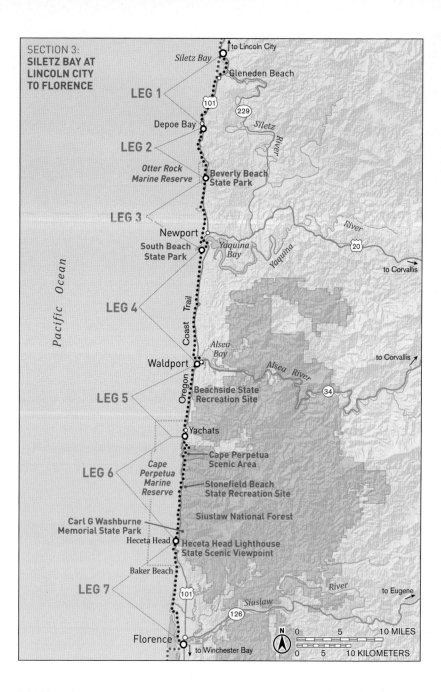

SECTION 3:
**SILETZ BAY AT
LINCOLN CITY
TO FLORENCE**

LEG 1

Siletz Bay

to Lincoln City

Gleneden Beach

101

229

Depoe Bay

LEG 2

Siletz

River

*Otter Rock
Marine Reserve*

Beverly Beach
State Park

LEG 3

Newport

South Beach
State Park

*Yaquina
Bay*

Yaquina

River

20

to Corvallis

Pacific Ocean

Coast Trail

LEG 4

*Alsea
Bay*

Waldport

Alsea River

34

to Corvallis

LEG 5

Beachside State
Recreation Site

Oregon

Yachats

Cape Perpetua
Scenic Area

LEG 6

*Cape
Perpetua
Marine
Reserve*

Stonefield Beach
State Recreation Site

Siuslaw National Forest

Carl G Washburne
Memorial State Park

Heceta Head

Heceta Head Lighthouse
State Scenic Viewpoint

Baker Beach

LEG 7

101

River

Siuslaw

to Eugene

126

Florence

to Winchester Bay

N

0   5   10 MILES

0   5   10 KILOMETERS

A cloud momentarily caps Heceta Head (Leg 6).

SECTION 3
Siletz Bay at Lincoln City to Florence

Distance
87.8 miles

Cumulative OCT miles
Miles 141.4 to 229.2

Elevation gain/loss
+5980/–5960 feet

Headland summits
Otter Crest (480 feet), Yaquina Head (160 feet), Cape Perpetua (960 feet), Heceta Head (530 feet), Sea Lion Point (550 feet)

Max distance between campgrounds
18.1 miles (Siletz Bay to Beverly Beach State Park, Legs 1 and 2; add 3.1 miles if starting at Devils Lake State Recreation Area, Lincoln City) and 17.8 miles (South Beach State Park to Beachside State Recreation Site, Legs 4 and 5)

Max distance between lodging
15.7 miles (Newport South Beach to Waldport, Leg 4)

Water availability
Good

Boat shuttle
None

Legs
1. Siletz Bay to Depoe Bay
2. Depoe Bay to Beverly Beach
3. Beverly Beach to Newport South Beach
4. Newport South Beach to Waldport
5. Waldport to Yachats
6. Yachats to Heceta Head
7. Heceta Head to Florence

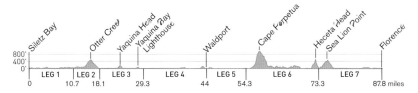

SECTION 3: SILETZ BAY AT LINCOLN CITY TO FLORENCE

Section 3 is the most civilized portion of the Oregon Coast Trail. The route is close to US 101 most of the way, though the ocean's roar tends to mask any traffic noise. On beach sections you'll frequently be walking past oceanfront homes, and you'll be ducking in and out of towns.

Long stretches of rocky coastline move the OCT onto side roads on parts of Leg 2 and onto US 101 on parts of Legs 6 and 7. The section begins and ends at big bays, with two more along the way, but none require (or provide options for) a boat shuttle; instead you'll be crossing the bays on bridges.

This is a good stretch for inn-to-inn hiking, with a lot of lodging options, though there are a couple of longer stretches (unless you can score vacation rentals to break them up). There are also a fair number of developed campgrounds, which is good: with all those towns, opportunities for legal beach camping are somewhat limited. But their spacing still requires some relatively long days; beach camping or a night at a motel can help shorten some hiking days.

Section 3 passes through the traditional homelands of the Tillamook, Yaquina, Alsi, and Siuslaw people.

ACCESS

At the north end of this section, I suggest parking on the street near where you want to start walking. Overnight parking is not allowed in the parking area at the north side of Siletz Bay, nor at Gleneden Beach State Recreation Site.

At the south end, you can park overnight at the Siuslaw River north jetty or nearby Harbor Vista County Park with a special use permit; request it at least ten days in advance from Lane County Parks (see Contacts); there may be a per-day charge. Harbor Vista might be a safer spot than the jetty to leave a vehicle for several days. Without a permit, overnight parking is not permitted at the north jetty, nor in Old Town or the Port of Siuslaw parking in Florence. You can leave a car overnight at South Jetty Beach at parking areas 1 through 7 with the proper permit from the Oregon Dunes National Recreation Area (see Contacts). For options for return travel by bus as far south as Yachats and for the bus schedule between Yachats and Florence, see Contacts.

Otter Crest Loop offers views of the rocky shoreline to the south (Leg 2).

SUGGESTED ITINERARIES

Mileage figures here reflect distances on the OCT route only; distance to lodgings or a developed campground may add up to 0.4 mile to your day's hike.

7 Days Camping		Miles
Consider breaking up the longer days with beach camping or a night in a motel.		
Day 1	Siletz Bay to Beverly Beach State Park	18.1
Day 2	Beverly Beach to South Beach State Park	11.7
Day 3	South Beach to Beachside State Recreation Site	17.8
Day 4	Beachside to Cape Perpetua Scenic Area campground	13
Day 5	Cape Perpetua to Carl G. Washburne Memorial State Park	9.5
Day 6	Washburne to Baker Beach Campground	7.3
Day 7	Baker Beach to Old Town Florence	10.4

9 Days Inn-to-Inn		Miles
You may be able to break up Day 5 of this itinerary with a vacation rental. Break up Day 8 by splurging on a night at Heceta Lighthouse B&B.		
Day 1	Siletz Bay to Gleneden Beach	3.6
Day 2	Gleneden Beach to Depoe Bay	7.1
Day 3	Depoe Bay to Otter Rock	5.3
Day 4	Otter Rock to Newport South Beach	12.3
Day 5	Newport South Beach to Waldport	15.7
Day 6	Waldport to Yachats	10.3
Day 7	Yachats to Stonefield Beach	10.6
Day 8	Stonefield Beach to Heceta Beach	16.6
Day 9	Heceta Beach to Old Town Florence	6.3

LEG 1   SILETZ BAY TO DEPOE BAY

Distance   10.7 miles
Elevation gain /loss   +380/−340 feet

From the mouth of Siletz Bay, the end of Gleneden Spit is excruciatingly close—but you need a boat to cross, and there are no commercial outfitters offering boat ferries in Siletz Bay. If you happen to arrive at the mouth of the bay when there are boats about, definitely try to hail one to give you a one-minute ride to the end of the spit, then walk south along the spit's ocean side. This is possible only around high tide; at low tide the bay nearly empties out.

It is more likely that you'll need to follow the highway around Siletz Bay—either on foot, by bus, or by car. From the parking area at the mouth of Siletz Bay, walk out SW 51st Street to US 101, then walk the highway shoulder to the traffic light at the Salishan Marketplace. If you're a guest of Salishan Coastal Lodge, you can follow the nature trail winding west 0.5 mile between the bay and the golf course to the beach. Otherwise, continue south through the parking area to get on Gleneden Beach Loop heading south. Turn right on Laurel Street and follow it west to the beach (BA 51).

If you've walked around Siletz Bay, you resume beach walking at Gleneden Beach.

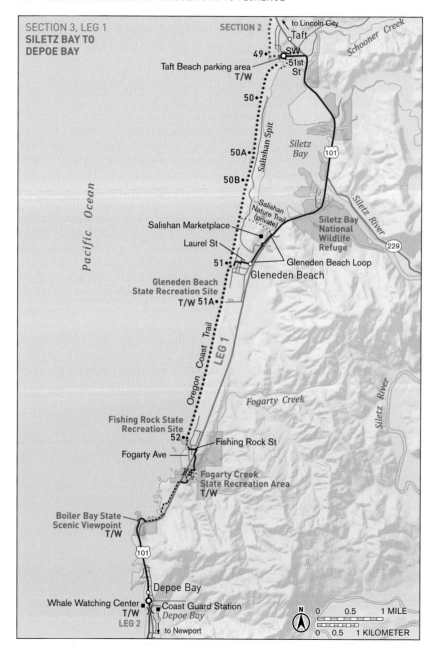

SECTION 3, LEG 1
SILETZ BAY TO DEPOE BAY

SECTION 2

to Lincoln City

Taft

Schooner Creek

49 • SW

Taft Beach parking area
T/W

51st St

50 •

Siletz Bay

101

50A •

50B •

Salishan Spit

Siletz Bay National Wildlife Refuge

229

Salishan Nature Trail (private)

Salishan Marketplace

Laurel St

Gleneden Beach Loop

51 •

Gleneden Beach

Gleneden Beach State Recreation Site
T/W 51A •

Oregon Coast Trail

LEG 1

Siletz River

Fogarty Creek

Fishing Rock State Recreation Site
52 •

Fishing Rock St

Fogarty Ave

Fogarty Creek State Recreation Area
T/W

Boiler Bay State Scenic Viewpoint
T/W

101

Depoe Bay

Whale Watching Center
T/W
LEG 2

Coast Guard Station
Depoe Bay

to Newport

Pacific Ocean

N

0   0.5   1 MILE

0   0.5   1 KILOMETER

A narrow path leads to a network of trails atop Fishing Rock, then out to US 101.

Walk the beach 2.7 mils to the base of Fishing Rock (BA 52), then follow informal trails (and a few OCT signs) to the top of the rock and east through dense vegetation to the west end of Fishing Rock Street. The map directs you across US 101 to Fogarty Creek State Recreation Area, but the following updated route is safer and more direct. After leaving the beach at Fishing

WATCH FOR WHALES

Plenty of whales live off or migrate past the Oregon Coast: grays, minkes, humpbacks, orcas, and in deeper water, sperm whales. But the species you're most likely to see during the hiking season is the gray whale. They're here in bigger numbers during their winter and spring migrations between Baja and the Bering Sea, but a population of gray whales tends to linger all summer offshore. Watch for spouts—exhalations of vaporous breath through the blowhole. High headlands with deep water below are best bets, but the seawall at Depoe Bay is also a good spot. Or splurge on a whale-watching—or "wildlife-watching"—charter boat trip out of Depoe Bay or another port town. There are no guarantees you'll see whales, but you'll certainly see something, from other marine mammals to summering seabirds.

Rock, turn right on Fogarty Avenue and follow it south to US 101. Then walk the highway shoulder just 0.1 mile, and veer right into a wide gravel path down to the beach. Wade the creek if you want; otherwise, go left on the paved path along the creek a short distance to a footbridge (at the park restrooms), cross the bridge, and take another paved path on the south bank east to stone stairs, leading uphill to where the OCT continues south.

The OCT winds through the woods for a ways, then follows close beside the highway before ducking back into the forest a couple of times and ending as a path just inside the highway guardrail north of Boiler Bay State Scenic Viewpoint. Follow the park road, then the highway shoulder, and finally a sidewalk south to make your way into Depoe Bay and reach the Whale Watching Center at the entrance to the harbor. This touristy little town is also a Coast Guard town; it claims the smallest natural navigable harbor in the world. Restaurants, shops, and lodgings are arrayed along US 101 facing the town's scenic seawall.

CAMPING

There is no developed tent camping on this leg. Beach camping is legal between Gleneden Beach and Fogarty Creek State Recreation Area, but with houses lining the oceanfront, it's not ideal.

LODGING

The Gleneden Beach area has some lodging, including the large Salishan Coastal Lodge resort. Depoe Bay offers lodging, including vacation rentals, at a range of prices.

BOAT SHUTTLE

If conditions are exactly right—if it's approaching or at high tide on a sunny day in mid- to late summer—you may be able to hail a recreational crabber to ferry

South of Fogarty Creek, pick up the OCT just west of the highway.

you across the narrow mouth of shallow Siletz Bay. Currently there are not any commercial outfitters available to provide a boat shuttle across this bay mouth.

FOOD RESUPPLY

There is a grocery store along US 101 just north of Fogarty Creek State Recreation Area. You'll find some mini-marts in Depoe Bay, and several restaurants and pubs, but no full-service grocery store.

Leg 1	Mileage between Waypoints
Taft Beach parking area (BA 49) to beach at Laurel Street in Gleneden Beach (BA 51) via US 101 and neighborhood roads	4.4
BA 51 to Fishing Rock (BA 52)	2.7
BA 52 to north entrance Fogarty Creek State Recreation Area	0.3
Fogarty Creek north entrance to south entrance	0.7
Fogarty Creek south entrance to Boiler Bay State Scenic Viewpoint	1.3
Boiler Bay to Whale Watching Center, Depoe Bay	1.3

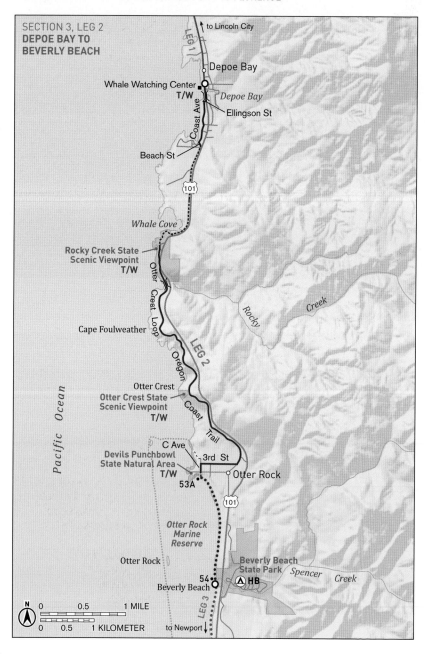

SECTION 3, LEG 2
**DEPOE BAY TO
BEVERLY BEACH**

to Lincoln City

LEG 1

Depoe Bay

Whale Watching Center
T/W

Depoe Bay

Coast Ave

Ellingson St

Beach St

101

Whale Cove

**Rocky Creek State
Scenic Viewpoint
T/W**

Otter Crest Loop

Cape Foulweather

LEG 2

Rocky   *Creek*

Oregon

Otter Crest

**Otter Crest State
Scenic Viewpoint
T/W**

Coast

C Ave

Trail

3rd St

**Devils Punchbowl
State Natural Area
T/W**

Otter Rock

53A

101

*Otter Rock
Marine
Reserve*

Pacific Ocean

Otter Rock

**Beverly Beach
State Park**   *Spencer*   *Creek*

54

⛺ HB

Beverly Beach

LEG 3

N

| 0 | 0.5 | 1 MILE |
| 0 | 0.5 | 1 KILOMETER |

to Newport

LEG 2 DEPOE BAY TO BEVERLY BEACH

Distance   7.4 miles
Elevation gain/loss +420/–470 feet

After crossing over the Depoe Bay harbor inlet on the highway bridge, turn right on Ellingson Street, walk one block, and turn left on Coast Avenue. Follow it 0.6 mile, turn left on gravel Beach Street, and follow Beach Street a short distance to US 101, where the OCT resumes as a narrow trail mostly in the powerline right-of-way alongside the highway. Along the way, enjoy a peek into pristine Whale Cove, a state-designated marine refuge.

The route crosses a hotel entrance road, then resumes as a trail on the right. At the **Y**, either bear left for a shortcut to the Rocky Creek State Scenic Viewpoint restroom or detour to the right on the trail that winds 0.2 mile west, accessing a viewing platform overlooking Whale Cove, then turns south to reach the Rocky Creek parking area.

Follow the park access road south to the highway, then bear right onto Otter Crest Loop, a quiet and scenic side road. It gradually ascends to Otter Crest State Scenic Viewpoint, a great whale-watching site, either outdoors or from inside the small park-run souvenir shop. Continue as the road descends to 3rd Street,

The OCT south of Depoe Bay offers a glimpse into otherwise unseen Whale Cove.

Stairs lead down to the beach from Devils Punchbowl State Natural Area. (Photo by Alix Lee)

turn right, and walk to C Avenue. For a detour to a pocket beach known for its extensive tide pools, walk north a half block on C Avenue and pick up the short asphalt trail heading downhill. Otherwise, turn left on C Avenue and continue to the restrooms and outdoor surfers' shower at Devils Punchbowl State Natural Area. Nearby are coffee and chowder shops.

The park's namesake punchbowl, a short walk west of the park's restrooms, is a hollow rock formation where the surf churns violently at high tide, especially during winter storms. On calm summer days, especially at low to mid-tide, there's not much action to observe, though at very low tide you can explore inside the punchbowl.

To continue on the OCT, walk down the stairs directly south of the restrooms to the beach. Walk the beach south 1.4 miles to the mouth of Spencer Creek and BA 54. Here a trail leads east, under US 101, to Beverly Beach State Park.

SEA OTTERS

Fur hunters wiped out sea otters along the Pacific Northwest coast more than a century ago; the last one caught off of Oregon was reportedly killed in 1907. They've since been reintroduced successfully off California, Washington, British Columbia, and Alaska—but not Oregon. And they have not spread to Oregon on their own. In 2020, a major study was launched to investigate what it would take to bring back the sea otters. This charismatic marine mammal feeds on sea urchins, which mow down kelp forests; if sea otters come back, kelp forests—which provide shelter and food for a lot of other sea life and sequester carbon like grasslands and forests do—will be reinvigorated.

CAMPING

Beverly Beach State Park has a hiker-biker camp ($). Alternately, you could probably beach camp at the bottom of the stairs below Devils Punchbowl.

LODGING

There is a hotel at Whale Cove, a large resort (the Inn at Otter Crest) along Otter Crest Loop, and a number of vacation rentals along Otter Crest Loop and in the vicinity of Devils Punchbowl State Natural Area.

FOOD RESUPPLY

There are no grocery stores on this leg.

Leg 2	Mileage between Waypoints
Whale Watching Center, Depoe Bay, to trail at Beach Street	0.9
Beach Street to entrance, Rocky Creek State Scenic Viewpoint	1.3
Rocky Creek to right turn on 3rd Street	3.5
3rd Street to beach stairs, Devils Punchbowl State Natural Area	0.3
Beach stairs to Beverly Beach State Park (BA 54)	1.4

LEG 3   BEVERLY BEACH TO NEWPORT SOUTH BEACH

Distance   11.2 miles
Elevation gain/loss +280/−280 feet

This nearly all-beach leg takes you past the bustling port town of Newport and three of its distinctive neighborhoods: Nye Beach, the Bayfront, and South Beach. Find restaurants, lodging, and other services in each.

From Beverly Beach State Park, continue south down the beach 2.8 miles to Moolack Beach (BA 55). If the tide is medium to high, leave the beach here to avoid getting stopped at Schooner Point, a minor headland 1 mile to the south; in that case, walk south along the highway to NW 55th Street, where you rejoin the main OCT route heading south on the highway shoulder. Otherwise, continue south from Moolack Beach, rounding the headland, and in another 1.7 miles look for an unsigned trail heading up a ravine in the hillside about 0.2 mile before reaching the foot of Yaquina Head. Follow it up to a neighborhood

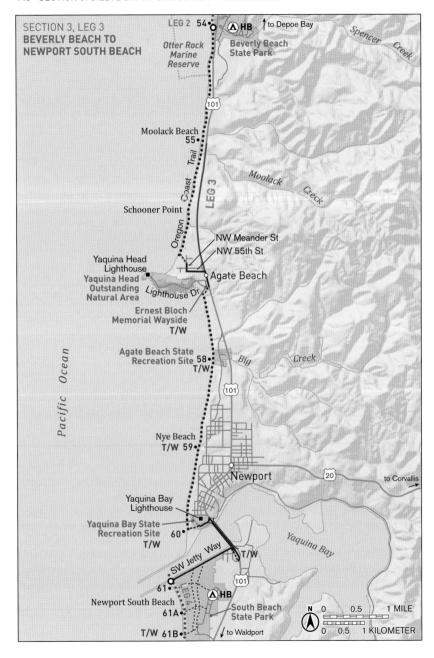

SECTION 3, LEG 3
**BEVERLY BEACH TO
NEWPORT SOUTH BEACH**

LEG 2 54

Ⓐ **HB**
↑ to Depoe Bay

*Otter Rock
Marine
Reserve*

Spencer Creek

Beverly Beach
State Park

101

Moolack Beach
55

Moolack Creek

LEG 3

Oregon Coast Trail

Schooner Point

NW Meander St
NW 55th St

Yaquina Head
Lighthouse
**Yaquina Head
Outstanding
Natural Area**

Agate Beach

Lighthouse Dr

Ernest Bloch
Memorial Wayside
T/W

Big Creek

Agate Beach State
Recreation Site 58
T/W

101

Pacific Ocean

Nye Beach
T/W 59

Newport

20

to Corvallis →

Yaquina Bay
Lighthouse

Yaquina Bay State
Recreation Site 60
T/W

Yaquina Bay

SW Jetty Way

T/W

101

61

LEG 4

Ⓐ **HB**

Newport South Beach
61A

South Beach
State Park

T/W 61B

↓ to Waldport

N
0   0.5   1 MILE
0   0.5   1 KILOMETER

and walk south on NW Meander Street for two blocks, then east on NW 55th Street to US 101.

Walk along the highway briefly, crossing Lighthouse Drive, and enter Ernest Bloch Memorial Wayside (with restrooms and an outdoor surfers' shower). Continue to the bottom of the parking area and pick up paved Lucky Gap Trail leading down to the beach. You may have to cross a stream here, on a well-placed drift log or just by wading.

Walk the beach 2.4 miles south to the beach access at Nye Beach (BA 59) and the lively neighborhood here with cafés, shops, and lodging. It's another 1.1 miles on the beach to a trail leading up the hillside to Yaquina Bay State Recreation Site and lighthouse; look for the bottom of the trail near the BA 60 sign as you approach the Yaquina Bay north jetty.

At the lighthouse, follow the park road out to US 101, at the north end of the Yaquina Bay Bridge. Here you can detour down to the Bayfront neighborhood with its shops, restaurants, and lodging. Otherwise walk the bridge's narrow sidewalk and take the pedestrian stairs down to a dirt path you'll follow a short distance north. If you don't detour east for a pint and a bite at Rogue Ales, swing west to follow the path leading to SW Jetty Way heading west along the south jetty. Where the road ends, follow the sand trail out to the beach.

Just north of Yaquina Head, watch for a ravine leading to the informal trail that takes you to the top of the headland.

A TALE OF TWO LIGHTHOUSES

The tallest lighthouse in Oregon stands at the end of Yaquina Head; you can't miss it as you walk south toward Newport. It's a 1-mile walk off the OCT; to visit, take Lighthouse Road west and consider stopping at the interpretive center in the former quarry along the road. The walk out to the Yaquina Head Lighthouse is worthwhile if only to get a close look at the dense nesting colony of common murres (and other seabirds) on the very near offshore rocks here.

South about 3.5 miles, on the hill just north of the mouth of Yaquina Bay, stands the Yaquina Bay Lighthouse. It's the only lighthouse in Oregon that combines living quarters and light, which juts out the top of the quaint two-story home. Commissioned in 1871, it was decommissioned just three years later. Officials had by then determined that a tall light at the end of Yaquina Head would better serve mariners at this point on the coast. It's open summer afternoons for self-guided tours.

CAMPING

There is a great hiker-biker campsite at South Beach State Park ($) and a couple of ways to get there on foot from the OCT:

If the tide is out, peek through this hole in Schooner Point. (Photo by Brandon Tigner)

» **From SW Jetty Way**, head west on either Old Jetty Trail, a sand path, or paved South Beach Jetty Trail and follow it to the intersection with the paved path leading toward the hiker-biker camp.

» **From the beach**, detour east where you see a big viewing platform in the dunes, at BA 61A (0.5 mile south of the south jetty), and follow the path 0.4 mile to where it ends at the campground near the hiker-biker camp.

LODGING

There is a wide variety of lodging available in Newport.

FOOD RESUPPLY

You'll find several supermarkets in Newport and a natural foods store; all are located along or near US 101, requiring you to detour up to 1 mile off the OCT. A large grocery store is about 1 mile east of the OCT at Nye Beach; Oceana Natural Foods is about four blocks farther.

Leg 3	Mileage between Waypoints
Beverly Beach State Park (BA 54) to Moolack Beach (BA 55)	2.8
BA 55 to trail leading off beach	1.7
Base of trail to US 101 via NW 55th Street	0.6
NW 55th Street to Ernest Bloch Memorial Wayside	0.2
Bloch Wayside to beach via Lucky Gap Trail	0.2
Beach at Lucky Gap Trail to Nye Beach (BA 59)	2.4
BA 59 to trail to Yaquina Bay State Recreation Site (BA 60)	1.1
BA 60 to north end of Yaquina Bay Bridge	0.5
Yaquina Bay Bridge to return to beach at south jetty	1.7

LEG 4 NEWPORT SOUTH BEACH TO WALDPORT

Distance	14.7 miles
Elevation gain/loss	+250/–240 feet

Enjoy a lot of beach walking on this leg. From Yaquina Bay's south jetty, walk the beach south 7.9 miles, crossing Beaver Creek along the way. It's easy to wade in summer; at BA 62B you can access a large footbridge that leads to restrooms at Ona Beach, part of Brian Booth State Park. Approaching the end of the beach

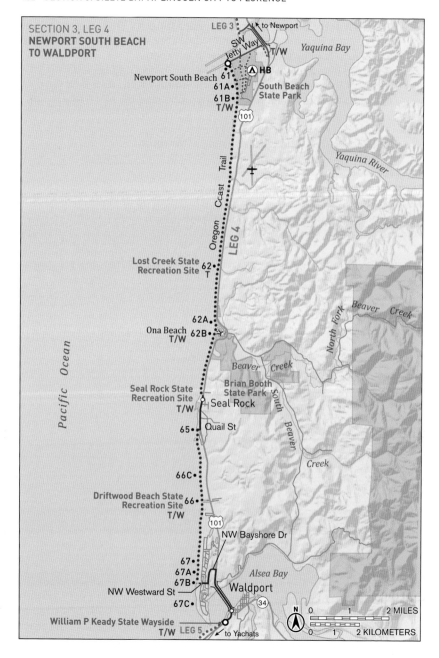

SECTION 3, LEG 4
**NEWPORT SOUTH BEACH
TO WALDPORT**

LEG 3
to Newport
SW Jetty Way
T/W
Yaquina Bay

Newport South Beach   61
61A
61B
T/W
Ⓐ HB
**South Beach
State Park**
101

Yaquina River

Oregon Ccast Trail

LEG 4

Lost Creek State
Recreation Site   62
T

62A
Ona Beach   62B
T/W

Beaver   Creek

North Fork

Beaver   Creek

South Beaver

Brian Booth
State Park

Seal Rock State
Recreation Site
T/W   Seal Rock

65   Quail St

Creek

66C

Driftwood Beach State
Recreation Site   66
T/W

101

NW Bayshore Dr

67
67A
67B
NW Westward St
Waldport

Alsea Bay

67C

William P Keady State Wayside   34
T/W   LEG 5
to Yachats

Pacific   Ocean

N
0   1   2 MILES
0   1   2 KILOMETERS

at a rocky bluff, look for a little trail leading up a creek ravine to US 101; it's unmarked and may be a little hard to find, but once you start up it, it's clear you're on an established route.

Follow the highway shoulder south 1.1 miles, bypassing Seal Rock State Recreation Site (which has a lovely beach but no legal way to return to the highway at its south end). At Quail Street, across the highway from Seal Rock Street, go west to return to the beach at BA 65. Walk the beach about 3 more miles to BA 67B, where a little trail leads through the dunes to Bayshore Beach Club. Follow NW Westward Street east, then go north and east on NW Bayshore Drive, following it up to US 101. Follow the highway a short distance to cross the soaring bridge that spans Alsea Bay and reach downtown Waldport.

An informal trail leads up a gully to US 101 just north of Seal Rock State Recreation Site.

CAMPING

As long as you're not adjacent to a state park, you can beach camp nearly anywhere along this stretch. There is a commercial KOA campground near the north end of the bridge at Waldport that allows tent camping, but it is expensive and reportedly not very accommodating to thru-hikers; I suggest continuing 4 miles more to the hiker-biker campsite at Beachside State Recreation Site (see Leg 5).

LODGING

Find budget lodging in Waldport and vacation rentals scattered throughout this route.

FOOD RESUPPLY

There is a supermarket in Waldport on State Route 34 about 0.4 mile east of US 101 and smaller grocery stores along US 101.

Leg 4	Mileage between Waypoints
Yaquina Bay south jetty to Lost Creek State Recreation Site (BA 62)	4.7
BA 62 to BA 62B, south of Beaver Creek	1.6
BA 62B to trail to US 101	1.6
Trail to US 101 to Quail Street (BA 65)	1.2
BA 65 to Driftwood Beach State Recreation Site (BA 66)	1.7
BA 66 to Bayshore Beach Club (BA 67B)	1.5
BA 67B to US 101 at NW Bayshore Drive	1.2
NW Bayshore Drive to downtown Waldport	1.2

LEG 5   WALDPORT TO YACHATS

Distance   10.3 miles
Elevation gain/loss +50/–20 feet

If the tide is low, return to the beach at William P. Keady State Wayside at the south end of downtown Waldport and follow the beach around the point. Otherwise, continue along US 101 to Governor Patterson Memorial State Recreation Site, where you can return to the beach.

Weather-sculpted shore pines mark the beach access at Governor Patterson Memorial State Recreation Site.

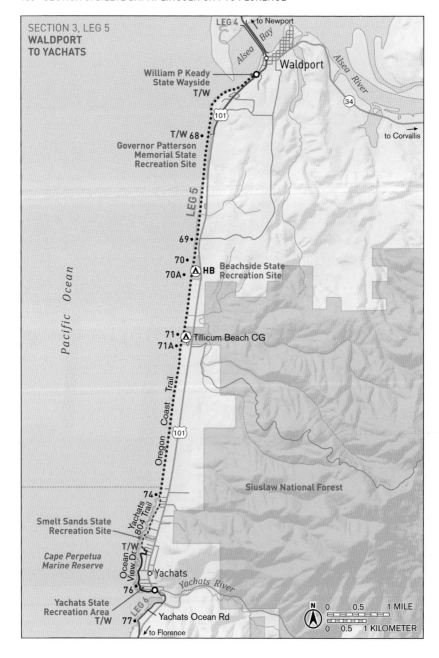

SECTION 3, LEG 5
**WALDPORT
TO YACHATS**

LEG 4 → to Newport

Alsea Bay

Waldport

Alsea River

34

to Corvallis

William P Keady
State Wayside
T/W

101

T/W 68 •
Governor Patterson
Memorial State
Recreation Site

LEG 5

69 •

70 •
70A • Ⓐ **HB**

Beachside State
Recreation Site

Pacific Ocean

71 • Ⓐ Tillicum Beach CG
71A •

Oregon Coast Trail

101

74 •

Yachats
804 Trail

Smelt Sands State
Recreation Site

*Cape Perpetua
Marine Reserve*

T/W

Ocean View Dr

Siuslaw National Forest

○ Yachats

Yachats River

76 •

Yachats State
Recreation Area
T/W   77 •

LEG 6

Yachats Ocean Rd

↙ to Florence

N

0   0.5   1 MILE

0   0.5   1 KILOMETER

Fences line the route of the Yachats 804 Trail south of Smelt Sands.

From here it's nearly 7 miles of beach walking to where the beach ends at a bluff north of Yachats (BA 74). Follow a path up a little ravine and continue south on what's known as Yachats 804 Trail to the parking area at Smelt Sands State Recreation Site. From here, the OCT continues south on a route that cuts across the grassy bluff, veers inland between a pair of fences, turns right at the street, and zigzags on a gravel path along neighborhood streets through the town of Yachats until reaching Ocean View Drive. Follow it to US 101 at the south end of town.

OREGON'S MARINE RESERVES

As you approach Yachats, you'll be walking past Cape Perpetua Marine Reserve, the largest of Oregon's five marine reserves. You've already passed three: off of Cape Falcon, Cascade Head, and Otter Rock north of Newport. Oregon's marine reserves are areas in the nearshore ocean dedicated to scientific research and conservation; all ocean development and removal of marine life is prohibited (though limited fishing is allowed in some adjacent marine protected areas). By closing these relatively small areas of the ocean to trolling and trawling, they serve as nurseries, replenishing populations of ocean flora and fauna all along the coast. They also serve as living laboratories where scientists can study the real-time impact of conservation on the marine environment.

CAMPING

Beachside State Recreation Site has a hiker-biker campground ($); to reach it, leave the beach at BA 70A. Tillicum Beach Campground ($$), 1.3 miles farther (at BA 71 and 71A), has reservable campsites but no drop-in hiker-biker camp.

LODGING

There are vacation rentals along this route and a lot of accommodation options in Yachats. One, the Drift Inn Hotel, has inexpensive "pedal out" rooms ideal for thru-hikers and touring cyclists.

FOOD RESUPPLY

There is a grocery store in Yachats.

Leg 5	Mileage between Waypoints
Waldport to Governor Patterson Memorial State Recreation Site (BA 68)	1.2
BA 68 to Beachside State Recreation Site (BA 70A)	2.4
BA 70A to Tillicum Beach Campground (BA 71 and 71A)	1.3
BA 71A to start of Yachats 804 Trail (BA 74)	3.4
BA 74 to Smelt Sands State Recreation Site parking area	0.8
Smelt Sands to US 101 at Yachats River	1.2

The view south from the OCT takes in the Cape Perpetua Scenic Area shoreline and forest.

LEG 6 YACHATS TO HECETA HEAD

Distance	19 miles
Elevation gain/loss	+3310/–3300 feet

Cape Perpetua Scenic Area offers great hiking, both on and off the OCT route. Consider a layover day here to explore further and rest up after your ascent and steep descent of the cape and after resupplying with food at Yachats. There's more forested hiking to the south. But there isn't much beach walking on this leg, and there is a long stretch of highway shoulder walking.

Cross the Yachats River and veer right onto Yachats Ocean Road. Just before the road meets US 101, turn right on an unsigned paved road and follow OCT

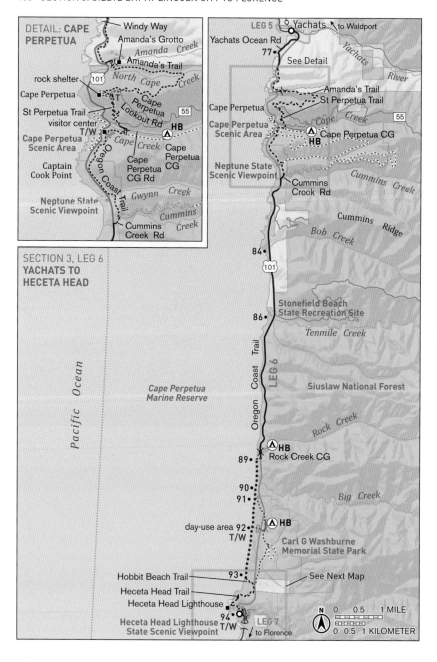

DETAIL: CAPE PERPETUA

Windy Way
Amanda's Grotto
Amanda Creek
Amanda's Trail
rock shelter
101
North Cape Creek
Cape Perpetua
St Perpetua Trail
Cape Perpetua Lookout Rd
visitor center
T/W
55
HB
Cape Perpetua Scenic Area
Cape Creek
Cape Perpetua CG
Cape Perpetua CG Rd
Captain Cook Point
Oregon Coast Trail
Gwynn Creek
Cummins Creek
Neptune State Scenic Viewpoint
Cummins Creek Rd

SECTION 3, LEG 6
YACHATS TO HECETA HEAD

LEG 5 Yachats   to Waldport
Yachats Ocean Rd
77
See Detail
Yachats River
Amanda's Trail
St Perpetua Trail
Cape Perpetua
Cape Creek
55
Cape Perpetua Scenic Area
HB
Cape Perpetua CG
Neptune State Scenic Viewpoint
Cummins Crook Rd
Cummins Creek
Cummins Ridge
84
101
Bob Creek
Stonefield Beach State Recreation Site
86
Tenmile Creek
Oregon Coast Trail
LEG 6
Siuslaw National Forest
Pacific Ocean
Cape Perpetua Marine Reserve
Rock Creek
HB
Rock Creek CG
89
90
91
Big Creek
day-use area 92
T/W
HB
Carl G Washburne Memorial State Park
93
See Next Map
Hobbit Beach Trail
Heceta Head Trail
Heceta Head Lighthouse
Heceta Head Lighthouse State Scenic Viewpoint
94
T/W
LEG 7
to Florence

N
0   0.5   1 MILE
0   0.5   1 KILOMETER

REMEMBERING AMANDA

As you start up Amanda's Trail, you'll pass through Amanda's Grotto, where a statue festooned with visitors' offerings honors the memory of the trail's name-sake and recalls the grim chapter of Oregon history she represents. In 1864, an elderly, blind Indigenous woman named Amanda De-Cuys lived near Coos Bay. That year, the US government rounded up members of the Coos and other tribes, including Amanda, and marched them north to a settlement in present-day Yach-ats, within what was then the Coast Indian Reservation. The trip took ten days. Walking over the sharp rocks at Cape Perpetua, Amanda reportedly "tore her feet horribly over these ragged rock [sic], leaving blood sufficient to track her by." There the written record of her life ends.

Many descendants of the coastal tribes who survived the US government's cruelty in the nineteenth century are today part of confederated tribes, such as the Siletz, the Grande Ronde, and the Coos, Lower Umpqua, and Siuslaw, whose current enterprises are helping to support their communities, restore Native lands, and improve life for others in Oregon through their charitable giving.

signs parallel to US 101 (but off of the highway shoulder). In 0.2 mile (at Windy Way Street), cross the highway and continue south as the OCT path climbs above but still parallel to the highway for another 0.2 mile to the bottom of Amanda's Trail. Follow Amanda's Trail 0.5 mile to where it crosses a gravel road and, soon, reaches a shrine known as Amanda's Grotto.

From here the trail crosses a creek and heads up rather steeply for about 1 mile, tops off, and then descends for most of the next mile to a junction with a short trail leading left to the road and lower parking area. Either make a left here and walk the road up a short distance to the parking lot atop the cape, or bear right and continue to the next junction, where a left turn leads to the upper parking area. Alternately, bear right at all trail junctions to reach the rock shelter viewpoint built by the Civilian Conservation Corps in the 1930s, then continue on that trail to the parking area.

Follow the steep St. Perpetua Trail south down the cape, crossing the lookout and campground access roads and Cape Creek, to the visitor center. Pick up the asphalt trail heading south; it crosses the visitor center access road and becomes a dirt trail that crosses Gwynn Creek shortly before ending at Cum-mins Creek Road; take this gravel road west out to US 101.

From here the OCT follows US 101 for 6 miles. Past Bob Creek you might be able to find a way down to the beach, but only briefly, as you have to get back on the highway at Stonefield Beach State Recreation Site at BA 86; past here you run into cliffs and won't be able to get off of the beach. Return to the beach just

Adorned with offerings, a sculpture honoring Amanda De-Cuys sits alongside her name-sake trail.

past the entrance to Rock Creek Campground; look for the BA 89 sign, where a little trail leads down to the sand.

From Rock Creek, walk the beach 2.8 miles to the Hobbit Beach Trail at BA 93, just north of Heceta Head. Follow the trail east 0.3 mile. Just before reaching US 101, turn right at the junction to pick up the trail up and over Heceta Head. After topping out, you'll pass Heceta Head Lighthouse (built in 1893) and the vintage lighthouse keeper's quarters, which are now a B&B. Continue down to the parking area and pocket beach at Heceta Head Lighthouse State Scenic Viewpoint.

The Heceta Head Trail provides glimpses of the coastline stretching north.

CAPE PERPETUA SCENIC AREA

Cape Perpetua Scenic Area may be best known to visitors for its tide pools and shoreline Spouting Horn, a rock formation that becomes a saltwater fountain at high tide. But its most important function is protection of some of the few remaining intact old-growth forests on the central Oregon Coast. Douglas-fir, western hemlock, and Sitka spruce blanket the steep hillsides rising from the rocky shoreline. Some of this forest, including parts of the forest along the route of the OCT, was logged in the past, but most of it has never been logged. Giant legacy trees, including a six-hundred-year-old Sitka spruce in Cape Perpetua Campground, are scattered throughout the area.

The scenic area includes much of Cape and Gwynn Creeks, which empty into the Pacific at Cape Perpetua Marine Reserve, creating the kind of habitat connectivity that is the gold standard of coastal conservation. If you camp here, consider taking a layover day to explore the shoreline and more of the trails, some of which were built by members of the Civilian Conservation Corps when it had a camp here in the 1930s. The map in this book isn't large or detailed enough to show you all 26 miles of trail in the scenic area, but you can find maps online (or stop by the visitor center).

A hiker makes her way among pools in the sand north of Heceta Head.

The beach west of Washburne State Park ends at forested Heceta Head.

CAMPING

Cape Perpetua Campground ($) offers a handful of hiker-biker sites, some more private and appealing than others; some hikers have said it was their favorite campsite on the entire OCT. There are no showers.

For dispersed camping south of Cape Perpetua, consider venturing up the road to the Cummins Creek trailhead or, to the south, the road to the Cummins Ridge trailhead to find a bivouac site.

Rock Creek Campground doesn't have a formal hiker-biker area but ask the campground host for a hiker-biker site ($) and you may be accommodated. The entrance is 0.2 mile north of Rock Creek BA 89; walk the access road 0.4 mile to the shady creekside campground. There are no showers.

Carl G. Washburne Memorial State Park has a hiker-biker campground ($) and is about a half mile off the OCT route. There are a couple of ways to reach it from the OCT. Leave the beach at BA 91, south of China Creek, and follow the trail leading into the dunes, under US 101, and along the creek to the campground's loop B; the hiker-biker site is in the middle of loop A. Or leave the beach at BA 92, the day-use parking area for the state park, and follow the road and trail east across US 101 to the campground entrance. To rejoin the OCT, return to the beach at BA 92 or pick up the trail heading south from the campground entrance road. Where it ends at US 101, cross the highway and pick up the OCT toward Heceta Head Lighthouse.

LODGING

A small number of mostly modestly priced accommodations can be found north and south of Stonefield Beach State Recreation Site, along the highway-walking portion of this leg.

The nineteenth-century Queen Anne–style lighthouse keeper's quarters perched on a bluff just south of Heceta Head Lighthouse now serves as a luxurious six-room bed-and-breakfast under concession from the Forest Service. A stay includes a seven-course breakfast.

FOOD RESUPPLY

There are no grocery stores on this leg past Yachats.

Leg 6	Mileage between Waypoints
Yachats River Bridge to start of Amanda's Trail	1.4
Amanda's Trail to top of Cape Perpetua	3.3
Top of Cape Perpetua to visitor center	1.9
Visitor center to US 101 at Cummins Creek Road	1.4
Cummins Creek Road to Stonefield Beach State Recreation Site (BA 86)	3.1
BA 86 to beach access at Rock Creek (BA 89)	2.9
BA 89 to Hobbit Beach Trail (BA 93)	2.8
BA 93 to junction with Heceta Head Trail	0.3
Heceta Head Trail to Heceta Head Lighthouse State Scenic Viewpoint parking area	1.9

LEG 7   HECETA HEAD TO FLORENCE

Distance	14.5 miles
Elevation gain/loss	+1290/–1310 feet

This leg starts with a highway shoulder walk and ends with a long beach walk at the northern end of the large dune sheet that stretches south 50 miles to the mouth of Coos Bay.

From the parking area at Heceta Head Lighthouse State Scenic Viewpoint, follow signs pointing to US 101 southbound. Walk US 101 south or try catching a ride with a southbound driver to avoid walking through the very narrow, 200-yard-long highway tunnel just to the south. There is no sidewalk and barely enough room for a large motor home to get through this two-lane tunnel, let alone a motor home plus an oncoming vehicle, plus you. Consider asking for a ride through the tunnel from a motorist parked at Heceta Head. Alternatively, push the "Bikes in Tunnel" button and sprint through.

SECTION 3, LEG 7
**HECETA HEAD
TO FLORENCE**

LEG 6

Heceta Head
Lighthouse

94

Cape Creek

to Yachats

Heceta Head Lighthouse
State Scenic Viewpoint

Sea Lion Point
Sea Lion Caves

See Detail

LEG 7

Cape Perpetua
Marine Reserve

95

101

Berry

Creek

Siuslaw National Forest

95A

▲T
Baker
Beach
CG

Sutton
Creek

Sutton
Lake

Mercer
Lake

Oregon Coast Trail

Sutton CG ⚑

Siuslaw
National
Forest

Pacific Ocean

96
96A

Heceta Beach Rd

Clear
Lake

97

T North Jetty Rd

⚑

Harbor Vista
County Park

Rhododendron Dr

101

to Eugene ↗

126

Oregon Dunes
National
Recreation
Area

Siuslaw River

Florence ○ T/W
⚑ Port of Siuslaw CG
Old Town

Sand Dunes

Sand Dunes Rd

106

to Winchester Bay

SECTION 4

DETAIL:
**HECETA
HEAD**

93

to Yachats

Heceta Head Trail

LEG 6

101

Heceta Head
Lighthouse
T/W

Cape Creek

94

Heceta Head
Lighthouse
State Scenic
Viewpoint

LEG 7

to Florence

N

0   0.5   1 MILE

0   0.5   1 KILOMETER

Whether walking or riding in a vehicle, continue south on US 101 for 3 miles along this rocky stretch of coastline. Shortly before reaching the high point on this road walk over Sea Lion Point, you'll pass the roadside attraction Sea Lion Caves, boasting "America's largest sea cave." Before you pay admission, note that the Steller sea lions found here don't normally hang out inside the cave in summer; they're outside on offshore rocks. Continue on the highway shoulder to where a spectacular view opens up to the south; look for a small OCT signpost just south of milepost 181 near the sign for the Southview housing development.

Follow the trail 0.2 mile down to the beach. From here the beach stretches 6 miles south to the Siuslaw River. You might need to take off your shoes to cross the mouth of Berry Creek at about 0.8 mile (near BA 95) and Sutton Creek 2.7 miles farther. At BA 97, angle off the beach and onto the north jetty of the Siuslaw and follow it inland to the parking area. There is no practical way to get a boat shuttle across the Siuslaw due to the long rock jetties on both banks. If you did, you would miss Florence and the opportunity to restock with food and water for the hike down the dunes. Instead, walk the road 5.3 miles into Old Town in Florence.

Begin by walking out N. Jetty Road, past Harbor Vista County Park, and turn right on Rhododendron Drive. Follow it until it curves left as it approaches the center of town. Stay on Rhododendron all the way to US 101 if you need to hit the supermarket; otherwise, start bearing right at street junctions and you'll end up at the bridge across the Siuslaw and in Old Town with its restaurants, shops, and possibly camping.

CAMPING

Beach camping is not allowed in summer from the base of Heceta Head to about a half mile south of the mouth of Sutton Creek due to snowy plover restrictions. There are no such restrictions on beach camping south of here to the north jetty of the Siuslaw River, but it's not very remote. Much of the dunes east of the beach in this area, north of BA 96, is Siuslaw National Forest land, where dispersed camping is allowed.

From BA 95A, a trail leads inland 0.4 mile to rustic Baker Beach Campground ($$). It's expensive given that all you get is a tent site, a vault toilet, and no water. South 1.5 miles, an unmarked trail leads through the dunes briefly to a spot where you can usually cross Sutton Creek on a fallen log; just past it is the end of the road leading 1.5 miles to Sutton Campground ($$), which takes reservations but has no hiker-biker camp (and no showers).

Harbor Vista County Park ($$), off N. Jetty Road, is a deluxe campground with showers and other amenities, but no hiker-biker area; make reservations in summer.

The Port of Siuslaw offers tent camping ($$) walking distance from restaurants and shops in Florence, 0.6 mile east of the Siuslaw River Bridge. The

Driftwood piles up on the beach near the north jetty of the Siuslaw River.

campground no longer has a hiker-biker area, but there is often room for drop-in hikers in the grassy tent camping area (or call ahead to make a reservation). It's not remote, but it's a convenient spot to lay over and celebrate having reached the halfway point on the OCT.

LODGING

There are vacation rentals and a large condominium complex—Driftwood Shores—in the Heceta Beach neighborhood north of Florence, accessed via BA 96 and BA 96A about 1 mile north of the north jetty. Among lodging options in Florence, look for inexpensive hostel rooms listed on AirBnB.com.

FOOD RESUPPLY

A supermarket on US 101 in Florence is a short walk from the bridge.

Leg 7	Mileage between Waypoints
Heceta Head Lighthouse State Scenic Viewpoint parking area to start of trail to beach	3
Beach trail to trail to Baker Beach Campground (BA 95A)	1.1
BA 95A to north jetty Siuslaw River (BA 97)	5.1
BA 97 to Siuslaw River Bridge, Florence	5.3

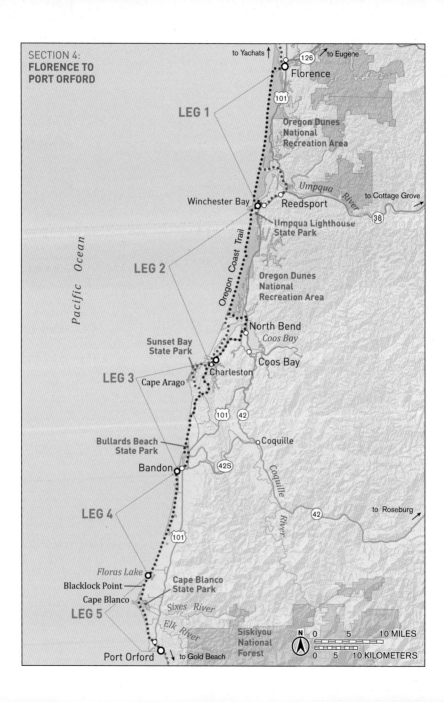

SECTION 4:
**FLORENCE TO
PORT ORFORD**

to Yachats ↑   ↗ to Eugene
126
Florence

LEG 1

101

Oregon Dunes
National
Recreation Area

Umpqua River   → to Cottage Grove

Winchester Bay   Reedsport
Umpqua Lighthouse   38
State Park

LEG 2

Oregon Coast Trail

Oregon Dunes
National
Recreation Area

North Bend
Coos Bay
Sunset Bay
State Park
Charleston   Coos Bay
LEG 3
Cape Arago

101 42

Bullards Beach
State Park   Coquille

Bandon
42S

LEG 4   42   → to Roseburg

101

Floras Lake
Blacklock Point   Cape Blanco
Cape Blanco   State Park
LEG 5   Sixes River
                         Elk River   Siskiyou
                                           National   N   0   5   10 MILES
                                           Forest
Port Orford ↓ to Gold Beach   0   5   10 KILOMETERS

Pacific Ocean

Heading over the foredune south of the Siuslaw south jelly (Leg 1)

SECTION 4
Florence to Port Orford

Distance
108.8 miles with Umpqua boat shuttle
(97.9 with Coos Bay boat shuttle)

Cumulative OCT miles
Miles 229.2 to 338

Elevation gain/loss
+2640/−2610 feet

Headland summits
Coos Head (165 feet), Seven Devils
(540 feet), Blacklock Point (184 feet),
Cape Blanco (240 feet)

Max distance between campgrounds
19.9 miles (Bullards Beach State Park to
Boice Cope County Park, Legs 3 and 4)

Max distance between lodging
23.7 miles with boat shuttle or 29.6
miles without boat shuttle (Florence
to Winchester Bay, Leg 1)

Water availability
Poor on some legs

Boat shuttle
Two (Legs 1 and 2)

Legs
1. Florence to Winchester Bay
2. Winchester Bay to Charleston
3. Charleston to Bandon
4. Bandon to Floras Lake
5. Floras Lake to Port Orford

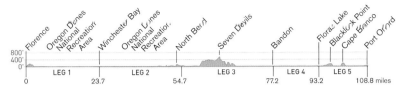

SECTION 4: FLORENCE TO PORT ORFORD

This is the most remote section of the entire OCT, requiring long days for inn-to-inn hikers but a lot of dispersed camping options for backpackers and *no* highway shoulder walking once you return to the beach south of Florence. This section begins at the Oregon Dunes National Recreation Area—a vast area of wild and undeveloped sand dunes stretching south to Coos Bay. Immediately south of Coos Bay is a rugged coastline of sheer cliffs known as the Seven Devils that must be skirted on back roads. Then you hit the charming town of Bandon and the long, remote beach to the south, followed by wild Blacklock Point and Cape Blanco, the westernmost point on the Oregon Coast.

Be aware that you may encounter (or at least hear) OHVs on parts of the beach adjacent to Oregon Dunes, particularly north of the Siltcoos River and between Winchester Bay and your beach exit north of Coos Bay. They mostly stick to the sand dunes, however, and not the beach. You also need to be aware of regulations protecting snowy plovers: mainly, avoid camping in known plover nesting areas, which are typically well signed.

Section 4 passes through the traditional homelands of the Siuslaw, Kuitsh, Coos, and Coquille people.

ACCESS

You can leave a car overnight at South Jetty Beach at parking areas 1 through 7 with the proper permit from the Oregon Dunes National Recreation Area (see Contacts). Alternately, leave your car on a neighborhood street in Florence and walk or take a taxi to the South Jetty Beach area to start your section hike.

Section 4 ends at Port Orford. Overnight parking is available at the Port of Port Orford, or call Port Orford Heads State Park (see Contacts for both) to inquire about getting a permit to leave your vehicle overnight at Tseriadun State Recreation Site.

Bus transportation is available to between Florence and Port Orford. Curry Public Transit's Coastal Express bus runs north and south three times a day between North Bend and Brookings (see Contacts).

Low-angled sunlight casts deep shadows in the Oregon Dunes National Recreation Area.

SUGGESTED ITINERARIES

Limited accommodations require some long days of walking for inn-to-inn hikers, but a wealth of dispersed camping opportunities make this an excellent section for backpacking or a camping and lodging combo. Section hikers will want to start at South Jetty Beach parking area 2 rather than in Florence to avoid a road walk; in that case, subtract 3.3 miles from Day 1. Mileage figures here reflect distances on the OCT route only; distance to lodgings or a developed campground may add 0.1 to 1 mile to your day's hike (or as much as 4.2 miles to camping near Charleston).

7 Days Camping		Miles
Day 1	Siuslaw River Bridge, Florence, to Threemile Lake	15.7
Day 2	Threemile Lake to Umpqua Lighthouse State Park hiker-biker camp (with boat shuttle across Winchester Bay)	9.2
Day 3	Umpqua Lighthouse State Park to Bluebill Campground	16.4
Day 4	Bluebill Campground to Charleston (access to nearby hiker-biker camps)	13.4
Day 5	Charleston to Bullards Beach State Park hiker-biker camp via Pearl's Trail (walking the route on Seven Devils Road)	18.6
Day 6	Bullards Beach State Park to Boice Cope County Park	19.9
Day 7	Boice Cope County Park to Port Orford	15.6

11 Days Camping		Miles
Day 1	Siuslaw River Bridge, Florence, to Waxmyrtle Campground	8.3
Day 2	Waxmyrtle Campground to beach camp near Sparrow Park Road	9
Day 3	Sparrow Park Road to Umpqua Lighthouse State Park hiker-biker camp (with boat shuttle across Winchester Bay)	7.6
Day 4	Umpqua Lighthouse State Park to beach 1.5 miles south of Tenmile Creek	8.9

Day 5	Beach south of Tenmile Creek to Bluebill Campground	7.5
Day 6	Bluebill Campground to Charleston Park (aoooou to nearby hiker-biker camps)	13.4
Day 7	Charleston to beach camp near Seven Devils State Recreation Site (walking the route on Seven Devils Road)	12.1
Day 8	Seven Devils beach to Bullards Beach State Park hiker-biker camp via Pearl's Trail	6.5
Day 9	Bullards Beach State Park to New River bivouac campsite	15.7
Day 10	New River bivouac to Cape Blanco State Park hiker-biker camp	12
Day 11	Cape Blanco State Park to Port Orford	7.8

7 Days Inn-to-Inn · Miles

Lack of lodging in, or even near, the Oregon Dunes NRA requires long days for inn-to-inn hikers, especially if you can't arrange boat shuttles. Section hikers could shorten their first day to 20.4 miles by starting at South Jetty Beach parking area 2. Shorten it further to a pleasant 11.3 miles by starting at Tahkenitch Campground trailhead. Walk the trail 0.25 mile to a junction, turn left, and follow signs to Threemile Lake (pausing for a swim if it's warm). Continue to the beach (3.3 miles), then continue south 8 more miles to your boat shuttle and lodgings on Winchester Bay. If you arrange for a boat shuttle across Coos Bay or a taxi ride through North Bend–Coos Bay, you can compress Days 2 and 3 into one.

Day 1	Siuslaw River Bridge, Florence, to Winchester Bay (with boat shuttle)	23.7
Day 2	Winchester Bay to North Bend (without boat shuttle across Coos Bay)	21.8
Day 3	North Bend to Charleston	9.2
Day 4	Charleston to Bandon Dunes Golf Resort	16.8
Day 5	Bandon Dunes to BA 152A (Face Rock area south of Bandon)	7.8
Day 6	Face Rock to Floras Lake	13.9
Day 7	Floras Lake to Port Orford	15.6

THE OREGON DUNES

South of Heceta Head and all the way to Coos Bay, the Oregon Coast Trail passes the largest expanse of active sand dunes in North America. Much of it is public land within the Oregon Dunes National Recreation Area.

A dune is a hill of sand formed by wind. Some dunes here are barren of plants and are constantly being sculpted anew by the wind. Others are barely recognizable as dunes; on some, plants hold the dune in place. Widespread planting of non-native European beachgrass early in the twentieth century (and continuing to this day) has changed this landscape. This plant's roots go deep and broad; as wind blows, sand piles up around the plant, and it grows upward, creating a mound. That dynamic is what has created tall foredunes—like sandy seawalls—all along this part of the coast. The foredune intercepts sand blowing off the beach, "starving" the active dunes inland of sand and creating freshwater depressions behind the foredunes. The changes to the active dune landscape inland multiply; as a result, the active dunes here are slowly disappearing.

The resulting landscape is today a mosaic of active sand hummocks, wetlands harboring a diversity of plant life, steep-sloped mini-forests (known as "tree islands") surrounded by active dunes, and a type of transitional forest dominated by shore pines lying between the active dunes and coastal forest—impenetrably dense in places. Among the dunes lie freshwater dune swale lakes, the most accessible to OCT hikers being Threemile Lake, an appealing spot for camping and a dip on a hot day.

Much of the beach here is closed to camping to protect nesting snowy plovers, but the dunes inland a short distance are available. You'll need to scout around to find the best bivouac sites in the dunes—not too sandy but not too wet. Or venture inland a mile or more to camp in a developed campground (you may need to reserve a campsite; there are no hiker-biker camps here).

LEG 1 FLORENCE TO WINCHESTER BAY

Distance   23.7 miles (29.6 without boat shuttle)
Elevation gain/loss   +260/−280 feet

From Florence, either get a ride or walk south across the Siuslaw River Bridge, down US 101, and west on South Jetty Road (becomes Sand Dunes Road). Where the road bends right at BA 106 (South Jetty Staging), continue straight over the foredune to reach the beach. If you are leaving a car, follow the road north a short distance to parking area 2. All the elevation gain on this leg is from the road walk from Florence to South Jetty Beach.

Winchester Bay Charters picks up hikers just inside the north jetty of the Umpqua River.

From here you have miles and miles of beach walking and camping opportunities, limited only by snowy plover restrictions (see Camping). You'll need to bring enough water to last you to Winchester Bay unless you are willing to detour inland a bit to a developed USFS campground (or you're willing to drink filtered surface water). These campgrounds have water and toilets; only one has showers, and they have no drop-in hiker-biker camps. You may see and hear OHVs on the beach between BA 106 and the Siltcoos River, though they're mostly in the adjacent dunes.

Your first obstacle is the Siltcoos River, 5.4 miles south of where you returned to the beach; you should be able to wade it at low to mid-tide in summer. South about 6 more miles is the mouth of Tahkenitch Creek; it should be wadeable at any tide in summer. For a freshwater swim, continue south and detour inland at BA 115A; the sand trail here leads east about a half mile to the north end of Threemile Lake. Threemile Creek, easily waded, is about 2 miles ahead, just south of the end of Sparrow Park Road at BA 116.

At Sparrow Park Road you have a choice. The best option is to call a day or two ahead to arrange a boat shuttle across the Umpqua River to the marina at Winchester Bay with Winchester Bay Charters (see Contacts). If you've made

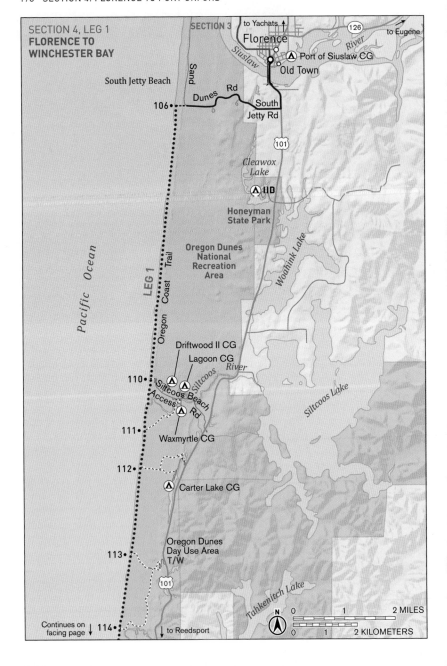

SECTION 4, LEG 1
**FLORENCE TO
WINCHESTER BAY**

SECTION 3

to Yachats ↑

Florence

126

to Eugene

River

Siuslaw

Port of Siuslaw CG

Old Town

Sand

South Jetty Beach

Dunes Rd

South
Jetty Rd

106

101

*Cleawox
Lake*

IID

**Honeyman
State Park**

Woahink Lake

**Oregon Dunes
National
Recreation
Area**

LEG 1

Oregon Coast Trail

Pacific Ocean

Driftwood II CG

Lagoon CG

Siltcoos River

110

Siltcoos Beach

Siltcoos Lake

Access Rd

111

Waxmyrtle CG

112

Carter Lake CG

**Oregon Dunes
Day Use Area**
T/W

113

101

Tahkenitch Lake

N

0   1   2 MILES

0   1   2 KILOMETERS

Continues on
facing page ↓ 114

↓ to Reedsport

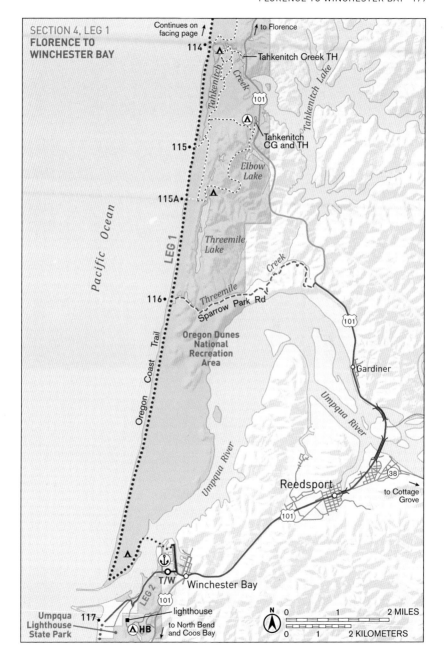

SECTION 4, LEG 1
**FLORENCE TO
WINCHESTER BAY**

Continues on
facing page ↑

↑ to Florence

114

Tahkenitch Creek TH

Tahkenitch Creek

101

Tahkenitch Lake

Tahkenitch
CG and TH

115

*Elbow
Lake*

LEG 1

115A

*Threemile
Lake*

Pacific Ocean

Creek

116

Threemile

Sparrow Park Rd

101

**Oregon Dunes
National
Recreation
Area**

Gardiner

Oregon Coast Trail

Umpqua River

Umpqua River

Reedsport

38

to Cottage
Grove

101

T/W   **Winchester Bay**

LEG 2

101   lighthouse

**Umpqua
Lighthouse
State Park**   117

HB

to North Bend
and Coos Bay

N

0   1   2 MILES

0   1   2 KILOMETERS

For a secluded campsite, hike 0.4 mile off the beach at BA 114 and wade Tahkenitch Creek to reach this oxbow.

this arrangement, continue south on the beach 5.4 miles to the north jetty of the Umpqua. Pick up the trail that curves north along the bay shore and follow the beach inside the jetty to the end of the jetty, about 0.9 mile. Continue north along the beach just 0.1 mile or so; this seems to be the preferred spot for Winchester Bay Charters to pick up passengers and shuttle them a short distance across the water to the marina at Winchester Bay. Alternately, park yourself on the river beach here and attempt to wave down a passing recreational boater.

The other option is to walk out Sparrow Park Road to US 101 (3.9 miles, 310 feet elevation gain) through not particularly scenic industrial timberlands. This road has a massive water-filled pothole 2.4 miles from US 101; you can wade it, but it's not passable with most passenger cars. Then walk south along US 101 for another 8.4 miles, with 580 feet of elevation gain, through the town of Reedsport to Winchester Bay. The town of Winchester Bay is oriented around the harbor and RV camping, but you'll find several motels and eateries.

HAZARDS

Crossing the Siltcoos River might be possible only at low to mid-tide.

CAMPING

Carry plenty of water. This leg is entirely within the Oregon Dunes National Recreation Area, where, theoretically, dispersed camping is allowed anywhere. But plover regulations set some restrictions, and the noise of OHVs may lead you to avoid certain areas. Some general guidelines:

>> North of BA 106 at the Siuslaw River south jetty: OHVs are not allowed on the beach or dunes here, making this a good area to beach camp if the beach is wide enough.

>> From BA 106 south nearly to BA 110 (Siltcoos Beach Day Use), north of Siltcoos River: Camping is allowed, but OHVs are allowed on the beach and in the dunes here, making this stretch less desirable for beach camping.

>> From BA 110 south to 0.6 mile north of BA 116 (Sparrow Park Road): Camping is not allowed on the beach here due to plover restrictions, but camping is allowed in the adjacent dunes (where OHVs are not allowed).

>> From BA 116 to 2.6 miles south of Sparrow Park Road: Camping is allowed; OHVs are not.

>> From 2.6 miles south of Sparrow Park Road to the Umpqua River north jetty: No camping due to plover restrictions, but follow the trail leading inland above the jetty a short distance and look for primitive campsites tucked in the trees.

Just north of the Siltcoos River, BA 110 leads to Siltcoos Beach Access Road. Follow the road to a series of campgrounds, the first two catering to OHV riders. One, Driftwood II ($$), has showers. Waxmyrtle ($$) and Lagoon ($$) cater to tent campers. Continuing south on the beach, BA 112 marks the start of the Carter Lake Trail, a series of posts in the dunes guiding you 0.75 mile to little Carter Lake Campground ($). Sites at all of these campgrounds can be reserved.

There are several attractive dispersed camping options in the vicinity of Tahkenitch Creek. Look for BA 114 and follow the trail inland a short distance to potential campsites along the creek. Or continue a total of 0.4 mile from the beach to an overlook above an oxbow in the creek; the bank drops off steeply here, so follow the trail north a bit to descend to a spot where you can more easily wade the creek to camp on a flat sandbar in the hook of the oxbow.

The next, and maybe best, dispersed campsite area is at the north end of swimmable Threemile Lake. At BA 115A take the sand trail inland 0.3 mile, crossing another little sand trail, and continue 0.1 mile to where the trail forks. Here, you can either continue straight to the lakeshore, where you will find several tent sites tucked in the trees, or go left up the trail another 0.1 mile to

Several primitive campsites are tucked in the pines near the north shore of Threemile Lake.
(Photo by Donna Scurlock)

the top of a sand knoll above the lake—a nice spot for several tents with a tiny ocean view, but lacking immediate access to the lake.

You may find car campers near Sparrow Park Road, but there are no toilets or water here. Continue south to the north jetty and look for a few flat tent sites along the trail that leads to the boat pickup spot on the bay past the north jetty.

The hiker-biker camp at Umpqua Lighthouse State Park ($) is located 1 mile off the OCT near Winchester Bay. Some hikers choose to bypass the state park and, after stocking up on water, head south down the beach to camp in seclusion. Get water at Windy Cove Campground (near the marina) or Umpqua Lighthouse State Park rather than at the other RV campgrounds down the road, where the water is high in iron and not recommended for drinking. Fishermans RV Park ($$) also offers tent camping in Winchester Bay.

LODGING

There are a number of motels and vacation rentals in Winchester Bay but no lodging adjacent to the OCT between Florence and Winchester Bay. Just west of the marina, Umpqua Dunes RV Park has laundry facilities and ten small reservable cabins, and nearby Windy Cove Campground has two tiny reservable cabins with bedding provided.

BOAT SHUTTLE

Winchester Bay Charters offers hikers a boat ferry from the Umpqua north jetty to Winchester Bay marina. The pickup spot is a short distance past where the rock jetty ends, about 1 mile after leaving the beach. Call one to two days ahead to arrange; rendezvous time may be affected by tide (or maybe not).

FOOD RESUPPLY

Find mini-marts and several casual eateries in Winchester Bay. There are no large grocery stores.

Leg 1	Mileage between Waypoints
Siuslaw River Bridge, Florence, to South Jetty Beach (BA 106)	3.3
BA 106 to Siltcoos Beach Day Use (BA 110)	5
BA 110 to mouth of Siltcoos River	0.4
Siltcoos River to Carter Lake Trail (BA 112)	1.3
BA 112 to North Oregon Dunes Overlook Trail (BA 113)	1.6
BA 113 to South Oregon Dunes Overlook Trail (BA 114)	1.1
BA 114 to Tahkenitch Creek mouth	1.8
Tahkenitch Creek mouth to Threemile Lake Trail (BA 115A)	1.2
BA 115A to Sparrow Park Road (BA 116)	1.6
BA 116 to Winchester Bay via beach and boat shuttle	6.4
ALT: BA 116 to Winchester Bay via Sparrow Park Road and US 101	*12.3*

LEG 2   WINCHESTER BAY TO CHARLESTON

Distance   31 miles (20.1 with boat shuttle)
Elevation gain/loss   +870/–870 feet

Much of this part of the Oregon Dunes National Recreation Area is designated for OHV use. It's probably the last time you'll encounter OHVs on an OCT thru-hike. For the first several miles south of Winchester Bay you'll hear dune buggies buzzing in the dunes, but they're not allowed on the beach. South of

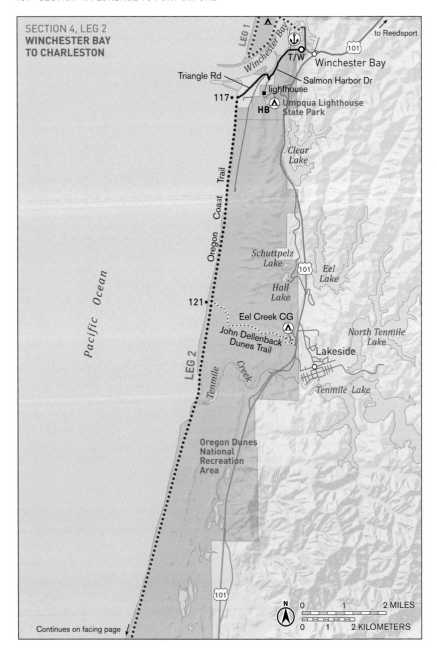

SECTION 4, LEG 2
**WINCHESTER BAY
TO CHARLESTON**

LEG 1

Winchester Bay

to Reedsport

101

T/W   Winchester Bay

Triangle Rd

Salmon Harbor Dr

lighthouse

117

HB   Umpqua Lighthouse
State Park

Clear
Lake

Oregon Coast Trail

Schuttpelz
Lake

101   Eel
Lake

Hall
Lake

121

Eel Creek CG

John Dellenback
Dunes Trail

North Tenmile
Lake

Lakeside

LEG 2

Tenmile   Creek

Tenmile Lake

Pacific Ocean

Oregon Dunes
National
Recreation
Area

101

N

0   1   2 MILES

0   1   2 KILOMETERS

Continues on facing page

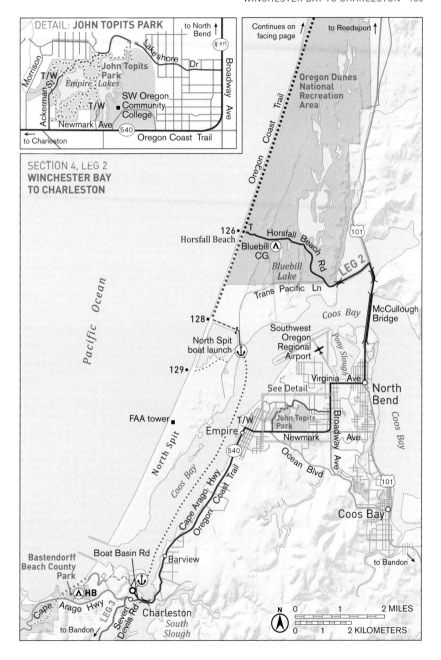

DETAIL: **JOHN TOPITS PARK**

to North Bend ↑

Lakeshore Dr

Morrison

Ackerman

T/W St

John Topits Park
Empire Lakes

T/W

Newmark Ave

Broadway Ave

SW Oregon Community College

to Charleston ←

540

Oregon Coast Trail

SECTION 4, LEG 2
WINCHESTER BAY TO CHARLESTON

Continues on facing page ↑

to Reedsport ↑

Oregon Coast Trail

Oregon Dunes National Recreation Area

101

126
Horsfall Beach

T

Horsfall Beach Rd

Bluebill CG

Bluebill Lake

LEG 2

Trans Pacific Ln

Coos Bay

McCullough Bridge

Pacific Ocean

128

North Spit boat launch

Southwest Oregon Regional Airport

Pony Slough

Virginia Ave

North Bend

129

See Detail

John Topits Park

Coos Bay

FAA tower

North Spit

T/W

Empire

540

Newmark Ave

Broadway Ave

Ocean Blvd

Cape Arago Hwy

Oregon Coast Trail

Coos Bay

101

Coos Bay

to Bandon

Bastendorff Beach County Park

Boat Basin Rd

Barview

△ HB

Cape Arago Hwy

LEG 3

Seven Devils Rd

Charleston
South Slough

to Bandon

N

0   1   2 MILES

0   1   2 KILOMETERS

Tenmile Creek to Horsfall Beach (BA 126), you're likely to encounter them motoring down the beach as well. In the middle of this leg, though, is a quiet, remote stretch of beach from about 2.5 miles north of the mouth of Tenmile Creek to about 1.5 miles south of it. No OHVs on the beach here, but also no camping; it's a plover nesting zone.

The leg ends at the little port town of Charleston, which you may be able to get to via boat; if not, you'll need to walk or drive through the cities of North Bend and Coos Bay. The elevation gain indicated above for this leg all comes from the walk through the towns; if you get a boat shuttle, you stay at sea level other than walking over the foredune.

To get started from the Winchester Bay marina area, follow Salmon Harbor Drive west and south; it becomes Triangle Road. Where it ends at the sign for BA 117, follow a sand trail over the dunes and down to the beach.

The only significant water crossing on this stretch is at Tenmile Creek, roughly 6.5 miles south of your return to the beach. It's an innocuous little stream at low tide, but it fills up at high tide and isn't wadeable. From here it's about 8.2 miles to the next beach access point at Horsfall Beach (BA 126). The "campground" here is a large paved parking lot with vault toilets (no water) used as a staging area for OHV riders; hikers can walk a little farther to Bluebill Campground (see Camping).

The sounds, and sometimes the sights, of dune buggies are common south of Winchester Bay.

Tenmile Creek can be waded, but only at low to mid-tide. (Photo by Donna Scurlock)

At Horsfall Beach you have a decision to make. There is no regular boat shuttle service for hikers seeking to cross the bay to Charleston at this writing. However, Winchester Bay Charters may be able to arrange a ride for you with a charter boat operator among their colleagues in Charleston. If you are able to make this arrangement, continue south down the beach 2.2 miles to BA 128. BA 128 may be hard to spot in the dunes; if you miss it, leave the beach at BA 129 and follow the sand road indicated on the map. From BA 128 there is a hard gravel road leading between a wetlands and the Port of Coos Bay's industrial waste ponds, which sounds, well, industrial and wasted, but it's pleasant and the bird-watching on this trail can be fabulous. It leads 0.6 mile to a fence and gate at Trans Pacific Lane. Walk around the fence and go south on Trans Pacific Lane 0.5 mile to the entrance to the Bureau of Land Management North Spit boat launch. Pick up your boat shuttle to Charleston here.

If you can't arrange a boat shuttle, you'll need to follow Horsfall Beach Road and Trans Pacific Lane to US 101, cross Coos Bay on McCullough Bridge, and walk through the towns of North Bend and Coos Bay to the smaller town of Charleston. See the map for a direct route on primary roads that leads past shopping centers for resupplying.

Detour past freshwater Lower Empire Lake in John Topits Park during your walk through North Bend.

Alternatively, pick your own route on secondary roads, possibly including a pleasant walk through John Topits Park, along the shore of freshwater Lower Empire Lake in North Bend. The route through the park is part of the 5.6-mile Sawmill and Tribal Trail, memorializing paths Native people once followed between bayside villages and hunting grounds. It's also a nod to the route that sawmill and shipyard workers in North Bend followed to reach watering holes in the town (now neighborhood) of Empire to the southwest. You can find maps of the route online, but it's unnecessarily complicated for a thru-hiker to want to follow step-by-step. The best part is the route through John Topits Park. There are toilets and even a swimming beach toward the east end of the park. It provides a pleasant break on this urban walk. Leaving the park, take Ackerman Street south to Newmark Avenue to continue toward Charleston.

Or, take a taxi from Horsfall Beach to Charleston. I've heard good and bad things about taxi rides here: some folks have had a quick, inexpensive ride and others finally gave up waiting for a taxi that never came.

HAZARDS

The mouth of Tenmile Creek must be crossed at low to mid-tide.

CAMPING

Dispersed camping is generally allowed in the Oregon Dunes National Recreation Area, but restrictions protecting snowy plovers and the (noisy) presence of off-highway vehicles mean you need to pick your beach or dunes camping site carefully:

» From the Umpqua south jetty to about 4 miles south, beach camping is allowed, and OHVs are not allowed on the beach (but you'll hear them in the adjacent dunes).

» No beach camping is allowed from the Douglas-Coos county line, about 2.5 miles north of the mouth of Tenmile Creek, to 1.5 miles south of the creek. Camping is allowed in the adjacent dunes, but OHVs are allowed in the dunes south of Tenmile Creek.

» From about 1.5 miles south of Tenmile Creek to Horsfall Beach (vicinity of BA 126), camping is allowed, but so are OHVs, both on beach and in dunes.

» Beach camping is allowed from Horsfall Beach to the sand road (near BA 129) about 1.3 miles south, and OHVs are not allowed in dunes

Bluebill Lake has a lovely trail around it as well as a rustic campground.

A hiker follows OHV tracks to Horsfall Beach.

year-round or on the beach here May 1 to September 30, making this a potentially good place for beach/dune camping. Vehicles are allowed on the beach from here south to the FAA tower.

Neither vehicles nor camping are allowed south of the FAA tower during the plover nesting season.

Bluebill Campground ($$) is a quiet developed campground (no showers) 0.8 mile east on Horsfall Beach Road. There's no hiker-biker camp, but it's unlikely to be full. For camping options in the vicinity of Charleston, see Leg 3.

LODGING

There are many lodging options in North Bend–Coos Bay and a couple of inexpensive motels in Charleston.

BOAT SHUTTLE

Coos Bay presents a formidable gap in the OCT. At this writing, there is no reliable shuttle service across the bay to Charleston, but Winchester Bay Charters may be able to arrange a boat ferry from the Bureau of Land Management North Spit boat launch to Charleston with one of the outfitters they work with in Charleston. It's worth a call; otherwise you must walk or take a taxi many miles through town. Prices are to be arranged. Expect to pay more than usual for this longer-than-usual shuttle.

FOOD RESUPPLY

There are plenty of restaurants and grocery stores in North Bend–Coos Bay. Pony Village Mall, off of Virginia Avenue, has groceries, sporting goods, and more. There are mini-marts and a handful of restaurants and cafés in Charleston.

Leg 2	Mileage between Waypoints
Winchester Bay marina to beach at south jetty (BA 117)	2.1
BA 117 to mouth of Tenmile Creek	6.5
Tenmile Creek to Horsfall Beach (BA 126)	8.2
BA 126 to Charleston marina via North Bend–Coos Bay	14.2
ALT: To Charleston marina via beach and boat shuttle	*3.3*

LEG 3 CHARLESTON TO BANDON

Distance	22.5 miles
Elevation gain/loss	+950/−960 feet

This stretch begins with a trek over the formidable Seven Devils, a craggy stretch of coastline with no beach and no public trail. It is dominated by industrial timberland, which you must either walk through or around, mostly on back roads. Once you return to sea level at Seven Devils State Recreation Site, you are back on the beach all the way to Bandon and well beyond.

Top off your water bottles in Charleston; there may be no drinking water access on this leg until you reach Bullards Beach State Park. From the marina at Charleston, the OCT route heads south a scant half mile on Boat Basin Road to Cape Arago Highway; follow it west 0.25 mile, then turn left onto Seven Devils Road. In 4.2 miles, you'll see a sign to South Slough National Estuarine Research Reserve, a vast natural area on the Coos estuary. The visitor center and restrooms are 0.2 mile off Seven Devils Road and are open weekdays from 8 AM to 4 PM; come back another day to explore the reserve's many miles of hiking trails.

Walk Seven Devils Road another 6.7 miles to the entrance to Seven Devils State Recreation Site, where you return to the beach. The route from Charleston is paved for the first 6.5 miles; just after it tops out at about 560 feet elevation, it veers right (at the junction with W. Beaver Hill Road) and turns to gravel. It stays gravel for 3.4 miles as it slowly descends, then turns back to pavement for the last mile before reaching the park entrance.

CAPE ARAGO: WORTH A LAYOVER

Southwest of Charleston lie a string of three state parks arrayed along a spectacular coastline. If you're well supplied with food, consider camping an extra night at Sunset Bay or Bastendorff Beach to explore this shoreline. The three parks are linked by the Shoreline Trail, which begins at Sunset Bay State Park with its protected and warmer (relatively speaking) waters. Next is Shore Acres State Park, the site of an elaborate formal garden. To the south is a view of Simpson Reef and Shell Island, a good place to spot nesting seabirds, seals, sea lions, and possibly elephant seals. At the end of the road is Cape Arago State Park, with short trails that lead to beaches at its north, middle, and south coves.

Shallow Sunset Bay has relatively warm water, attracting paddlers and even swimmers.

If you want to camp near Charleston, you'll need to detour at least a couple of miles toward Cape Arago (see sidebar, "Cape Arago: Worth a Layover"), an exceptionally scenic and off-the-beaten-path stretch of coastline. Two parks offer hiker-biker camping here: Sunset Bay State Park and Bastendorff Beach County Park.

The simplest way to reach them is to walk the shoulder of Cape Arago Highway (State Route 540); there's not much traffic, as it's essentially a back road dead-ending at Cape Arago. From Charleston Marina via the highway it's about 2.1 miles to the entrance to the campground at Bastendorff Beach and 1.5 miles farther to the entrance to Sunset Bay.

However, I prefer the following off-highway route: From the marina, follow Boat Basin Road north a short distance to the campus of the Oregon Institute of Marine Biology and turn left up gravel Coos Head Loop. Follow it 0.7 mile, bearing left at the first junction. When it meets paved Coos Head Road, turn right, walk 0.4 mile, bear left, and continue 0.3 mile more to a beach access parking area with vault toilets at Bastendorff Beach (BA 133A). To reach Bastendorff Beach County Park campground, continue on the road 0.5 mile and turn left up the park access road.

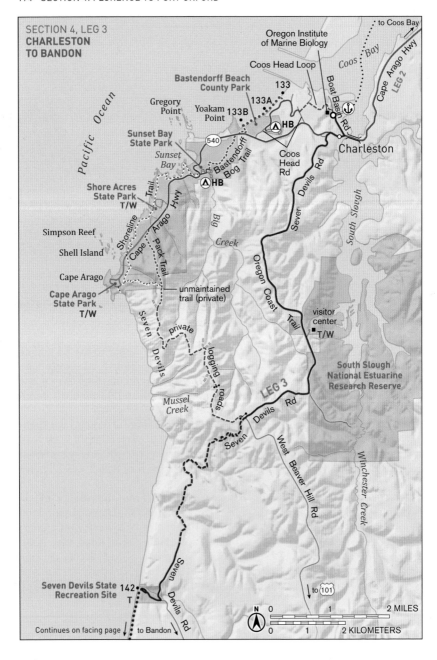

SECTION 4, LEG 3
**CHARLESTON
TO BANDON**

to Coos Bay

Coos Bay

Oregon Institute
of Marine Biology

Coos Head Loop

Cape Arago Hwy

LEG 2

Bastendorff Beach
County Park   133

Gregory   133A
Point   Yoakam
Point   133B

Boat Basin Rd

⚓

Pacific Ocean

Sunset Bay
State Park

(540)

⛺ **HB**

Charleston

Coos
Head
Rd

Bastendorff
Bog Trail

Sunset
Bay

⛺ **HB**

Coos Head Rd

Sever Devils Rd

South Slough

**Shore Acres
State Park
T/W**

Shoreline Trail

Cape Arago Hwy

Pack Trail

Big

Creek

Simpson Reef

Shell Island

Cape Arago

**Cape Arago
State Park
T/W**

unmaintained
trail (private)

Oregon Coast Trail

visitor
center
■
T/W

Seven Devils

private

logging roads

LEG 3

Seven Devils Rd

**South Slough
National Estuarine
Research Reserve**

*Mussel
Creek*

West Beaver Hill Rd

Winchester Creek

↓ to (101)

**Seven Devils State
Recreation Site 142
T**

Seven Devils Rd

N   0   1   2 MILES

◈   0   1   2 KILOMETERS

Continues on facing page ↓ to Bandon ↓

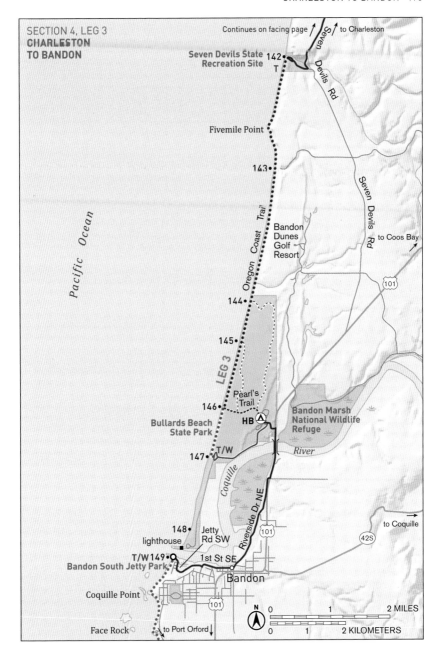

SECTION 4, LEG 3
CHARLESTON TO BANDON

Continues on facing page → Seven Devils Rd / to Charleston

Seven Devils State Recreation Site 142 • T

Fivemile Point

143 •

Seven Devils Rd

to Coos Bay

Pacific Ocean

Oregon Coast Trail

Bandon Dunes Golf Resort

144 •

145 •

LEG 3

Pearl's Trail

146 •

HB ⛺

Bullards Beach State Park

Bandon Marsh National Wildlife Refuge

River

T/W

147 •

Coquille

Riverside Dr NE

101

to Coquille

42S

148 • Jetty Rd SW

lighthouse

T/W 149 •

Bandon South Jetty Park

1st St SE

101

Bandon

Coquille Point

Face Rock

to Port Orford ↓

101

N

0   1   2 MILES
0   1   2 KILOMETERS

OVER THE SEVEN DEVILS? IT'S COMPLICATED

Some OCT thru-hikers choose to go through, rather than around, the forest south of Cape Arago. This requires you to walk on logging roads through private timberland. Many timber companies in Oregon and across the country allow hikers, hunters, and anglers to access their property as long as they behave themselves and don't camp, build fires, or leave garbage. I have tried to inquire about whether that is the case here, but after tracking the property through two changes of ownership, I gave up. This is a very volatile time in the timber industry, with TIMOs—timber investment management organizations—buying up huge swaths of industrial forest on behalf of investors, often with minimal thought to the local impact, from availability of sawmill jobs to recreational opportunities. Even if I tracked down the current owner and inquired about its rules regarding recreational access, the land may well have changed hands by the time you read this.

The upshot: consider this alternative route as long as there aren't "No Trespassing" signs or other indications that the current owner does not allow hikers access. From the Charleston marina, this route and the official route down Seven Devils Road are roughly comparable in mileage and elevation gain, but if you're camping at Bastendorff or Sunset Bay campgrounds, you save a few miles by not needing to backtrack to Charleston.

The route: From Sunset Bay State Park, continue south on Cape Arago Highway 1.4 miles to the Pack Trail trailhead on your left; follow that trail up to its high point at 1.3 miles. Here the trail bends sharply right; instead, continue straight on an unmaintained trail 0.3 mile to a broad clearing. Across the clearing, pick up the trail leading out of the southwest corner of the clearing. If you've picked the right trail, it will very quickly open up to become a gravel logging road. Stay on what appears to be the main road for about 4.8 miles, heading south-south-east. You'll walk around one gate and then, in a bit more than a mile, hit a final gate where the road ends near the junction of Seven Devils and West Beaver Hill Roads. From here, follow the main OCT route down to Seven Devils State Recreation Site.

To reach Sunset Bay State Park from BA 133A, follow the beach south 1 mile, wading a small creek. Where the beach ends at a rocky point just north of larger Yoakam Point, you will see trails leading to an RV park. Don't take these; rather, look for a couple of wooden steps leading up to a crude, narrow trail that heads steeply up the hillside to the south before leveling off. Continue on the trail, bearing left at a confusing series of spur trails, to where you spill out onto Cape Arago Highway. Cross the highway and walk a short distance to reach the start of the Bastendorff Bog Trail (look carefully; it might not be signed), which leads 1.25 miles to Sunset Beach State Park campground. At my last visit this trail was no longer signed, but the trail was maintained and easy to follow. Total distance from Charleston marina via this route is 4.2 miles.

From Seven Devils State Recreation Site, head south on the beach. Ahead 1.2 miles is Fivemile Point, which is passable only at low to mid-tide. If you plan to camp at Bullards Beach State Park, continue 4.5 miles from Fivemile Point to Pearl's Trail at BA 146. Follow Pearl's Trail 0.8 mile to the park campground. Even if you're not planning to camp here, this route via the campground shaves almost 1 mile off the standard route, which takes you down the beach another 0.8 mile to the park's day-use area at BA 147 and out the park road to US 101.

It would be lovely if there were a boat ferry option at the end of Coquille spit, allowing you to walk on the beach a little longer. But there isn't, as of this writing. So, from the entrance to Bullards Beach State Park, follow the highway shoulder south 0.3 mile to the bridge across the Coquille River. This is probably the scariest road bridge on the OCT: there's no real sidewalk for pedestrians, so timing is everything. In another 0.5 mile, turn right onto Riverside Drive NE and follow it south 1.6 miles to 1st Street SE. Turn right onto 1st and follow it a couple of blocks into Bandon's Old Town. Continue on 1st Street around the bay as it turns into Jetty Road SW and leads you to Bandon South Jetty Park, where you return to the beach.

HAZARDS

Take care crossing the US 101 bridge over the Coquille River on foot.

CAMPING

South of Charleston there are two campgrounds with hiker-biker areas. Camping is not allowed at the Coos Bay south jetty. Bastendorff Beach County Park

The hiker-biker camp at Sunset Bay is a few miles off the OCT but is worth a detour and maybe even a layover day.

($) campground has an informal, grassy hiker-biker area across the road from restrooms with showers; it's on the bluff above Bastendorff Beach. Note that there are no power outlets to recharge phones at the campground. Two tiny camping cabins are available by reservation. A couple of miles farther is the hiker-biker camp at Sunset Bay State Park campground ($), a short walk from the beach at Sunset Bay.

Consider camping on the beach north or south of Seven Devils State Recreation Site. Note that the site has toilets but no drinking water.

Bullards Beach State Park ($) has a very attractive hiker-biker area about 2 miles north of Bandon; see narrative above for quickest route from the beach.

LODGING

Bandon Dunes is a luxurious golf resort on the bluff south of Seven Devils State Recreation Site. It is accessible via a 1-mile unsigned trail 3.5 miles south of Fivemile Point. Bandon has many other lodging options. To cut a couple of miles off your next day's hiking, consider staying in the Face Rock area at the south end of town (near BA 152A, Inn at Face Rock) after stocking up on food in the center of town. There are two hotels here.

BOAT SHUTTLE

You might search online or check with the Bandon Visitors Center (see Contacts) about whether an outfitter is offering a boat ferry across the Coquille River into downtown Bandon, either by motorboat or kayak.

FOOD RESUPPLY

There is a supermarket on US 101 at the north end of town and a number of cafés and restaurants in Bandon, which is a popular tourist destination.

Leg 3	Mileage between Waypoints
Charleston marina to beach at Seven Devils State Recreation Site (BA 142)	12.1
BA 142 to Fivemile Point	1.2
Fivemile Point to Pearl's Trail at Bullards Beach State Park (BA 146)	4.5
BA 146 to US 101 at Bullards Beach State Park entrance via Pearl's Trail and park roads	1.4
Park entrance at US 101 to Bandon South Jetty Park (BA 149)	3.3

LEG 4   BANDON TO FLORAS LAKE

Distance	16 miles
Elevation gain/loss	0 feet

From Bandon's south jetty, walk the wide beach south around Coquille Point and past huge boulders studding this spectacular shore. If you intend to rough camp along the New River north of Floras Lake (see Camping), your last option for topping off water bottles is at Devils Kitchen beach access (BA 154). The mouth of the New River is about 4.7 miles south of the south jetty at this writing, but it is notorious for moving north or south (and, some years, for breaching the dune and creating a second river "mouth"). In any case, to be able to wade the mouth, you'll need to cross it as close to low tide as possible.

Past the mouth of the New River, the beach narrows and steepens. Many hikers consider this the toughest leg of the OCT. It is also very remote. The toughness is from the beach itself; coarse-grained sand, a narrow beach, and a steep gradient make for slow going. My best advice is to time your day's walk to reach the mouth of the New River before low tide; if it's not yet wadeable, it

A hiker contemplates crossing the "breach"—a second river mouth—in the New River.
(Photo by Donna Scurlock)

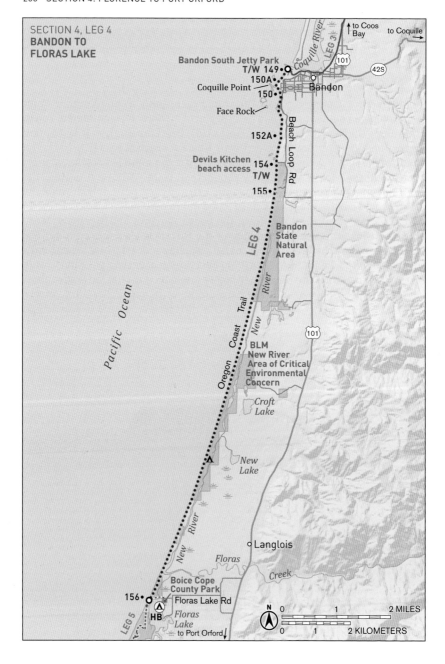

SECTION 4, LEG 4
**BANDON TO
FLORAS LAKE**

will be soon. That will put you in the best position to wade any possible river breach to the south, and it also gives you the widest beach, which doesn't help much with the walking, but some.

You'll know you're getting close to Floras Lake when you start to see people, or at least footprints in the sand. You may also see distant sails in the air, as Floras Lake is a popular kiteboarding venue. If you plan to spend the night here (camping or lodging), pick up the 0.5-mile sand trail heading east just north of Floras Lake at BA 156.

HAZARDS

The New River may be wadeable only at low tide, and it may have a second "outlet" that needs to be crossed.

CAMPING

The beach is too narrow to camp on, but the managing agency here, the Bureau of Land Management, has identified a site about 4 miles north of Floras Lake where bivouac camping is allowed in the dunes alongside the New River. There is no toilet or water. There is room for about three tents to fit comfortably, but summer weekends sometimes see more tents than that crowding the site. Watch for a sign in the dunes.

A primitive campsite lies between the beach and the New River north of Floras Lake.

Boice Cope County Park ($$) is a small campground frequented mostly by board sailors and kiteboarders; the park offers tent camping in the middle of the single grassy campground loop above the lake. It's possible hiker-biker camping will be offered in the future.

LODGING

Floras Lake House Bed & Breakfast hosts kiteboarders and the occasional hiker. For more options, search online for a vacation rental. Bring your own food; the café and grocery store in Langlois are almost 4 miles away.

FOOD RESUPPLY

There are no grocery stores or eateries between Bandon and Port Orford (Legs 4 and 5).

Leg 4	Mileage between Waypoints
Bandon South Jetty Park to Face Rock (BA 52A)	2.1
BA 152A to mouth of New River	2.6
New River mouth to primitive campsite	7.1
Primitive campsite to Floras Lake Trail (BA 156)	4.2

LEG 5   FLORAS LAKE TO PORT ORFORD

Distance   15.6 miles
Elevation gain/loss   +560/−500 feet

Ascend two headlands (neither very tall) and wade two rivers in this leg that follows a remote stretch of shoreline not seen by many visitors to the Oregon Coast. Floras Lake State Park is completely undeveloped (other than its hiking trails): there are no restrooms or campground, and there is just enough signage to keep you on the OCT route, unless vandals have been through. It includes Blacklock Point—remote and forested and gorgeous. There's an airstrip here, one large enough to land commercial aircraft, but you won't see it without a detour. Cape Blanco is the westernmost point in Oregon, with the winds to prove it. The lighthouse here is the oldest on the coast; it's open for tours in summer for a small fee.

From the end of the beach trail at Floras Lake (BA 156), head south on the beach. There are various ways to connect to the trail system on Blacklock Point, but the official and simplest route is to leave the beach in just 0.3 mile at the trail sign in the dunes. Follow the sand and then sandstone trail a short distance to

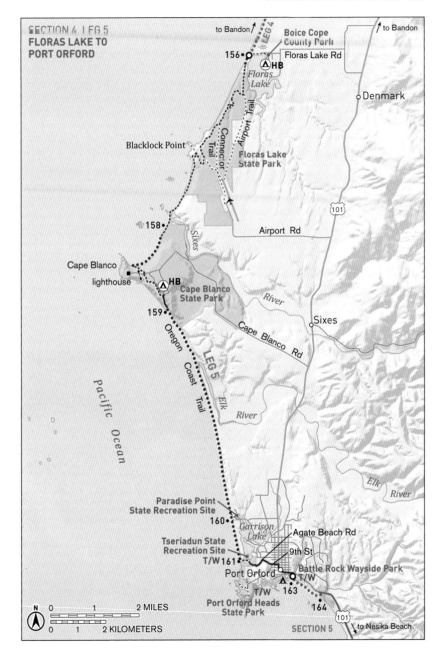

SECTION 4 | LEG 5
FLORAS LAKE TO
PORT ORFORD

to Bandon↗

LEG 4

to Bandon↗

Boice Cope
County Park

156● Floras Lake Rd

HB

Floras Lake

○ Denmark

Airport Trail

Connector Trail

Blacklock Point

Floras Lake
State Park

158●

Sixes

Airport Rd

101

Cape Blanco
lighthouse

HB

159●

Cape Blanco
State Park

River

Oregon Coast Trail

LEG 5

Cape Blanco Rd

○ Sixes

Pacific Ocean

Elk

River

Elk
River

Paradise Point
State Recreation Site

160●

Garrison
Lake

Agate Beach Rd

Tseriadun State
Recreation Site

T/W 161●

9th St

Battle Rock Wayside Park

Port Orford

T/W
163

T/W

T/W

Port Orford Heads
State Park

164●

101

N

0   1   2 MILES
0   1   2 KILOMETERS

SECTION 5

to Nesika Beach↘

the forest's edge, then between two boulders; at the trail junction here, continue heading south.

Take a right at the junction with the Airport Trail, 0.6 mile after leaving the beach (should be signed), cross a footbridge, and continue straight where a path angles up from the beach. The trail drops down to cross a creek (possibly with no footbridge) and climbs back up. You'll meet a couple of spur trails coming in from the west; ignore them and continue on the main trail heading south. At the junction with the Connector Trail (which might be signed, or might not), bear right with the main OCT route.

Continue heading south, past some spectacular viewpoints worth a detour. At 0.7 mile past the Connector Trail junction is another junction; bear left here, then right in 0.3 mile at the junction with the main trail leading to the trailhead at the end of Airport Road. Turn right in 0.2 mile more; you're now heading northwest. In 0.4 mile you'll reach the last junction at what would be a lovely bivouac site among the trees if camping were allowed here. Continue straight to get a view of the ocean from the end of Blacklock Point. Otherwise turn left and wind down the hillside 0.2 mile to the beach.

The Sixes River is about 1.2 miles ahead; it can generally be waded only from low to mid-tide, though conditions vary considerably. From here continue south

A hiker gingerly crosses a creek on the trail that travels up and over Blacklock Point. (Photo by Vickie Skellcerf)

CAPE BLANCO: A HABITAT INFLECTION POINT

Pay attention and you'll notice subtle changes to the landscape after you cross over Cape Blanco, the westernmost point in Oregon. The rocks on the beach are different colors, a testament to the south coast's complicated geology. The mix of tree species changes. You're even a little less likely to get rained on after you get past Cape Blanco. What you cannot see (without scuba gear) are changes in the mix of plants and animals in the ocean. Cape Blanco represents a biogeographic break within the ocean's California Current System, where the north–south extent of some marine species begins or ends. That's what makes Redfish Rocks Marine Reserve, south of Port Orford, so important to scientists studying the dynamics of Oregon's nearshore ocean.

on the beach to the base of Cape Blanco and look for the trail leading up the hillside to the lighthouse access road at the top. Cross the road and pick up the trail at the post a short distance east of the parking area near the gate. It starts as a mowed path and turns into a forest trail leading about a half mile to the Cape Blanco State Park campground and hiker-biker camp. Continue south on the beach access road another 0.5 mile to reach the beach on the south side of the cape (BA 159).

The Elk River is less than 2 miles ahead; it's not as large as the Sixes, so it can be waded at mid-tide or possibly higher. Continue down the beach to the base of Port Orford Heads, where a trail leads off the beach to Tseriadun State Recreation Site. Follow Agate Beach Road east (it becomes 9th Street) 0.8 mile to US 101 and turn right to reach the center of Port Orford. Battle Rock Wayside Park, where you return to the beach, is 0.3 mile to the south off US 101.

Downhill from downtown Port Orford is the town's unusual commercial fishing port, one of only two "dolly docks" in the country (the other is in Los Angeles). The harbor here is too shallow for safe mooring. So, between trips to sea, boats are lifted in and out of the ocean with two yellow cranes and stored on trailers parked in rows on the dock. It's something to see; the best time to enjoy the action is late in the afternoon on fine weather days, as fishermen return with their catch. Visitors are welcome to watch boats being lifted and their catch unloaded: cabezon, Dungeness crab, black cod, lingcod, rockfish, salmon, and sea urchins, a local specialty.

HAZARDS

Plan to cross the mouth of the Sixes River at low to mid-tide. Elk River can usually be crossed at mid-tide or higher.

As the westernmost point in Oregon, Cape Blanco was an ideal headland on which to locate a lighthouse in the nineteenth century.

PORT ORFORD'S LIVESAVING HISTORY

A detour of 0.9 mile off US 101 (and nearly 300 feet in elevation) takes you to Port Orford Heads State Park, dedicated to preserving the memory of the Port Orford Lifeboat Station. Its staff of up to a hundred surfmen kept watch over 40 miles of coastline from Cape Blanco to Cape Sebastian from 1934 to 1970. Short trails lead past a view down to Nellie's Cove, where lifeboats were launched, and out to the site of the observation tower. The station's unsinkable thirty-six-foot motor lifeboat is on display outside an interpretive center (check the park's website for open days and hours; see Contacts).

CAMPING

Cape Blanco State Park has a hiker-biker camp ($). It's possible to camp in town at Port Orford, at the informal RV campsite/gravel parking area operated by the Port of Port Orford that overlooks the port on 5th Street and Dock Road ($). Erect your tent at the grassy edge of the lot. There are no toilets on-site; walk down Dock Road 0.3 mile to use the toilets and showers at the port.

LODGING

There are a number of motels and other lodgings at a wide range of prices in and around Port Orford.

FOOD RESUPPLY

The largest grocery store in town is on US 101 and 15th Street, six blocks north of 9th Street. There are several choices of eateries, ranging from a great fish-and-chips shop to an elegant ocean-view restaurant.

Leg 5	Mileage between Waypoints
Floras Lake Trail (BA 156) to junction with Airport Trail	0.9
Airport Trail junction to Connector Trail junction	1.2
Connector Trail junction to main trail junction	1
Main trail junction to beach	0.8
Beach to mouth of Sixes River	1.2
Sixes River to Cape Blanco State Park campground	2.7
Cape Blanco campground to mouth of Elk River	1.8
Elk River to Tseriadun State Recreation Site (BA 161)	4.9
BA 161 to Battle Rock Wayside Park, Port Orford (BA 163)	1.1

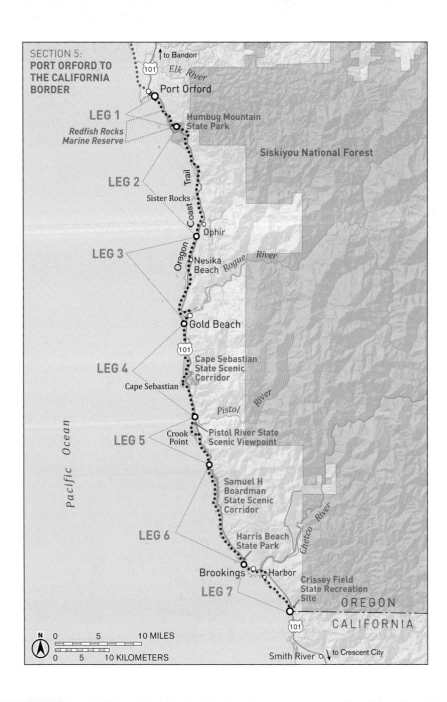

SECTION 5:
**PORT ORFORD TO
THE CALIFORNIA
BORDER**

↑ to Bandon

Elk River

101

Port Orford

LEG 1

*Redfish Rocks
Marine Reserve*

Humbug Mountain
State Park

Siskiyou National Forest

LEG 2

Sister Rocks

Coast Trail

Oregon

Ophir

LEG 3

Nesika
Beach

Rogue River

Gold Beach

101

Cape Sebastian
State Scenic
Corridor

LEG 4

Cape Sebastian

River

Pistol

Crook
Point

Pistol River State
Scenic Viewpoint

LEG 5

Samuel H
Boardman
State Scenic
Corridor

Chetco River

LEG 6

Harris Beach
State Park

Brookings   Harbor

LEG 7

Crissey Field
State Recreation
Site

OREGON

101

CALIFORNIA

Pacific Ocean

N

0   5   10 MILES

0   5   10 KILOMETERS

Smith River ○   ↓ to Crescent City

Cloud-capped Humbug Mountain dominates the view south from Battle Rock Wayside Park in Port Orford (Leg 1).

Port Orford to the California Border

Distance
74.3 miles

Cumulative OCT miles
Miles 338 to 412.3

Elevation gain/loss
+ 7320/–7370 feet

Headland summits
Devils Backbone (460 feet), Otter Point (310 feet), Cape Sebastian (676 feet), Sand Hill (470 feet)

Max distance between campgrounds
36.2 miles (Gold Beach to Harris Beach State Park, Legs 4, 5, and 6)

Max distance between lodging
27.5 (Gold Beach to Whaleshead Beach Resort, Legs 4 and 5)

Water availability
Poor on some legs

Boat shuttle
None

Legs
1. Port Orford to Humbug Mountain
2. Humbug Mountain to Ophir
3. Ophir to Gold Beach
4. Gold Beach to Pistol River
5. Pistol River to Boardman State Scenic Corridor
6. Boardman State Scenic Corridor to Brookings
7. Brookings to the California Border

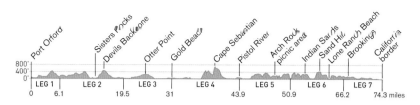

SECTION 5: PORT ORFORD TO THE CALIFORNIA BORDER

Scenery-wise, this is a spectacular stretch of the OCT; however, it is not very remote—the highway is never far away. In fact, the highway is often right at your elbow; it includes more highway shoulder walking than any other section. It is also logistically difficult and impossible for a backpacker to walk without some very long days, a motel or two, some stealth camping, a little bus or taxi assist, or a combination of all four. And water is a problem; there is no public water source between Gold Beach and Harris Beach State Park, Legs 4 through 6, although you can buy water at Whaleshead Beach Resort in Leg 6.

So, why hike it? It's part of the thru-hike. It has some memorable highlights including Sisters Rocks, the hike over Cape Sebastian and the beaches at either side, remote Crook Point, and the hike through Boardman State Scenic Corridor. Honestly, especially for a thru-hiker who's come this far, the highway shoulder walking isn't bad, especially if you can get an early start. The views are great, and there's much less traffic here than on the north coast. You also have the option of hopping on Curry Public Transit's Coastal Express bus.

There is no lodging between Port Orford and Gold Beach. An inn-to-inn hiker could take the bus from Port Orford to Nesika Beach; you wouldn't miss much (the off-road route from Arizona Beach to Sisters Rocks can be done only at low tide anyway). In so doing, you could collapse these three legs into one 10- to 11.5-mile day by starting at Ophir Wayside Rest Area or Nesika Beach and walking to Gold Beach.

Section 5 passes through the traditional homelands of the Coquille, Tututni, Chetco, and Tolowa people.

ACCESS

Overnight parking is available at the Port of Port Orford, or leave your vehicle on the street. At the south end, call Harris Beach State Park to inquire about leaving a vehicle overnight at either Harris Beach State Park, where the OCT effectively

The rocky shoreline at Boardman State Scenic Corridor keeps the trail off the beach and offers great views (Legs 5 and 6).

ends (the rest is mostly road walking), or Crissey Field State Recreation Site, which is the official end of the OCT, just north of the California border. (See Contacts for parking information.)

This section of the Oregon Coast is served by Curry Public Transit, whose Coastal Express bus runs north and south three times a day between North Bend, Coos Bay, and Brookings (see Contacts).

SUGGESTED ITINERARIES

Mileage figures here reflect distances on the OCT route only; distance to lodgings or a developed campground may add 0.1 to 1 mile to your day's hike.

5 Days Camping		Miles
Day 1	Battle Rock Wayside Park (BA 163), Port Orford, to Humbug Mountain State Park hiker-biker camp	6.1
Day 2	Humbug Mountain to Indian Creek RV Park campground, Gold Beach	23.9
Day 3	Gold Beach to Pistol River Middle (BA 185)	12.6
Day 4	Pistol River Middle to Harris Beach State Park hiker-biker camp	23.6
Day 5	Harris Beach to California border	8.1

8 Days Camping and Lodging		Miles
This itinerary breaks up the walk through Boardman State Scenic Corridor with one night of lodging; otherwise you're forced to stealth camp or hike a very long day.		
Day 1	Port Orford to Humbug Mountain State Park hiker-biker camp	6.1
Day 2	Humbug Mountain to Honey Bear by the Sea RV Resort and Campground, Ophir	13.4
Day 3	Ophir to Indian Creek RV Park campground, Gold Beach	10.5
Day 4	Gold Beach to beach north of Cape Sebastian	4.6
Day 5	Cape Sebastian to Pistol River Middle (BA 185)	8
Day 6	Pistol River Middle to Whaleshead Beach Resort	15.9
Day 7	Whaleshead Beach to Harris Beach State Park hiker-biker camp	7.7
Day 8	Harris Beach to California border	8.1

5 Days Inn-To-Inn		Miles

There are no motels between Port Orford and Gold Beach (31 miles), nor between Gold Beach and a single "resort" with cabins in the middle of Boardman State Scenic Corridor (27.5 miles). Consider taking the bus from Port Orford to Ophir Wayside Rest Area or Nesika Beach and walk 10 to 11.5 miles into Gold Beach, collapsing two or three days into one. Then consider expanding Day 3 into two days by calling a cab to fetch you at Pistol River and take you to lodgings in Brookings, then return you to Pistol River the next day to finish your hike into Brookings. Mileage will vary depending on proximity of lodgings to the OCT.

Day 1	Port Orford to Nesika Beach vacation rental	21.1
Day 2	Nesika Beach to Gold Beach	9.9
Day 3	Gold Beach to Whaleshead Beach Resort	27.5
Day 4	Whaleshead Beach to Brookings	10.2
Day 5	Brookings to California border	5.6

LEG 1 PORT ORFORD TO HUMBUG MOUNTAIN

Distance   6.1 miles
Elevation gain/loss   +820/–800 feet

From Battle Rock Wayside Park in Port Orford, follow the trail down to the beach and head south for 1.9 miles, crossing Hubbard Creek (BA 164) at 1.1 miles. Look for a narrow path, possibly unsigned, 0.8 mile past BA 164 (leaving the beach about 0.4 mile north of Rocky Point) and follow it a short distance up to the highway. It would be nice to stay on the beach 0.8 mile more to the next beach access (BA 165), but you'd have to round the boulder field at Rocky Point, which is not recommended; it would require a hazardous scramble even at low tide. Instead, from the top of the path off the beach, follow the highway shoulder 1.5 miles to the entrance sign for Humbug Mountain State Park. A side road east of the highway leads 0.1 mile to a gate and the start of the old coast road, which is now a hiker's path—the Old Coast Highway—into the state park campground.

Follow the old asphalt road as it hugs the hillside above US 101. It ends at the state park campground entrance road just south of the hiker-biker camp. Avoid touching any overhanging vines or branches of poison oak; this leg is likely the first place you will encounter it on the OCT. (See Coastal Hazards in How to Use This Guide for information on poison oak.)

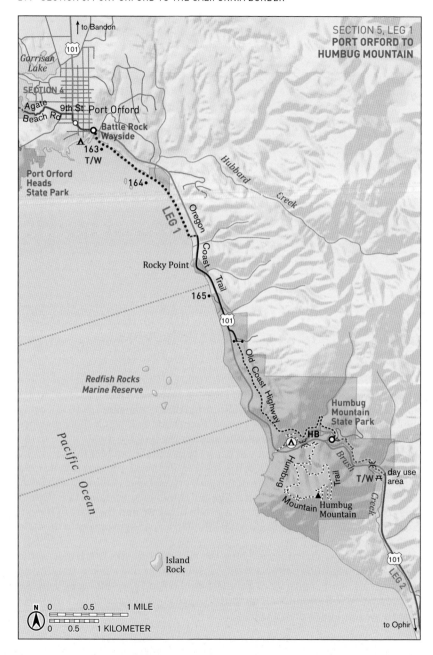

SECTION 5, LEG 1
PORT ORFORD TO HUMBUG MOUNTAIN

to Bandon

Garrison Lake

SECTION 4

Agate Beach Rd

9th St Port Orford

Battle Rock Wayside

163 T/W

164

Port Orford Heads State Park

LEG 1

Oregon Coast Trail

Rocky Point

165

Hubbard Creek

Old Coast Highway

Redfish Rocks Marine Reserve

Humbug Mountain State Park

HB

Humbug Mountain Trail

T/W

Brush Creek

day use area

Pacific Ocean

Humbug Mountain

Island Rock

N

0   0.5   1 MILE

0   0.5   1 KILOMETER

to Ophir

LEG 2

CAMPING
Humbug Mountain State Park has a hiker-biker camp ($).

LODGING
No lodging is available on this short leg.

FOOD RESUPPLY
There are no stores or cafés on this leg.

Leg 1	Mileage between Waypoints
Battle Rock Wayside Park, Port Orford, to path off beach	1.9
Path to start of Old Coast Highway in Humbug Mountain State Park	1.7
Old Coast Highway to Humbug Mountain State Park campground road	2.5

A hiker crosses Hubbard Creek. In the distance are the boat-lifting cranes at the Port of Port Orford.

CLIMB HUMBUG MOUNTAIN

The Oregon Coast Trail bypasses Humbug Mountain; private land on the mountain's south flank rules out an up-and-over OCT route for now. But if you're not in a hurry, consider a detour to the summit. To reach the trailhead from Humbug Mountain State Park, take the short access trail that leads under US 101 from the campground's B loop. It's 5.5 miles round-trip, with 1730 feet of elevation gain. Just past 1 mile the trail splits; bear left for a more gradual 2-mile ascent to a junction with the spur trail that leads to the summit. The view from the top isn't as spectacular as other vistas you've had, but it's a pleasant hike in a lovely southern Oregon coastal forest. Enjoy the scent of bay leaves as you crunch them underfoot. To return to the trailhead, complete the loop or return as you came.

LEG 2 HUMBUG MOUNTAIN TO OPHIR

Distance	13.4 miles
Elevation gain/loss	+1180/–1240 feet

More than half of this leg is on road, with most of it on the shoulder of US 101, though there are ways to reduce that highway walking. If you're not attached to hiking every inch, you could take Curry Public Transit's Coastal Express bus for some or all of it. If you call at least an hour ahead (see Contacts), the bus will stop for you at the Humbug Mountain trailhead parking area, the park's day-use area, or another flagstop that you request.

On foot, pick up the OCT on the south side of the Humbug Mountain State Park campground entrance road. It crosses a creek on a footbridge, crosses a paved road, and then rolls along the hillside above Brush Creek. Watch carefully for overhanging poison oak. Shortly after leading under US 101, the OCT reaches the picnic area at Humbug Mountain State Park. From here, cross the lawn to US 101 and walk south on the highway shoulder for 5 miles to the entrance to Arizona Beach State Recreation Site.

I don't advise detouring onto what appears on Google Maps as Highlands Drive (1.8 miles south of the park picnic area); the entrance to the road has a gate that, while it may be open, bristles with "No Trespassing" signs. Some 2.5 miles farther down US 101 at a pair of mailboxes across the highway from Lookout Rock, you could consider getting off the highway to walk Arizona Ranch Road. This road's first 0.9 mile is private even if you don't see No Trespassing signs, so walk at your own risk. From the highway, walk up a short distance, turn right onto an old asphalt road and follow it 0.2 mile to a gate you can walk around. A brushy 0.7 mile farther there's another gate, and from here

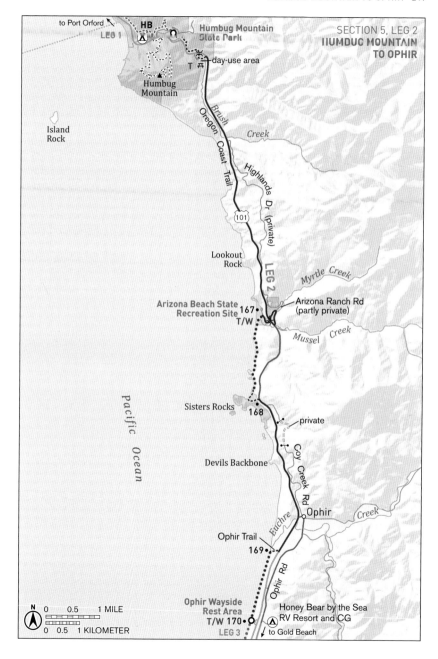

to Port Orford

LEG 1

HB

Humbug Mountain
State Park

T

day-use area

Humbug
Mountain

Island
Rock

Brush

Creek

Oregon Coast Trail

Highlands Dr (private)

101

LEG 2

Lookout
Rock

Myrtle Creek

Arizona Beach State
Recreation Site   167
T/W

Arizona Ranch Rd
(partly private)

Mussel   Creek

Pacific   Ocean

Sisters Rocks   168

private

Devils Backbone

Coy Creek Rd

Euchre

Ophir

Creek

Ophir Trail
169

Ophir Rd

N

0   0.5   1 MILE

0   0.5   1 KILOMETER

Ophir Wayside
Rest Area
T/W 170

Honey Bear by the Sea
RV Resort and CG

LEG 3   to Gold Beach

the road is a public, paved county road that leads 0.6 mile to the access road for Arizona Beach State Recreation Site.

From Arizona Beach, if it's mid-tide or higher, use the alternate route and stick to the highway for another 2.5 miles; the main route on the beach is accessible only at low tide and requires some careful climbing over big boulders.

If you decide to try the beach route, from the highway look around for a spot where you can scramble directly down to the beachside park. If it's too brushy, follow the entrance road, which loops east of the highway (a footbridge offers a little shortcut) and ducks back under the highway to reach the beach. Wade or hop across Mussel Creek and head south, rounding a headland to reach a spectacular secret beach. Ahead is a boulder pile you must scramble carefully over. Down the beach is Sisters Rocks: three rocks, one in the ocean and two connected by a narrow neck. There's a lot to explore here, including a sea cave accessible only at low tide. In the nineteenth century this was a townsite; rock quarried here was used for local roads. The land is now an undeveloped state park.

Continuing, follow a rocky jeep trail east up the neck of the southernmost of the Sisters Rocks. About halfway up to the highway, bear right on a footpath and follow it up to a parking area on the highway (BA 168). From here, walk south on the highway shoulder and return to the beach at BA 169 via the Ophir Trail in 2.9 miles.

CAN YOU WALK ON PRIVATE ROADS?

More than 8 miles of this leg is on the shoulder of US 101, even more if it's high tide and you must skip the 2.6-mile beach walk from Arizona Beach to Sisters Rocks. There are quiet back roads east of and above the highway, but they are partly or all privately owned. The OCT experience on this leg would be vastly improved if you could walk these side roads instead of the highway shoulder, though it would add some elevation and mileage.

Can you? Legally, no. They're private property, period. But as a practical matter, it's up to you. Often private roads are commonly used by the public on foot, and the owners don't mind. Sometimes the owners' concern is more about drivers using the road rather than hikers quickly passing through. The maps indicate the location of those private roads here. I would not advise hiking on Highlands Drive, which is clearly marked with "No Trespassing" signs. The north end of Arizona Ranch Road has no such signage, and this private stretch doesn't pass any homes. Coy Creek Road is iffy; the short private stretch makes it very tempting to walk it to get to the long public stretch. Let the presence (or absence) of "No Trespassing" signs be your guide. But the bottom line is: these are private roads and you have no legal right to use them.

Be prepared to scramble over boulders if you take the beach route south from Arizona Beach. (Photo by Vickie Skellcerf)

Alternatively, consider walking up Coy Creek Road, again at your own risk. This 2.4-mile off-highway detour is private for only 0.4 mile and is otherwise public. It's 0.6 mile longer than walking the highway, and it reduces your highway shoulder walking by nearly 2 miles. If you choose to try it, look for an unsigned but possibly mown path leading east from US 101 about 0.3 mile south of the top of the jeep road leading up from Sisters Rocks at BA 168. You'll soon hit a gate. The path is brushy and overgrown for just the next 0.15 mile before becoming a gravel road. From here it continues south, alternating gravel and pavement and hitting another gate at 0.5 mile, which signals the start of the public road.

Rocks stud the beach on the walk toward Sisters Rocks. (Photo by Vickie Skellcerf)

Continue on Coy Creek Road 1.9 miles more to a road junction at "downtown" Ophir—it's really just a crossroads. From here walk west a short distance to US 101, then south on the highway 1 mile to the Ophir Trail, a path that leads across the dunes just south of Euchre Creek and back to the beach at BA 169. Ophir Wayside Rest Area is just off of the beach 1.4 miles ahead. If you plan to spend the night at Honey Bear (see Camping), you could skip the highway and beach walk and, from the crossroads at Ophir, just continue south on what becomes Ophir Road to the campground.

CAMPING

Honey Bear by the Sea RV Resort and Campground ($$) has some of the finest tent camping on the Oregon Coast. An individual hiker will pay at least three times what state parks charge for hiker biker sites, but you get to camp at one of a handful of tent sites scattered at the edge of a huge meadow out of sight of the RV park. There are lovely, clean showers and a restaurant that may be open on weekends only. Advance reservation advised. Use the resort's shortcut to return to the beach at Ophir Wayside Rest Area.

LODGING

There is no motel lodging between Port Orford and Gold Beach (31 miles). You could take the bus from Port Orford to Nesika Beach, most of which is highway shoulder walking anyway, so you wouldn't miss much. In this way you could collapse these three legs into one 10- to 11.5-mile day by starting at Nesika Beach (or Ophir Wayside Rest Area) and walking to Gold Beach.

FOOD RESUPPLY

Aside from the restaurant at Honey Bear, there are no restaurants or stores on this leg.

Leg 2	Mileage between Waypoints
Humbug Mountain State Park campground road to day-use area	1.2
Humbug day-use area to beach at Arizona Beach State Recreation Site (BA 167)	5.3
BA 167 to US 101 at Sisters Rocks (BA 168) via beach	2.6
BA 168 to Ophir Trail to beach (BA 169)	2.9
BA 169 to Ophir Wayside Rest Area	1.4

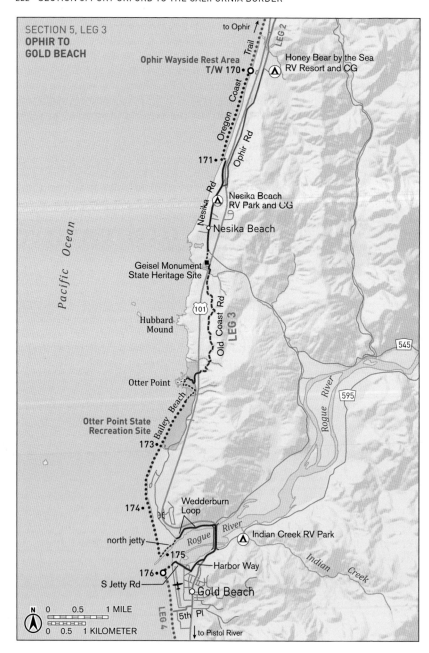

SECTION 5, LEG 3
**OPHIR TO
GOLD BEACH**

to Ophir

LEG 2

Oregon Coast Trail

Ophir Wayside Rest Area
T/W 170

Honey Bear by the Sea
RV Resort and CG

Ophir Rd

171

Nesika Rd

Nesika Beach
RV Park and CG

Nesika Beach

Geisel Monument
State Heritage Site

Pacific Ocean

101

Old Coast Rd

LEG 3

Hubbard
Mound

545

Otter Point

Bailey Beach

Rogue River

595

Otter Point State
Recreation Site

173

174

Wedderburn
Loop

Rogue River

Indian Creek RV Park

north jetty

175

Indian Creek

176

Harbor Way

S Jetty Rd

Gold Beach

N

0   0.5   1 MILE
0   0.5   1 KILOMETER

LEG 4

5th Pl

to Pistol River

LEG 3   OPHIR TO GOLD BEACH

Distance	11.5 miles
Elevation gain/loss	+890/−890 feet

This leg is mostly a combination of beaches, back roads, and short trails. From Ophir Wayside Rest Area, follow the beach south to Nesika Beach (BA 171) and pick up the little trail leading up to Nesika Road, which runs through the community of Nesika Beach. Watch carefully for this little path, as south of here the beachfront up to the next rocky headland is privately owned, with no more public beach access.

Follow Nesika Road south until it bends left, approaching US 101 at the south end of the community; here take a right on a little OCT link leading through the woods a short distance to Geisel Monument State Heritage Site. Follow the park road back out to US 101, cross the highway, walk the highway shoulder south 0.1 mile, and pick up the Old Coast Road. It quickly turns south, passes some houses, turns to gravel, and enters private timberland. It ducks in and out of clear-cuts for 2 miles until it meets and crosses US 101. Follow it west 0.4 mile into the trailhead parking area for Otter Point State Recreation Site.

A 1-mile trail leads south and down to Bailey Beach. Walk the beach to BA 175 at the Rogue River's north jetty, climb up on the jetty, and follow it 0.4 mile to the road. Follow Wedderburn Loop upriver to US 101 and the bridge over the Rogue. After crossing the bridge, follow the highway back downriver 0.2 mile to Harbor Way. Turn right off the highway, then take another right onto S. Jetty Road, which leads to Oceanside Drive and to the south jetty, where you return to the beach.

Alternately, stay on US 101 to reach lodging, a sporting goods store for camping supplies, food, and other services in Gold Beach. To return to the OCT, walk along US 101 south to 5th Place and follow it out to the beach. (The fencing around an airport runway blocks beach access north of 5th Place.)

CAMPING

Nesika Beach RV Park and Campground ($$) has tent sites. At the north end of Gold Beach, Indian Creek RV Park ($$) has a lovely tent camping area with twenty-six sites; you might want to call ahead to reserve one. The on-site café serves breakfast and dinner; another restaurant and bar serving lunch and dinner is just 0.2 mile up the road.

LODGING

Gold Beach has plenty of lodging choices.

Follow a gravel road on the north jetty toward the Rogue River Bridge.

FOOD RESUPPLY

Nesika Beach has a mini-mart. There are two supermarkets in Gold Beach, one north and one south of 5th Place. There are several eateries, including a brewpub in the harbor area and a coffeehouse inside a stellar bookstore.

Leg 3	Mileage between Waypoints
Ophir Wayside Rest Area to Nesika Beach (BA 171)	1.6
BA 171 to Geisel Monument State Heritage Site path	1.7
Geisel Monument path to Otter Point trailhead	2.7
Otter Point trailhead to Bailey Beach	1
Bailey Beach to Wedderburn Loop at Rogue River north jetty	2.4
Wedderburn Loop to beach at Rogue River south jetty	2.1

LEG 4 GOLD BEACH TO PISTOL RIVER

Distance   12.9 miles
Elevation gain/loss   +1160/−1130 feet

Top off your water bottles in Gold Beach; it's the last place to get tap water before hitting Harris Beach State Park at the end of Leg 6.

The last big headland to summit on the OCT is Cape Sebastian. From the Rogue River south jetty, walk the beach about 2 miles to the mouth of Hunter Creek at BA 179. Here the highway veers away from the beach; continue down the now-remote beach 2.8 miles more. Watch for what looks like a grassy ramp angling up the hillside about 0.7 mile north of the base of the cape; as you approach it through the dunes, you should see an OCT trail post and a footpath clearly heading up the hill.

Hikers emerge from the forest shortly before reaching the top of the trail at the Cape Sebastian State Scenic Corridor south parking area.

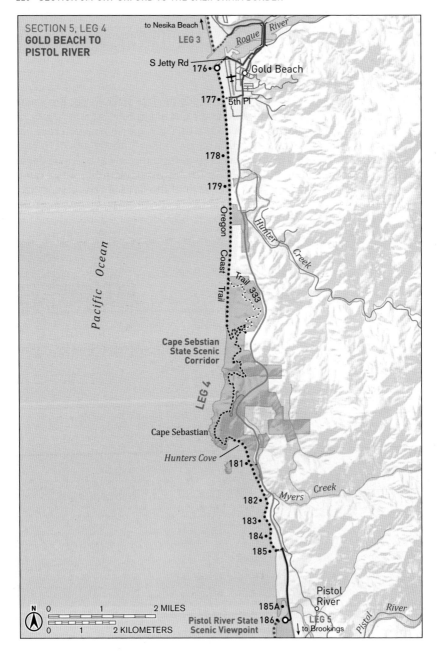

SECTION 5, LEG 4
**GOLD BEACH TO
PISTOL RIVER**

to Nesika Beach ↑
LEG 3
Rogue River

S Jetty Rd 176•○
Gold Beach

177• 5th Pl

178•

179•

Oregon Coast Trail

Trail 333

Hunter Creek

Cape Sebastian
State Scenic
Corridor

LEG 4

Pacific Ocean

Cape Sebastian

Hunters Cove 181•

182•
Myers Creek

183•
184•
185•

185A•
Pistol River

186•○ LEG 5
Pistol River State
Scenic Viewpoint ↓ to Brookings
Pistol River

N
0   1   2 MILES
0   1   2 KILOMETERS

The trail to the top of Cape Sebastian can be confusing at times; signage isn't always where you need it to be. After a gradual ascent for 1 mile you'll reach a gate and a junction with Trail 333; walk around the gate and go right to stay on the OCT. From here the trail rolls up and (mostly) down for a couple more miles, then makes a final climb to reach the south parking lot for Cape Sebastian State Scenic Corridor at the top of the cape. From here it's a pleasant 1.6-mile descent on a better maintained and easy-to-follow trail through a Sitka spruce forest to the beach. The last drop to the beach at Hunters Cove is very steep and slippery; use the rope here to back your way down.

Walk the beach south toward Pistol River. Conditions may change, but Pistol River can't be waded under typical summer (or winter) conditions. I recommend leaving the beach at Pistol River Middle (BA 185). You may not see a beach access sign, so look for a house-sized rock and a trail leading through the dunes to the highway. Walk the shoulder of US 101 south 1.3 miles, cross the river on the highway bridge, and enter the parking area for Pistol River State Scenic Viewpoint (BA 186).

HAZARDS

The trail down the south side of Cape Sebastian ends with a slippery drop-off to the beach.

CAMPING

No developed camping spots are available; consider camping on the beach south of BA 179. Carry water.

LODGING

No lodging is available on this leg, not even vacation rentals near the OCT.

FOOD RESUPPLY

There are no stores or cafés on this leg.

Leg 4	Mileage between Waypoints
South jetty Rogue River to start of Cape Sebastian Trail	4.8
Cape Sebastian Trail to summit at Cape Sebastian State Scenic Corridor south parking area	3.8
Cape Sebastian summit to beach at foot of cape	1.6
Foot of cape to Pistol River Middle (BA 185)	1.4
BA 185 to Pistol River State Scenic Viewpoint parking area (BA 186)	1.3

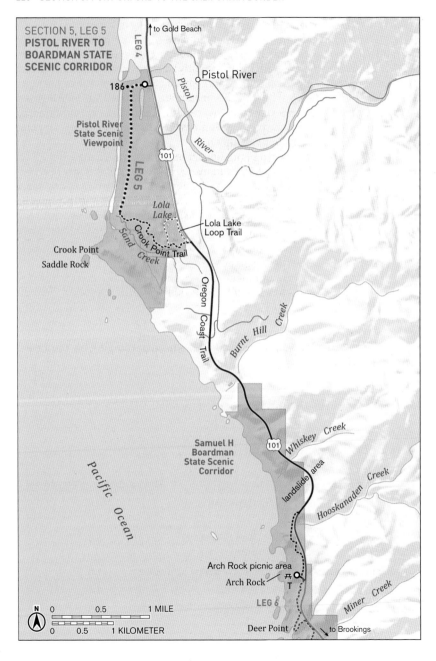

SECTION 5, LEG 5
PISTOL RIVER TO BOARDMAN STATE SCENIC CORRIDOR

↑ to Gold Beach

LEG 4

Pistol River

186

Pistol River State Scenic Viewpoint

Pistol River

101

Lola Lake

LEG 5

Lola Lake Loop Trail

Crook Point Trail

Crook Point

Saddle Rock

Sand Creek

Oregon Coast Trail

Burnt Hill Creek

101

Whiskey Creek

Samuel H Boardman State Scenic Corridor

landslide area

Hooskanaden Creek

Pacific Ocean

Arch Rock picnic area

Arch Rock

Miner Creek

LEG 6

N

0   0.5   1 MILE

0   0.5   1 KILOMETER

Deer Point

to Brookings →

LEG 5 PISTOL RIVER TO BOARDMAN STATE SCENIC CORRIDOR

Distance	7 miles
Elevation gain /loss	+770/–590 feet

From the parking area at Pistol River State Scenic Viewpoint, cut west across a lagoon (dry in summer) and a dune to reach the beach, then head south to where the beach ends north of Crook Point. It's a lovely, remote beach. Look for the mouth of Sand Creek and follow it over a pile of driftwood and into the dune grass, where a trail leads uphill. The trail is not formally signed, but it's not hard to follow. It leads into a sandy bowl, then into a spruce-and-pine-forested dune. At the trail junction, continue straight (or add 0.5 mile by taking a detour left around Lola Lake, also dry in summer). The trail ends at US 101 at what amounts to a tiny parking pullout.

Walk the highway shoulder south for 3.2 miles. There have been attempts to build OCT connector trails between the north boundary of Samuel H. Boardman State Scenic Corridor (at about milepost 342.5) and Arch Rock picnic area, but most have deteriorated as a result of landslides. The first opportunity to get off US 101 in the Boardman Corridor may come at about milepost 344; look for the trail leading west and then immediately south. This route leads through the dunes and forest west of the highway and ends at Arch Rock picnic area, the first developed site in the scenic corridor. Alternately, stay on the shoulder of US 101 for 0.7 mile more.

OREGON ISLANDS NATIONAL WILDLIFE REFUGE

Crook Point is part of Oregon Islands National Wildlife Refuge—a vast refuge composed of every rock, reef, and island off the coast of Oregon and a handful of mainland sites. Hundreds of thousands of seabirds nest on these rocks every summer; for some bird species, it's the only time of year they come ashore.

Tufted puffins burrow into the soil on Haystack Rock at Cannon Beach and Face Rock at Bandon from May to August. Vast colonies of common murres nest on bare rock ledges all along the coast, including on the rocks off the end of Yaquina Head (one of the best sites to see them), at Three Arch Rocks off Oceanside, and on Tillamook Rock. Mack Reef, off of Crook Point, has the second-largest concentration of nesting seabirds along the Oregon Coast. To protect the wildlife here, Crook Point is off-limits to humans.

Driftwood piles up at the mouth of Sand Lake, just north of Crook Point.

CAMPING

Because of the proximity of the Pistol River State Scenic Viewpoint, beach camping is not technically allowed on this leg, nor is camping allowed in the dunes within the state park itself. In other words, there is no legal camping on this leg.

LODGING

There is no lodging on this leg.

FOOD RESUPPLY

There are no stores or cafés on this leg.

Leg 5	Mileage between Waypoints
Pistol River State Scenic Viewpoint parking area (BA 186) to mouth of Sand Creek	1.8
Sand Creek to US 101	1
US 101 at Crook Point Trail to trailhead at milepost 344	3.2
Milepost 344 trailhead to Arch Rock picnic area, Boardman State Scenic Corridor	1

LEG 6 BOARDMAN STATE SCENIC CORRIDOR TO BROOKINGS

Distance 15.3 miles
Elevation gain /loss +2200/–2230 feet

This is the landscape that launched the Oregon Coast Trail: the shoreline of natural bridges and arch rocks and pocket beaches that inspired geographer Sam Dicken to begin promoting the notion of a border-to-border coast trail in Oregon.

There is no major headland to summit on this leg, but the trail through Samuel H. Boardman State Scenic Corridor is constantly ascending and descending, which adds up to a lot of elevation gain. This spectacular stretch of coastline can't be seen from a car window, but a series of short trails allows motorists to stop along US 101 and access several viewpoints. The OCT knits those trails together to get you from Arch Rock picnic area to the southern border of the Boardman Corridor. A network of social trails in addition to the formal trails, and a lack of signage, make wayfinding momentarily confusing in places. Time your hike to avoid hitting China Beach at high tide.

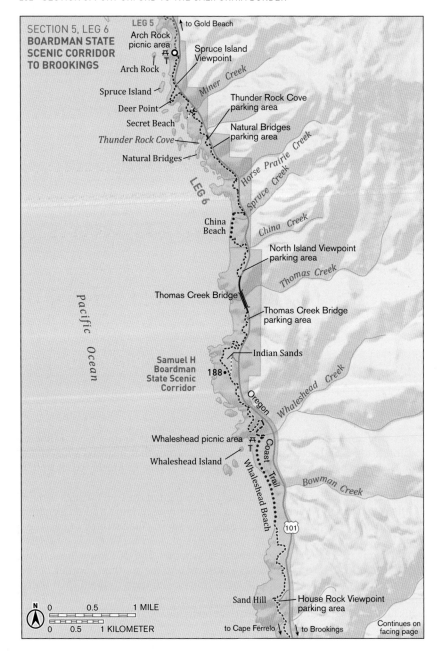

SECTION 5, LEG 6
BOARDMAN STATE SCENIC CORRIDOR TO BROOKINGS

LEG 5

to Gold Beach

Arch Rock picnic area

Spruce Island Viewpoint

Arch Rock

Miner Creek

Spruce Island

Thunder Rock Cove parking area

Deer Point

Secret Beach

Natural Bridges parking area

Thunder Rock Cove

Natural Bridges

Horse Prairie Creek

Spruce Creek

LEG 6

China Beach

China Creek

North Island Viewpoint parking area

Thomas Creek

Thomas Creek Bridge

Thomas Creek Bridge parking area

Indian Sands

Samuel H Boardman State Scenic Corridor

188

Pacific Ocean

Oregon Coast Trail

Whaleshead Creek

Whaleshead picnic area

Whaleshead Island

Whaleshead Beach

Bowman Creek

101

Sand Hill

House Rock Viewpoint parking area

N

0   0.5   1 MILE

0   0.5   1 KILOMETER

to Cape Ferrelo   to Brookings

Continues on facing page

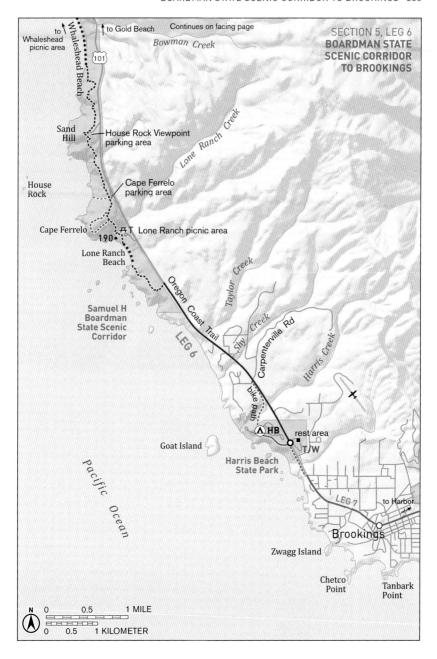

SECTION 5, LEG 6
BOARDMAN STATE SCENIC CORRIDOR TO BROOKINGS

Continues on facing page

The trails through Boardman State Scenic Corridor are typically well maintained but hardly ever level.

The OCT heads south from the top of the parking loop at Arch Rock picnic area. It winds west and south and returns to US 101 at Spruce Island Viewpoint. Pick up the trail at the south end of the parking lot. It leads out to Deer Point, with a view of flatiron-shaped Spruce Island, then back nearly to the highway before leading down to a footbridge across Miner Creek at 1.6 miles. An informal trail leads up to the highway and down to Secret Beach, one of the sweetest spots in the Boardman Corridor.

The trail continues to a view of Thunder Rock Cove before leading back to the Thunder Rock Cove parking area and resuming at its south end. Just 0.25 mile later it hits the Natural Bridges parking area. The trail resumes as a combination of paved path and wooden boardwalk and leads to a viewpoint. It continues nearly to the highway, crosses Horse Prairie Creek, and leads to a highway turnout just north of Spruce Creek. Walk inside the guardrail, then follow the trail down to the beach. Round the rock point (may not be possible at high tide) and you're on China Beach.

About halfway down the beach, pick up the trail leading up the hillside and continue south. At the junction, go right (left leads to the North Island Viewpoint parking area). Continue on the main trail until it hits US 101 near the north end of Thomas Creek Bridge, the tallest bridge in Oregon. There is no sidewalk; walk in the bike lane.

At the end of the bridge, continue past a former parking area now blocked by a guardrail and return to the trail at the actual parking area just ahead. Bear south on the trail as it descends and then leads back to the highway guardrail before veering west to a viewpoint. The trail then plunges down a steep draw, over a saddle, and up to the dunes at scenic Indian Sands, an unusual dune landscape whose sand comes from eroding sandstone.

Stay on the main trail heading south. Eventually it leads out to the highway; walk the shoulder for about 40 yards, then return to the trail before hitting the gravel access road down to Whaleshead Beach. Walk the road to the day-use area and follow a short trail to the beach, then walk south about 1 mile to the end of the beach.

Here the OCT heads up Sand Hill, but it requires a scramble to reach the trail; the land has slid in several places, taking parts of the trail with it. It leads about 1.4 miles to the top of Sand Hill. The trail picks up across the access road. Follow it down to where it rolls past a detour to a nude beach (to your right) and a parking area (on your left) then to a trail junction at the top of Cape Ferrelo. From here a right turn would give you a 0.3-mile detour west to the tip of Cape Ferrelo and a grand view. The trail sort of loops south back to the main trail on a secondary trail, but it's unmaintained and very brushy; it is best to just hike

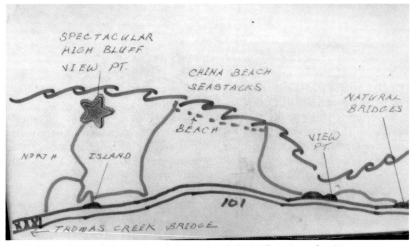

Locals have taken trail signage into their own hands in the Boardman Corridor.

Unless there's been some major trail work, prepare for careful climbing around a landslide to reach the bottom of the trail to the top of Sand Hill. (Photo by Vickie Skellcerf)

out and back if you like, then return to the main trail for another 0.5 mile to reach Lone Ranch Beach.

Walk south to the end of Lone Ranch Beach and look for a trail leading up the headland. Shortly after it tunnels into the trees, the trail seems to split; take the more well-traveled path bearing left to avoid head-height poison oak. You'll reach US 101 and the end of the trail 0.8 mile from the beach, near the southern border of Boardman State Scenic Corridor. The trail portion of the OCT ends here; some hikers consider it the end of the OCT. If you do, congratulations! Otherwise, follow the highway shoulder 1.6 miles south and look for a bike path west of US 101 just past Carpenterville Road and Dawson Road. If you are heading to Harris Beach State Park, follow it south 0.7 mile to the campground entrance. Otherwise, follow the highway into Brookings.

THANK SAM BOARDMAN

Without Sam Boardman, there would be no Oregon Coast Trail.

In 1929, Boardman, a highway engineer in eastern Oregon, was tapped to become Oregon's first state parks supervisor. At that time the state park system consisted of a handful of highway rest stops. During his twenty-one years as parks director, Boardman brought more than fifty thousand additional acres into state park protection, including thirty-six new coastal parks, and expanded the very definition of a state park in Oregon. Among those parks he created or at least launched—later to be enlarged—are those containing most of the coastal headlands you've hiked: Ecola, Oswald West, Cape Meares, Cape Lookout, and Cape Sebastian. He took advantage of low land prices during the Great Depression, while generous Oregon families also donated land to the park system. Most of those coastal headlands he acquired had already been logged, which reduced their value. Today they are lush second-growth forests, on a trajectory toward becoming mature temperate rainforests again, with trails now serving as links in the OCT—all thanks to Sam Boardman.

Boardman saw the recreation potential in Curry County's rugged shoreline and urged the federal government to create a national park here. That didn't happen. But he started the ball rolling on acquiring the land for what would ultimately become his namesake state park. A monument to Boardman stands alongside the OCT atop Sand Hill.

HAZARDS

Plan to hit China Beach at low to mid-tide, so you're able to get around the rock at the north end of the beach. Watch for bikes and vehicles while crossing Thomas Creek Bridge in the bike lane. The bottom of the trail at the south end of Whaleshead Beach is washed out and requires a steep climb.

CAMPING

There is no legal camping in this entire leg until you get to Harris Beach State Park, which has a hiker-biker camp ($). Whaleshead Beach Resort does not offer tent camping.

LODGING

Whaleshead Beach Resort offers lodging in comfortable, cabin-like RVs arrayed on the hillside above US 101. Brookings offers a wide array of lodging.

FOOD RESUPPLY

Whaleshead Beach Resort offers beverages (including water) and snack foods for sale off of the lobby; during some years it also operates a small restaurant.

Treeless Cape Ferrelo gives you your first look at Lone Ranch Beach.

Leg 6	Mileage between Waypoints
Arch Rock picnic area to Miner Creek	1.6
Miner Creek to Natural Bridges parking area	0.9
Natural Bridges parking area to north end of China Beach	1.2
China Beach to north end of Thomas Creek Bridge	1.3
Thomas Creek Bridge to Indian Sands (BA 188)	1.3
BA 188 to Whaleshead Beach access road	1.3
Whaleshead Beach access road to top of Sand Hill	2.7
Sand Hill to trail junction at summit of Cape Ferrelo	1.2
Cape Ferrelo to south end Lone Ranch Beach	0.7
Lone Ranch Beach to US 101	0.7
Lone Ranch Beach Trail junction at US 101 to entrance to Harris Beach State Park	2.4

LEG 7 BROOKINGS TO THE CALIFORNIA BORDER

Distance 8.1 miles
Elevation gain/loss +300/−490 feet

Reaching the California border, and thus truly hiking the entire Oregon Coast Trail, mainly requires a road walk through Brookings. The coastline here is mostly cliffs, and there is no bluff-top road or path.

Follow the paved bike path out of Harris Beach State Park and south alongside US 101 for 0.4 mile. Hike the highway shoulder and sidewalk along US 101 for 2.1 miles, crossing the Chetco River on the highway bridge. Immediately turn right onto Lower Harbor Road and follow it 1 mile to where it rises and turns left. Here, take a sharp right onto Oceanview Drive. Follow Oceanview Drive 2.2 miles more to the entrance to McVay Rock State Recreation Site.

If the tide is high, you won't be able to get around a rock outcropping 0.4 mile down the beach; in that case, continue south on Oceanview Drive to US 101. Follow it across the Winchuck River and look for a trail leading to the river beach (or follow trails through the dunes to the ocean beach). Passing the visitor center at Crissey Field State Recreation Site, walk the beach south. The California state line is about a half mile south of the Winchuck River; as of this writing it is unmarked, but state park officials plan to install an end-of-the-Oregon-Coast-Trail marker complementing the marker at the start of the trail at Fort Stevens State Park, some 400 OCT miles to the north.

The porch outside Crissey Field is a fitting spot for your I-did-it photo. (Photo courtesy of James Viscardi and Griff Owen)

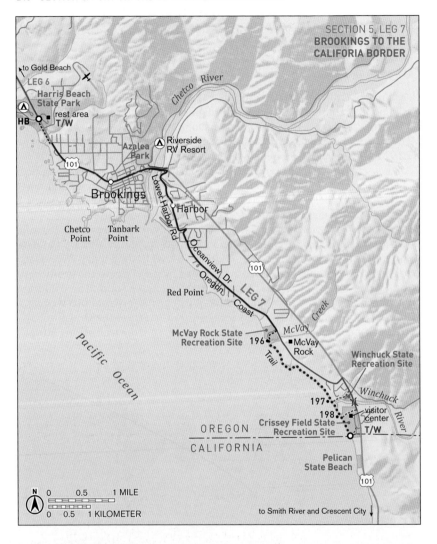

If the tide is low, or even at mid-tide, you may be able to walk from McVay Rock to California on the beach. From the parking area, take the left-hand path down to the beach and walk 1.6 miles to the Winchuck River. The wadeability of this river varies widely from year to year and even from week to week: the mouth may be blocked by sand and there is nothing to wade, or it may be narrow enough to just hop across, allowing you to stroll another 0.5 mile to the California border.

WHAT'S NEXT FOR YOU?

In 2016, brothers Harry and Dub Bludworth, ages sixty-five and seventy-five, achieved an accomplishment they called the Oregon Triple Crown: completion of the Oregon Coast Trail, the Pacific Crest Trail through Oregon, and a 300-mile untrailed route roughly following inside Oregon's eastern border. It took them six years, hiking each trail section by section. At the time they didn't know of anyone else who had done something like it, but they hoped others would follow in their footsteps. Maybe you? If such an achievement calls to you, you could consider trekking the Oregon Desert Trail—a 750-mile route, still rough in places, crafted and promoted by the Oregon Natural Desert Association—rather than bushwhacking along the eastern Oregon border as the Bludworth brothers did.

If the river is too high to wade, make your way up to the parking turnout at the BA 197 sign, walk out to the highway, cross the river on the highway bridge, cut through the woods to the south bank of the river just north of the Crissey Field State Recreation Site visitor center, and continue down the beach as described above.

Be sure to stop inside the visitor center, sign the OCT completion roster, take some pictures, and allow the staff to celebrate your achievement!

CAMPING

Riverside RV Resort ($$) offers tent camping 0.4 mile off of US 101 along the north bank of the Chetco River.

LODGING

Brookings and the adjacent town of Harbor have a lot of lodging options. South of the trail's end in California, you'll find more lodging options in Smith River and Crescent City.

FOOD RESUPPLY

Your walk from Harris Beach south through Brookings takes you past numerous restaurants and grocery stores.

Leg 7	Mileage between Waypoints
Harris Beach State Park to beach at McVay Rock State Recreation Site (BA 196)	6
BA 196 to mouth of Winchuck River (BA 197) via beach	1.6
BA 197 to the California border	0.5

The multicolored rocks on McVay Beach represent the complicated geology of the mountains fronting the beach here (Section 5, Leg 7).

ACKNOWLEDGMENTS

Thanks to all the Oregon Coast Trail hikers and prospective hikers who have contacted me in the past several years through my website, hikingtheoct.com, with questions or updates from their own experiences; just when I think I know everything about the OCT, I learn some tidbit about the trail that I wouldn't have guessed. Many thanks to my "hiking interns," Erin, Shannon, Donna, and Vickie—four friends who have accompanied me on scouting trips, section hikes, and a thru-hike. Their company was grand, and their help allowed me to be more efficient in scouting out every nook and cranny.

My husband, Charlie, is always a willing companion on coast hikes as time allows (and as long as we can bring the dog); he's an enthusiastic cheerleader for all of my projects, including this one.

I am indebted to the staffs of Oregon State Parks, the US Forest Service, and other managing agencies for working with me to provide accurate information, particularly about what's planned for the near future, as well as for their efforts in expanding the trail. Thank you to Robin Wilcox for her efforts on behalf of the Oregon Coast Trail Action Plan and to the Oregon Coast Visitors Association and Trailkeepers of Oregon for picking up trail construction and maintenance on the OCT.

A number of friends have allowed me to use their photographs in the book; thank you, Neal, Carolyn, Donna, Vickie, Jeanne, and others. Jack Urness double-checked my elevation and mileage figures.

And I so appreciate the editors at Mountaineers Books, who are as dedicated to getting it right as I am. I particularly thank them for taking a chance on a book whose audience is still building.

Sunset from a shoreline trail in Ecola State Park; Section 1, Leg 4 (Photo by Randall Henderson)

CONTACTS

GENERAL

Oregon Coast Trail Information and Updates

» Visit stateparks.oregon.gov; under "Things to Do," click "Oregon Coast Trail"
» Visit the Oregon Coast Visitor's Association's OCT website, oregoncoasttrail.org
» Visit author Bonnie Henderson's website, hikingtheoct.com.

Bus Transportation

» Astoria to Yachats (Sections 1, 2, and 3): NW Connector, nworegontransit.org
» Yachats to Florence (Section 3): Lane Transit District, ltd.org
» Florence to Coos Bay (Section 4): Pacific Crest Bus Lines, pacificcrestbuslines.com; Coos County Area Transit, coostransit.org
» North Bend to Brookings and into California (Sections 4 and 5): Curry Public Transit, currypublictransit.org
» To and from the coast: The Point bus, Oregon-point.com for information and schedules; buy tickets at amtrak.com
» Portland International Airport to Portland Union Station: MAX light rail, trimet.org/max

Overnight and Day-Use Parking

For parking at US Forest Service sites, including the Oregon Dunes National Recreation Area (Sections 2, 3, and 4), visit fs.usda.gov/detail/siuslaw /passes-permits/recreation.

Find general information and information about day-use passes at stateparks.oregon.gov. Overnight parking is by permit only through advance arrangement with the specific park. See the park listings below for contact information.

Oregon State Parks Camping

Make campground reservations at 800-452-5687 or oregonstateparks .reserveamerica.com. Reservations are not needed for hiker-biker camping.

SECTION 1: COLUMBIA RIVER TO GARIBALDI

To Prearrange Overnight Parking
- » Fort Stevens State Park: 503-861-3170 x21
- » Nehalem Bay State Park: 503-368-5943
- » Port of Garibaldi: 503-322-3292 or admin@portofgaribaldi.org

Camping
- » Barview Jetty County Park: Information at 503-322-3522 or co.tillamook.or.us/gov/parks/campgrounds.htm; reservations by phone or online at reservations.co.tillamook.or.us
- » Jetty Fishery: 503-368-5746 or jettyfishery.com
- » Old Mill RV Park: 503-322-0322 or oldmill.us
- » Sea Ranch Resort: 503-436-2815 or searanchrv.com
- » Twins Ranch: 541-418-1460 or twinsranchllc.com
- » Wright's for Camping: 503-436-2347 or wrightsforcamping.com

Lodging
- » McMenamins Gearhart Hotel: 503-717-8159 or mcmenamins.com /gearhart-hotel
- » Seaside Lodge and International Hostel: 503-738-7911 or seasidehostel.net

Boat Shuttle
- » Jetty Fishery: 503-368-5746 or jettyfishery.com

Other
- » Camp Rilea Armed Forces Training Center: oregon.gov/omd/rilea /Pages/Range-Operations.aspx
- » Oregon Coast Scenic Railroad: 503-842-7972 or oregoncoastscenic.org

SECTION 2: GARIBALDI TO SILETZ BAY AT LINCOLN CITY

To Prearrange Overnight Parking
- » Cape Lookout State Park: 503-842-4981
- » Devils Lake State Recreation Area: 541-994-2002
- » Port of Garibaldi: 503-322-3292 or admin@portofgaribaldi.org

Camping
- » Cascade Head primitive camping: Information at fs.usda.gov/recmain /siuslaw/recreation
- » Neskowin Creek RV Resort: 503-392-3355 or soundpacificrv .com/neskowin/creek

» Sandbeach Campground: Information on campground and hiker-biker camping at 877-444-6777 or recreation.gov
» Tillamook Bay City RV Park: 503-377-2124 or tillamookbaycityrv.com
» Webb County Campground: Information at 503-965-5001 or co.tillamook.or.us/gov/parks/campgrounds.htm; reservations by phone or online at reservations.co.tillamook.or.us
» Whalen Island County Campground: Information at 503-965-6085 or co.tillamook.or.us/gov/parks/campgrounds.htm; reservations by phone or online at reservations.co.tillamook.or.us

Boat Shuttle

» Big Spruce RV Park: 503-501-5434
» Garibaldi Marina: 503-322-3312 or garibaldimarina.com
» Nestucca Adventures: 503-965-0060 or nestuccaadventures.com

Other

» Siuslaw National Forest (Cascade Head): fs.usda.gov/recarea /siuslaw/recarea/?recid=42717

SECTION 3: SILETZ BAY AT LINCOLN CITY TO FLORENCE

To Prearrange Overnight Parking

» Beachside State Recreation Site: 541-563-3220
» Beverly Beach State Park: 541-265-9278
» Carl G. Washburne Memorial State Park: 541-547-3416
» Harbor Vista County Park or Siuslaw River north jetty: Call Lane County Parks at 541-682-2000 or visit lanecounty.org/parks, navigate to "Applications and Permits," then to "Special Use Permit Application"
» Oregon Dunes National Recreation Area: Visit fs.usda.gov/siuslaw and click on "Passes and Permits"
» South Beach State Park: 541-867-4715

Camping

Make campground reservations for the following US Forest Service sites at 877-444-6777 or recreation.gov. Except where noted, USFS campgrounds do not have drop-in hiker-biker camping areas. Advance reservations are not available for Baker Beach Campground.

» Cape Perpetua Campground (drop-in hiker-biker sites available)
» Rock Creek Campground (hiker-biker sites may be available)
» Sutton Campground
» Tillicum Beach Campground

Other Campgrounds
- » Baker Beach Campground: Information at fs.usda.gov/recarea/siuslaw /recarea/?recid=42341
- » Harbor Vista County Park: For information call 541-997-5987; reserve campsites at 541-682-2000 or reservations.lanecounty.org
- » Port of Siuslaw Campground & Marina: Reserve campsites at 541-997-3040 or portofsiuslaw.com

Lodging
- » Drift Inn Hotel: 541-547-4477 or the-drift-inn.com
- » Heceta Lighthouse Bed & Breakfast: 866-547-3696 or hecetalighthouse.com
- » Salishan Coastal Lodge: 541-764-2371 or salishan.com

SECTION 4: FLORENCE TO PORT ORFORD

To Prearrange Overnight Parking
- » Bullards Beach State Park: 541-347-2209
- » Cape Blanco State Park: 541-332-6774
- » Harbor Vista County Park or Siuslaw River north jetty: Call Lane County Parks at 541-682-2000 or visit lanecounty.org/parks, navigate to "Applications and Permits," then to "Special Use Permit Application"
- » Oregon Dunes National Recreation Area: Visit fs.usda.gov/siuslaw and click on "Passes and Permits"
- » Port of Port Orford: 541-332-7121
- » Port Orford Heads State Park: 541-332-6774
- » Sunset Bay State Park: 541-888-3778
- » Umpqua Lighthouse State Park: 541-271-4118

Camping
Make campground reservations for the following Oregon Dunes National Recreation Area and Siuslaw National Forest sites at 877-444-6777 or recreation.gov. No USFS campgrounds in this section have drop-in hiker-biker camping areas.
- » Bluebill Campground
- » Carter Lake Campground
- » Driftwood II Campground
- » Lagoon Campground
- » Waxmyrtle Campground

Other Campgrounds
  » Bastendorff Beach County Park: 541-396-7755 or co.coos.or.us
    /departments/cooscountyparks/bastendorff.aspx (hiker-biker sites
    available)
  » Boice Cope County Park: 541-373-1555 or webreserv.com/currycounty
    (hiker-biker sites available)
  » Fishermans RV Park: 541-271-3535 or fishermansrvpark.com
  » Port of Port Orford: 541-332-7121 or portofportorford.org (drop-in
    camping available)

Lodging
  » Bandon Dunes Golf Resort: 855-220-6710 or bandondunesgolf.com
  » Floras Lake House Bed & Breakfast: 541-348-2573 or floraslake.com
  » Umpqua Dunes RV Park: 541-957-7001; info and cabin reservations at
    travel.camping.com
  » Windy Cove Campground: 541-957-7001; info and cabin reservations at
    travel.camping.com

Boat shuttle
  » Bandon Visitors Center: 541-347-9616 or bandon.com
  » Winchester Bay Charters: 541-361-0180 or winchesterbaycharters.com

Other
  » Sawmill and Tribal Trail: coasttrails.org/SawmillTribalTrail.html

SECTION 5: PORT ORFORD TO THE CALIFORNIA BORDER

To Prearrange Overnight Parking
  » Harris Beach State Park: 541-469-0224
  » Humbug Mountain State Park: 541-332-6774
  » Port of Port Orford: 541-332-7121

Camping
  » Honey Bear by the Sea RV Resort and Campground: 541-247-2765 or
    honeybearbythesea.com
  » Indian Creek RV Park: 541-247-7704 or indiancreekrv.com
  » Nesika Beach RV Park and Campground: 541-247-6077 or nbrvp.com
  » Riverside RV Resort: 541-469-4799 or riverside-rv.com

Lodging
  » Whaleshead Beach Resort: 541-469-7446 or whalesheadresort.com

On a clear day the view from Cape Blanco stretches north to Blacklock Point and beyond.

INDEX

ABOUT THE AUTHOR

Bonnie Henderson is a journalist and an avid hiker. She is the author of two other guidebooks, *Day Hiking: Oregon Coast* and *Best Hikes with Kids: Oregon* (with Zach Urness), both in their second editions. She is also the author of *The Next Tsunami: Living on a Restless Coast* and *Strand: An Odyssey of Pacific Ocean Debris*. Follow her work at bonniehendersonwrites.com and get updates on the Oregon Coast Trail at her website hikingtheoct.com.

MOUNTAINEERS BOOKS

SKIPSTONE   **BRAIDED RIVER**

recreation • lifestyle • conservation

MOUNTAINEERS BOOKS, including its two imprints, Skipstone and Braided River, is a leading publisher of quality outdoor recreation, sustainability, and conservation titles. As a 501(c)(3) nonprofit, we are committed to supporting the environmental and educational goals of our organization by providing expert information on human-powered adventure, sustainable practices at home and on the trail, and preservation of wilderness.

Our publications are made possible through the generosity of donors, and through sales of more than 700 titles on outdoor recreation, sustainable lifestyle, and conservation. To donate, purchase books, or learn more, visit us online:

MOUNTAINEERS BOOKS

1001 SW Klickitat Way, Suite 201 • Seattle, WA 98134 • 800-553-4453
mbooks@mountaineersbooks.org • www.mountaineersbooks.org

An independent nonprofit publisher since 1960

Leave No Trace strives to educate visitors about the nature of their recreational impacts and offers techniques to prevent and minimize such impacts. Leave No Trace is best understood as an educational and ethical program, not as a set of rules and regulations. For more information, visit www.lnt.org or call 800-332-4100.

YOU MAY ALSO LIKE

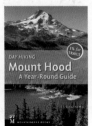